Joint Investigation Teams in the European Union:

From Theory to Practice

JOINT INVESTIGATION TEAMS IN THE EUROPEAN UNION:

FROM THEORY TO PRACTICE

Edited by

Conny RIJKEN

and

Gert VERMEULEN

T·M·C·ASSER PRESS
The Hague

Published by T·M·C·ASSER PRESS,
P.O.Box 16163, 2500 BD The Hague, The Netherlands

<www.asserpress.nl>

T·M·C·ASSER PRESS' English language books are distributed exclusively by:

Cambridge University Press, The Edinburg Building, Shaftesbury Road,
Cambridge CB2 2RU, UK,
or
for customers in the USA, Canada and Mexico:
Cambridge University Press, 100 Brook Hill Drive, West Nyack, NY 1094-2133, USA

<www.cambridge.org>

ISBN 10: 90-6704-215-3
ISBN 13: 978-90-6704-215-4

All rights reserved.
© 2006, T·M·C·ASSER PRESS, The Hague, The Netherlands and the authors

No part of the material protected by this copyright notice may be reproduced or utilized in any form or by any means, electronic or mechanical, including photocopying, recording, or by any information storage and retrieval system, without written permission from the copyright owner.

INTRODUCTION

Law enforcement authorities have long been convinced that they are not able to fight cross-border crime solely on the national level. In more recent times and actually since the early 1990s, the political level has become aware of this as well. This resulted in the adoption of a vast number of documents within the EU with the aim of facilitating cross-border activities to fight cross-border crime. One of the relevant instruments produced within the EU is that of the Joint Investigation Team (JIT). A JIT is considered a possible instrument to facilitate judicial cooperation within the European Union (EU). Until recently, the instrument of a JIT has not been used in practice although it was believed that there were a large number of cases in which the instrument could be applied. During the Dutch EU presidency (the second half of 2004), the establishment of an operational JIT was adopted as one of its goals in the field of police affairs. This JIT project was initiated with the aim being to use the instrument of a JIT as a possibility for a more intensive and efficient cooperation in the fight against Trafficking in Human Beings (THB) from and through Bulgaria (further on referred to as the THB-JIT project). As THB from and through Bulgaria was felt to be a common problem by most countries involved in this project (Belgium, Bulgaria, Germany, the Netherlands, and the United Kingdom), this crime was chosen as the subject for this project. Another aim of the project was to gain an insight into the way a JIT could function and the obstacles and conditions to be met for a JIT to be effective. To identify these obstacles and conditions and to make the information gathered available to future JITs, scientific research was conducted by an international and interdisciplinary research group, being given the possibility to monitor and analyse the whole project.[1] For various reasons, an operational JIT could not be established within the THB-JIT project. However, meanwhile an operational JIT was initiated between the Netherlands and the United Kingdom in a drugs case (referred to as the Drugs JIT). The research group was invited to monitor and analyse this process as well.

---

[1] This research was conducted with the financial support of the Dutch Ministry of Internal Affairs, the Dutch Ministry of Justice, the National Crime Squad in the United Kingdom, the *Bundeskriminalamt* in Germany, the Dutch Police and Science Programme, the Research and Documentation Centre of the Dutch Ministry of Justice, and the Netherlands Police EU Presidency 2004.

[2] These written sources consist of: a. relevant literature, b. legal documents such as relevant EU documents and instruments such as treaties, recommendations, Framework Decisions etc., c.

The three main sources for the gathering of the necessary information on both JIT projects were: written sources,[2] interviews (both live and telephone interviews) and questionnaires, and monitoring and observation of the meetings of the Steering Group, the so-called Joint Intelligence Group (JIG), the JIT and other meetings that were held in the context of both JIT projects.[3] The research was assigned to Tilburg University by the international steering group.[4] The international steering group consisted of representatives from all five countries involved in the THB-JIT project, and was managed by a project board from the Netherlands Police EU Presidency 2004.[5] The research group consisted of academic researchers from three of the different states involved in the THB-JIT project, namely, Belgium, Germany, and the Netherlands.[6] Consultations with a researcher from the United Kingdom took place on an *ad hoc* basis. Different professional backgrounds (legal, criminological, and sociological) were represented in the research group. It was counselled by a Scientific Advisory Board (SAB),[7] with academics from universities and academic institutions in different countries. All the researchers have adapted the result of their part of the research to contribute to this book.

This book provides a more analytical approach to the projects subject to the scientific research mentioned above. It is exceptional that academics are given the opportunity to be so closely involved in the operational field at such an early stage of testing and using new methods to fight cross-border crimes. Consequently, this book provides an insight into the obstacles met and remedies adopted when resorting to a JIT. It shows the complexity of factors that influence criminal cooperation and that have to be in place when this form of cooperation is initiated. Players in the field are not always aware of (the lack of) these factors.

---

policy documents of the countries involved in the JIT for the understanding of how things work out in practice in these countries, and d. reports of meetings from the Joint Intelligence Group, Analysis Group, JIT, Steering Group and other bodies, Europol documents, Eurojust documents, etc.

[3] The information that was gathered during these meetings concerned, for instance, the way in which the participants cooperated, how the interests in participating played a role in the cooperation, etc.

[4] See Chapter I.

[5] The members of the project board were Bas Barendregt, Timo Kansil, Jaco Vos and Jan Wiarda.

[6] Ghent University (Institute for International Research on Criminal Policy), Max Planck Institute, and Tilburg University respectively.

[7] The Scientific Advisory Board was chaired by Prof. Dr. Ernst Hirsch Ballin (Tilburg University). The other members of the SAB were Prof. Dr. Gert Vermeulen (Ghent University, Belgium), Prof. Dr. Hans Jörg Albrecht (Max Planck Institute), Prof. Dr. Monica den Boer (Free University Amsterdam), Prof. Dr. Willy Bruggeman (Benelux University Eindhoven Centre), Prof. Dr. Lazar Gruev (Sofia University and a member of the Constitutional Court of Bulgaria), Prof. Dr. Frans Leeuw and Roelof Jan Bokhorst, LL.M (Scientific Research and Documentation Centre, Dutch Ministry of Justice), Prof. Dr. Gert Vermeulen (Ghent University) and Frits Vlek, LL.M (Dutch Police and Science Program).

This book helps to identify these factors and does not leave the practitioners empty-handed. Conditions are formulated that have to be met before more intensified cooperation following the JIT concept can be successful. Furthermore, recommendations are made throughout the book and in the concluding chapter in particular for the application of these conditions.

The legal framework to start a JIT is a first prerequisite for the establishment of a JIT. Without such a framework, a JIT can never achieve its full potential. This legal framework within the EU was provided for in the first place by Article 13 of the EU Convention on Mutual Assistance and in the second place by the Council Framework Decision on JITs, which is an exact copy of Article 13. The way in which the different Member States involved in the THB-JIT project, have dealt with the obligation to implement the Framework Decision and Article 13 EU Convention on Mutual Assistance, if bound by it, is analysed in depth in Chapter I. However, it is thought that, especially on the operational level, with persons who must be considered able and qualified to make decisions to set up a JIT, there is a particular need for awareness as regards the practical consequences of the establishment of a JIT. This book attempts to meet this need.

The process of the establishment and the functioning of a JIT can be divided into three steps, corresponding with the different stages of an ordinary investigation, namely, the pre-operational phase, the operational phase, and the judicial phase. The possibilities and limitations concerning the exchange of law enforcement information within these phases is therefore elaborated upon in Chapters II, III and IV. Since they are two important bodies on the European level in facilitating police and judicial cooperation, Europol and Eurojust can be involved in JITs in several ways. The implications of their involvement on the practical as well as the juridical level are dealt with in Chapter V. The more practical aspects as well as the requirements for effective cooperation within a JIT form valuable information for practitioners who have to deal with JITs in the future. An insight is given into the way the two initiatives (the THB-JIT project and the operational Drugs JIT) were organised, who participated, and how relations developed (Chapter VI).

The analysis of the theoretical background of the instrument of a JIT, the efforts to establish a JIT within the THB-JIT project, and the establishment of the first operational JIT form the basis for the formulation of conditions and recommendations for the use of the instrument of a JIT and for the establishment of future JITs. Therefore, we believe that this book will be valuable to all those involved in criminal cooperation as well as to the national legislator, as it will show the importance of a clear and effective implementation of legislation.

The central question throughout the various stages of cooperation in criminal matters discussed in the book is what added value a JIT can bring. The results of the scientific research are used as illustrative material and operational input for a more theoretical reflection on the various aspects of a JIT. The book is composed in such a way that the chapters can be read separately, thus allowing the reader to focus on parts corresponding to his or her particular interest.

March 2006　　　　　　　　　　　　　　　　　　　　　　　　Conny RIJKEN
　　　　　　　　　　　　　　　　　　　　　　　　　　　　　　Gert VERMEULEN

SUMMARY OF CONTENTS

Introduction	V
Table of contents	XI
List of abbreviations	XIX

Chapter I
The legal and practical implementation of JITs: The bumpy road from EU to Member State level – *Conny Rijken and Gert Vermeulen* 1

1. Introduction 1
2. The THB-JIT project and the Drugs JIT 2
3. General introduction to the legal framework of JITs 10
4. To what extent has the legal framework on JITs properly been implemented in the participating Member States? 24
5. What can be the added value of a JIT and how can it be achieved? 50
6. Conclusion 51

Chapter II
Law enforcement information exchange in the pre-operational phase of a JIT – *Eveline De Wree* 53

1. Sharing of intelligence and information 54
2. The use of a JIG 72
3. Towards conclusions: how should information exchange take place in this phase? 78

Chapter III
Law enforcement information exchange in the operational phase of a JIT – *Annelies Balcaen* 85

1. Information exchange between the members of a JIT 86
2. Information exchange with other EU Member States not party to the JIT 107
3. Information exchange with third countries 110
4. Data protection guarantees within a JIT 110
5. Conclusions and recommendations 114

Chapter IV
Judicial cooperation in criminal matters: mutual legal assistance –
Els De Busser 119

1. Mutual legal assistance in criminal matters 119
2. Special aspects of the (use of the) JIT 143
3. Prosecution 156
4. Conclusion 157

Chapter V
The role of Europol and Eurojust in Joint Investigation Teams –
Annette Herz 159

1. Introduction 159
2. Europol and Eurojust as institutions 161
3. Legal framework for participation in JITs 165
4. Involvement in the THB-JIT project 177
5. Excursus: involvement in the JIT on drug trafficking 187
6. Conclusions and recommendations 195

Chapter VI
Sociological aspects regarding the set up and management of a Joint Investigation Team – *Markus Mayer* 201

1. The three cornerstones for the establishment of a JIT 201
2. Legal basis 202
3. Selection of a case – the setting up of a JIT 204
4. Management of a JIT 209
5. Conclusion 217

Chapter VII
Conclusions and Recommendations – *Conny Rijken* 219

1. Conclusion 219
2. Recommendations for the use of the JIT instruments 225
3. Final remarks 229

TABLE OF CONTENTS

Introduction	V
Summary of contents	IX
List of abbreviations	XIX

Chapter I
The legal and practical implementation of JITs: The bumpy road from EU to Member State level – *Conny Rijken and Gert Vermeulen* — 1

1.	Introduction	1
2.	The THB-JIT project and the Drugs JIT	2
2.1	The THB-JIT project	2
2.1.1	The Europol initiative	2
2.1.2	The Dutch initiative	3
2.1.3	The relation between the two initiatives	4
2.1.4	The organisational structure of the THB-JIT project	5
2.2	The Drugs JIT	8
2.2.1	The establishment of the Drugs JIT	8
2.2.2	The composition of the Drugs JIT	9
3.	General introduction to the legal framework of JITs	10
3.1	International legal instruments providing a legal basis for operating JITs	10
3.2	The legal framework of the instrument of a JIT	13
3.2.1	The involvement of Europol	18
3.2.2	Involvement of Eurojust	20
3.2.3	Legal implications for the Member States	20
4.	To what extent has the legal framework on JITs properly been implemented in the participating Member States?	24
4.1	Belgium	24
4.2	Germany	29
4.3	The Netherlands	34
4.4	The United Kingdom	44

5.	What can be the added value of a JIT and how can it be achieved?	50
6.	Conclusion	51

Chapter II
Law enforcement information exchange in the pre-operational phase of a JIT – *Eveline De Wree* — 53

1.	Sharing of intelligence and information	54
1.1	The identification of a JIT-worthy case	54
1.1.1	In a bottom-up initiative	54
1.1.2	In a top-down project	55
1.2	Finding possible partners for a JIT	58
1.3	The scope of shared intelligence	59
1.3.1	In a bottom-up initiative	59
1.3.2	In a top-down project	61
1.4	Type of data shared	63
1.5	Practical organisation	63
1.5.1	Sharing intelligence through national law enforcement agencies	63
1.5.2	Sharing intelligence through Europol	70
2.	The use of a JIG	72
2.1	A new instrument	72
2.2	What is a JIG? Two perspectives	73
2.2.1	The JIG as an enforcement of the AWF	73
2.2.2	The JIG as an addition to the AWF	74
2.3	Problems and concerns relating to the use of a JIG	75
2.3.1	A JIG existing next to an AWF	75
2.3.2	What about a JIG in a bottom-up procedure?	77
2.3.3	Efficiency of a JIG	77
3.	Towards conclusions: how should information exchange take place in this phase?	78
3.1	Recommendable characteristics	78
3.1.1	Rapidly and efficiently	78
3.1.2	Using available information and instruments	79
3.1.3	Aimed at identifying links	80
3.1.4	With the involvement of judicial actors	81
3.2	Challenges and questions to be answered	81
3.2.1	Bilateral or centralised?	81

3.2.2	Stimulating information flows	82
3.3	A stepping-stone to the operational phase	83

Chapter III
Law enforcement information exchange in the operational phase of a JIT – *Annelies Balcaen* 85

1.	Information exchange between the members of a JIT	86
1.1	Legal basis of the right for seconded members to provide the JIT with information which is available in the home country	86
1.1.1	Implementation legislation	87
1.1.2	The Netherlands	87
1.1.3	The United Kingdom	88
1.1.4	Belgium	88
1.1.5	Germany	89
1.1.6	Information available to seconded members	89
1.1.7	The Netherlands	89
1.1.8	The United Kingdom	91
1.1.9	Belgium	92
1.1.10	Germany	94
1.2	Obstacles in the information exchange between the members of a JIT	96
1.2.1	Differences in national legislation	96
1.2.2	Lack of availability of information to the members of the JIT	101
1.2.3	Differences in the categorisation of information	103
1.2.4	Reluctance to share information	104
1.3	Right to use information lawfully obtained within the JIT in the home country	104
1.3.1	The Netherlands	105
1.3.2	The United Kingdom	106
1.3.3	Belgium	106
1.3.4	Germany	106
2.	Information exchange with other EU Member States not party to the JIT	107
3.	Information exchange with third countries	110
4.	Data protection guarantees within a JIT	110
4.1	The Netherlands	113

4.2	The United Kingdom	113
4.3	Belgium	114
4.4	Germany	114
5.	Conclusions and recommendations	114

Chapter IV
Judicial cooperation in criminal matters: mutual legal assistance –
Els De Busser 119

1.	Mutual legal assistance in criminal matters	119
1.1	Traditional mutual legal assistance	119
1.2	Legal bases of joint investigation teams	122
1.2.1	General	122
1.2.2	Legal basis of the THB-JIT project	125
1.2.2.1	A challenging legal basis	125
1.2.2.2	Added value	129
1.2.3	Legal basis of the Drugs JIT	131
1.3	Setting up a JIT	132
1.3.1	Formalities fulfilled in setting up the Drugs JIT	132
1.3.2	The relationship between the Drugs JIT and the 'mother case' in the United Kingdom	133
1.3.3	Model agreement for EU Member States	135
1.3.4	Model agreement for third states	136
1.3.5	Scope	137
1.3.5.1	Objective(s) of the JIT	137
1.3.5.2	Police or judicial cooperation in criminal matters?	140
1.3.5.3	The nature of the offence	141
2.	Special aspects of the (use of the) JIT	143
2.1	Presence of foreign police officers in a state	143
2.2	Investigative measures	146
2.2.1	Problems concerning investigate measures	147
2.2.2	Number and variety of investigative measures	148
2.3	Evidence	148
2.3.1	Disclosure	149
2.3.1.1	General	149
2.3.1.2	THB-JIT project	149
2.3.1.3	Drugs JIT	152
2.3.2	Telephone interception	152

2.3.3	Civilian and criminal infiltration and the use of informers	154
2.3.4	Use of information gathered in the context of a JIT	154
3.	Prosecution	156
4.	Conclusion	157

Chapter V
The role of Europol and Eurojust in Joint Investigation Teams –
Annette Herz — 159

1.	Introduction	159
2.	Europol and Eurojust as institutions	161
2.1	Europol	161
2.2	Eurojust	163
3.	Legal framework for participation in JITs	165
3.1	Europol	165
3.1.1	Europol Convention	165
3.1.2	Treaty on European Union	166
3.1.3	EU Convention on Mutual Assistance/Framework Decision on JITs	166
3.1.4	Council Recommendations	169
3.1.5	Amendment of Europol Convention	169
3.1.6	Agreement between Eurojust and Europol	171
3.2	Eurojust	172
3.2.1	Treaty on European Union	172
3.2.2	Council Decision 2002	172
3.3	National legislation	173
3.3.1	The Netherlands	173
3.3.2	The United Kingdom	174
3.3.3	Belgium	175
3.3.4	Germany	175
4.	Involvement in the THB-JIT project	177
4.1	Europol	177
4.1.1	Role and responsibilities	177
4.1.2	Information exchange/Europol as a facilitator	179
4.1.3	Problems met by Europol	181

4.2	Eurojust	185
4.2.1	Role and responsibilities	185
4.2.2	Information exchange/Eurojust as a facilitator	186
4.2.3	Problems met by Eurojust	186
5.	Excursus: involvement in the JIT on drug trafficking	187
5.1	Europol	188
5.1.1	Information exchange/Europol as a facilitator	188
5.1.2	Role of the Europol analyst	190
5.1.3	Problems met by Europol	191
5.2	Eurojust	193
5.2.1	Information exchange/Eurojust as a facilitator	193
5.2.2	Problems met by Eurojust	194
6.	Conclusions and recommendations	195
6.1	Europol	196
6.2	Eurojust	198

Chapter VI
Sociological aspects regarding the set up and management of a Joint Investigation Team – *Markus Mayer*   201

1.	The three cornerstones for the establishment of a JIT	201
2.	Legal basis	202
2.1	Implementation of the EU Convention on Mutual Assistance on a national level	202
2.2	Review of the possibilities to cooperate with other countries	203
3.	Selection of a case – the setting up of a JIT	204
3.1	Specifications made by the EU Convention on Mutual Assistance	204
3.2	How can a JIT be initiated?	204
3.2.1	Top-down: identifying a field of crime and selecting a case	204
3.2.2	Bottom-up: processing a demand related to an ongoing investigation	207
3.2.3	Outside-in: processing of a demand from abroad	207
3.3	Conclusion	208
4.	Management of a JIT	209

4.1	Location and organisational structure	209
4.2	Finance and funding	210
4.3	Labour law aspects	211
4.4	Other legal aspects	211
4.5	Hierarchical structure	212
4.6	Language and culture in JITs	213
4.6.1	Emergence of subgroups	213
4.6.2	The need for translation	215
4.6.3	Restrictions due to a lack of language skills	215
4.7	Team building	216
4.7.1	Inauguration of new team members	216
4.7.2	Pairing	217
5.	Conclusion	217

Chapter VII
Conclusions and Recommendations – *Conny Rijken* 219

1.	Conclusion	219
1.1	The evaluation of the results of the projects under research	220
1.2	Conditions on the operational level for the establishment of a successful JIT	221
1.2.1	Conditions in the preparatory phase of a JIT	221
1.2.2	Conditions in the operational phase of a JIT	223
1.2.3	Conditions for the involvement of Europol and Eurojust in a JIT	224
2.	Recommendations for the use of the JIT instruments	225
2.1	Recommendations for the police	225
2.2	Recommendations for the prosecution	226
2.3	Recommendations for policy makers	227
2.4	Recommendations for the legislator	228
3.	Final remarks	229

LIST OF ABBREVIATIONS

ACPO	Association of Chief Police Officers
APB	Action Plan Bulgaria
APBWG	Action Plan Bulgaria Working Group
AWF	Analysis Work File
BDSG	Bundesdatenschutzgesetzes
BGBl	Bundesgesetzblatt
BKA	Bundeskriminalamt
BKAG	Bundeskriminalamtgesetz
CBP	College bescherming persoonsgegevens
CCP	Code of Criminal Procedure
CJA	Criminal Justice Act
CoE	Council of Europe
CPIA	Criminal Procedure and Investigations Act
CPS	Crown Prosecution Service
DIN	International Network Service (Dienst Internationale Netwerken)
DNRI	National Criminal Intelligence Service (Dienst Nationale Recherche Informatie)
ECJ	European Court of Justice
EDU	European Drugs Unit
EEC	European Economic Community
EJN	European Judicial Network
ELO	Europol Liaison Officers
ENU	Europol National Unit
EPCTF	European Police Chiefs Task Force
EU	European Union
Eurojust	European Judicial Cooperaton Unit
EUROPOL	European Police Office
IGO	Intergovernmental organisation

JIG	Joint Intelligence Group
JIT	Joint Investigation Team
KLPD	Korps Landelijke Politiediensten
LKA	Länder Kriminal Amter
LRT	Landelijk Recherche Team
MoU	Memorandum of Understanding
MRO	Meldingen Recherche Onderzoeken
NCIS	National Crime Intelligence Service
NCS	National Crime Squad
NCSEW	National Crime Squad of England and Wales
NGO	Non-Governmental Organisation
NSPIS	National Strategy for Police Information Systems
PII	Public interest immunity
PV	Proces-verbaal
RIPA	Regulation of Investigatory Powers Act
SAB	Scientific Advisory Board
SIC	Schengen Implementation Convention
SIRENE	Supplementary information request at the national entry
SIS	Schengen Information System
SOCA	Serious Organised Crime Agency
TEU	Treaty on European Union
THB	Trafficking in Human Beings
TOC	Transnational Organised Crime
TREVI	Terrorism, Radicalism, Extremism, Violence International

CHAPTER I
THE LEGAL AND PRACTICAL IMPLEMENTATION OF JITS: THE BUMPY ROAD FROM EU TO MEMBER STATE LEVEL

Conny Rijken and Gert Vermeulen*

1. INTRODUCTION

In this first chapter a general introduction will be given to two initiatives on the establishment of a Joint Investigation Team (JIT), namely, the THB-JIT project and the Drugs JIT, undertaken by Belgium, Bulgaria, Germany, the Netherlands, and the United Kingdom and by the Netherlands and the United Kingdom, respectively. Furthermore, in this chapter the reader will be introduced to the legal framework of the JIT and provided with an insight into the legal complications of and obstacles to adopting a sufficient basis for operational JITs. The obligations for the Member States following the various European and international instruments providing legal ground for JITs will be focused upon. The national implementing legislation of the countries involved will be thoroughly discussed concerning the issues relevant for law enforcement and will be provided with some critical remarks on the choices made by these Member States when implementing these instruments. This assessment gives a good impression of the consequences for practitioners when using these implementing provisions to operate a JIT. More general questions as regards the functioning and possibilities of a JIT will be answered, as well as the added value of operating a JIT.

This first chapter can be divided into four sections. The THB-JIT project and the Drugs JIT are introduced first. In order to have a better understanding of the problems and obstacles identified in the following chapters and to be able to properly compare the two initiatives, the establishment and the organisational structure of both projects will be explained. Then the international instruments

---

* Conny Rijken is Researcher and Lecturer at Tilburg University (the Netherlands) and Gert Vermeulen is Professor of Criminal Law at Ghent University (Belgium).

C. Rijken and G. Vermeulen (Eds.), *Joint Investigation Teams in the European Union*
© 2006, T·M·C·ASSER PRESS, The Hague, The Netherlands and the Authors

providing a basis for the establishment of a JIT will be reviewed. The most important instrument by far for Europe is the EU Convention on Mutual Assistance,[1] which includes an elaborate provision on JITs in Article 13. This article, together with the provisions in the Framework Decision on JITs,[2] which is an exact copy of Article 13, will be examined in detail. This exercise is followed by an assessment of the implementation legislation for the instrument of the JIT in the national law in the Member States participating in the THB-JIT project (Belgium, Germany, the Netherlands, and the United Kingdom). After this exercise, the possible added value of a JIT will be indicated on the basis of the assessment.

2. THE THB-JIT PROJECT AND THE DRUGS JIT

In this section, the background of two initiatives, namely, the THB-JIT project and the Drugs JIT will be described for a better understanding of the implications of and the reasons for the problems identified in the following chapters.

2.1 **The THB-JIT project**

The THB-JIT project originates from two initiatives to combat more effectively Trafficking in Human Beings (THB) from and through Bulgaria, namely, an initiative taken by Europol and one by the Netherlands.

2.1.1 *The Europol initiative*

During the European Police Chiefs Task Force (EPCTF) meeting on 22 and 23 July 2002 in Copenhagen, the EPCTF requested Europol to finalise the Action Plan for combating illegal immigration and trafficking in human beings.
The THB expert group from the Member States agreed that Bulgaria should be the focus and developed the Specific Action Plan. Germany, the Netherlands, and Belgium, with the support of the United Kingdom, volunteered to establish a working group, the Action Plan Bulgaria Working Group (APBWG). The United Kingdom offered the services of its liaison officer to facilitate the implementation of the Action Plan Bulgaria (APB). The supporting role of Europol is

---

[1] Council Act of 29 May 2000 Establishing in Accordance with Article 34 of the Treaty on European Union the Convention on Mutual Assistance in Criminal Matters between the Member States of the European Union, *OJ* C 197, 12.07.2000, p. 1. The Convention entered into force for the ratifying Member States on 23 August 2005.
[2] Framework Decision of 13 June 2002 on Joint Investigation Teams, *OJ* L 162, 20.06.2002, p. 1.

stressed in the APB. As regards intelligence activities, a central role in coordinating, analysing, and continuously updating information is played by Europol. A JIT as such was not explicitly referred to as one of the instruments for the implementation of the APB at the time the plan was adopted. In the APB, the actions to be undertaken were not yet made operational because they required additional efforts.

During the second meeting of the APBWG on 29 July 2003, Germany formally proposed the opening of an Analysis Work File (AWF)[3] called Maritsa, which was concerned with THB from Bulgaria in support of the Action Plan. This proposal was endorsed by the Netherlands and Belgium, and provisionally supported by the United Kingdom.

2.1.2 The Dutch initiative

A meeting between police officers from the United Kingdom and the Netherlands, in which the seeds for this initiative were sown, took place on 6 December 2002. The theme of one of the workshops during that meeting was Prostitution and Trafficking in Women and Children. In this workshop, the United Kingdom Chief Constables and the Dutch representative at the EPCTF decided to link efforts to set up a joint team to fight THB. They agreed that the setting up of a JIT was the best tool to combat trafficking in persons.

Following this meeting, an action plan was formulated including the following steps:

– Developing a plan of communication.
– Setting up a Joint Investigation Team with the participation of Germany, Belgium, the United Kingdom, the Netherlands, and Europol.

Because Germany and Belgium were already involved in other initiatives aimed at combating THB in Bulgaria, it was decided that the development of a JIT should involve those two countries. Bilateral meetings were held with representatives of these two countries to find out whether they were willing to participate. During the summer of 2003, more formal meetings on a tactical level were held to discuss further the possibilities of combating trafficking together by setting up a JIT. A meeting took place between Dutch and British Police Forces

---

[3] Within the Europol framework, data can be stored in an analysis work file on groups or persons who are suspected or have been convicted of, and for whom there are reasonable grounds to believe that they will commit, offences that fall within the competence of Europol (offences mentioned in Article 2 of the Europol Convention; see Articles 8 and 10 of the Europol Convention). For more details, see Scientific Research JIT, Second Report, 16 January 2005, p. 41-44.

on 7 May 2003. In this meeting, it was agreed that a Joint Intelligence Group (JIG) between the United Kingdom and the Netherlands would be set up in order to identify criminals involved in the trafficking of human beings for sexual purposes.

In a bilateral meeting between Germany and the Netherlands (8 July 2003 in Warnsveld), Germany stated that it was willing to support the THB-JIT project subject to the condition that it could focus on THB into central Europe with Bulgarian victims and Bulgarian perpetrators, because this had been detected as being a real crime problem for Germany.

2.1.3 *The relation between the two initiatives*

On 2 July 2003, a meeting took place between representatives of the two initiatives in order to exchange information. Although the start of the AWF Maritsa was agreed on, the Netherlands approached Europol in order to initiate intelligence gathering, and to establish a Joint Intelligence Group (JIG) and possibly a Joint Investigation Team (JIT) to support the APB. The APBWG had the same set up as the THB-JIT project and consisted of representatives from the United Kingdom, Belgium, Germany, and the Netherlands. It was agreed upon and seemed natural to link the JIT initiative to the ongoing APBWG. However, at that time, the representatives refrained from clarifying the relation between these two initiatives, although both the representatives of the THB-JIT project and the director of Europol were aware of the overlap of the two initiatives. Several reasons can be given as to why they were not able to reach an agreement on the linking of the two initiatives. Both were eager to profile their own project and organisation. Although Europol wanted to engage in the THB-JIT project, it wanted to continue with the APB as well. There was some reluctance to cooperate on both sides. For practical reasons, it was impossible to contact the director of Europol for some months after this meeting to continue discussions on the issue.

At that time, the representative of the THB-JIT project did not realise the consequences of not finding a solution to the situation in the long term. In practice, this failure to link the two initiatives led to repeating discussions at a later stage of the project and confusion as regards the functions of the different actors involved. For instance, in his Project Initiation Document the project manager stated that there was considerable risk of duplication of efforts across the JIT steering group and the APB. He suggested that consideration should be given to merging certain aspects of the two initiatives in order to avoid duplication.

At a later stage, another effort to clarify the relation between the two initiatives was made by Europol. On 3 February 2004, Europol sent a draft document to the members of the THB-JIT project with a proposal for the relation between the THB-JIT project and the APB. It suggested that the APB would be the main point of reference for coordination and management of the activities to engage in and that the THB-JIT project would fulfil some of the proposed activities of the APB, as would the Analysis Group and the APBWG. The structure of the THB-JIT project was seen as a solid basis for the management of all activities, but not in a hierarchical structure. It was proposed to place the steering group in a central position, implying all the functional relations with the Analysis Group and the APBWG. This seemed to be impossible, however, if the steering group was not placed in a hierarchical structure with the Analysis Group of the AWF and the APBWG.

The confusion as regards the functions of the different actors involved also follows from the fact that, within the steering group, the opening order of the AWF, which was proposed to Europol to follow the APB, was considered at length and agreed upon. However, the steering group did not formally have any competence in this respect as the states that are members of the Analysis Group of the AWF decide on its scope.

Finally, after many and lengthy discussions and numerous different proposals for the relation between the THB-JIT project and the Action Plan Bulgaria, the authorities involved were not able to reach agreement on this point. Even now, much remains unclear as regards the coordination of the activities conducted within the two initiatives. As we will see below, this caused friction and duplication at later stages in the project.

2.1.4 *The organisational structure of the THB-JIT project*

A follow-up strategic meeting on the initiation of a joint investigation team focusing on THB from and through Bulgaria was held on 17 September 2003 at Warnsveld, the Netherlands. The Member States that were indicated as potential candidates to participate in a JIT for this purpose were invited. Representatives of the National Crime Squad (*Dienst Nationale Recherche*) in the Netherlands, the Federal Police of Belgium, the National Crime Squad of the United Kingdom, the *Bundeskriminalamt* of Germany, Eurojust, and Europol were present and the meeting was led by the Dutch chair of the EPCTF. Bulgaria did not formally participate at that time. The structure of the THB-JIT project was decided upon in this meeting. The JIG was formally installed and the German JIG team leader appointed. In order to harmonise intelligence flows, it was agreed that the proposed AWF should be incorporated in the JIG. However, Belgium was of the opinion that the JIG should be a member of the Analysis Group of the AWF. The United Kingdom appointed the general project manager responsible for the overall operational management of the JIG and (when appropriate) the JIT team. He was to act as the point of contact for the team leaders of the JIG, the JIT, and the steering group. His task was to be the channel for any queries and to ensure that constraints were strictly adhered to within the agreed framework and objectives. He would not be directly responsible for the daily operational management of the JIG and the JIT as this was the task of the team leaders.

In this meeting, the steering group was established. Although it was decided that the steering group would be set up at police level, it became heterogeneous since persons from both the strategic as well as the operational level were participating in the meeting. The steering group would act as a coordination committee at the strategic operational level and be composed of delegates from the participating countries, delegates from Eurojust and Europol to participate as observers. Only some of the representatives in the steering group described themselves as particularly concerned with Trafficking in Human Beings in their regular field of work. This concerned delegates from Belgium and Germany as well as the leader of the AWF Maritsa and the representative of Europol. The other members did not mention any responsibility in this field of crime, which might have led to different motivations to participate in the steering group. It was agreed that the Dutch chair of the EPCTF would be the president of the steering group and would be assisted in this task by the project board.

The steering group had three main challenges.[4] First, it had to clarify whether the setting up of a JIT according to Article 13 EU Convention on Mutual Assistance was possible between the countries represented in the steering group. Second, a criminal case on Trafficking in Human Beings, ongoing in the respective countries, had to be identified. Finally, a JIT had to be established and managed. As we will see in this report, it is obvious that the management of the project intertwined these tasks instead of performing them separately, which unnaturally protracted the progress of the project and led to redundancies in the steering group.[5]

Hardly any of the members of the steering group would have been involved in the Joint Investigation Team had it been established. This is particularly interesting since it might indicate that the members of the steering group probably did not have the same agenda as the persons involved in the subsequent investigation.

---

[4] In some respects, these challenges reflect the terms of macro, meso and micro levels of police cooperation proposed by Benyon. See J. Benyon, et al., 'Understanding Police Cooperation in Europe Setting a Framework for Analysis', in M. Anderson and M. den Boer; *Policing Across National Boundaries*, London, Pinter Publishers, 1994, p. 46-65.

[5] During the first meeting of the steering group, it was already discussed how to establish a Joint Intelligence Group and a Joint Investigation Team, whereas the question of whether a JIT was feasible between the countries involved does not appear in the report. See the minutes of the meeting of the steering group on 17 September 2003.

It was further agreed that an action research team (later changed into Scientific Research JIT) would be set up.
The role and tasks of the different groups and functions within the THB-JIT project were confirmed and laid down in the 'letter of intent'.

The letter of intent was drafted in February 2004 after long discussions on its content and various rounds of amendments from September 2003. There were different views on the importance of the wording of this document. Some said that it was simply a declaration of intent and could be amended at any time in the future, while others saw it as the basis for the THB-JIT project and, therefore, felt that the text had to be optimal. During the negotiations, national interests were strongly defended. Furthermore, the participants differed in their opinions on the general scope of the project. The harm caused during the negotiations on the scope of the AWF (see below) affected the negotiations on the letter of intent in the sense that the negotiators were keen on its exact wording. Some of the negotiators were not included as signatories of the letter of intent and/or did not have the authority to decide on the final wording of the letter of intent. They had to contact the competent authorities in their home countries before they could agree on a text. This delayed the process and gave other participants the feeling that things could not be solved during the meeting for which they had travelled to the Netherlands. Furthermore, the agreements set down in the letter of intent demanded follow-up action on a national level and not all negotiators were in the position to make this demand, also because some of these demands had to be made on the judicial level. Negotiations on the wording of the letter of intent gave the impression that there was a reluctance to cooperate closely.
Finally, the purpose of the THB-JIT project was formulated in the letter of intent as follows:[6]

> In order to contribute to an effective combat of serious crime in the European Union, the Director General of the Criminal Department of the Federal Police in Belgium, the Director General of the National Crime Squad in the United Kingdom, the President of the Bundeskriminalamt (BKA) in Germany, the Chief of the National Dutch Police Agency, the Director of Europol and the President of Eurojust, have recognised a common wish to enter into closer and more structural cooperation on the areas of:
>
> – combating trafficking in human beings for the purpose of commercial and/or sexual exploitation(s), identifying Bulgaria as a source and/or transit country by means of joint investigations,

---

[6] Letter of Intent, February 2004, point 1 (internal document, not published).

- testing and evaluating the concept of the initiation and set-up of a Joint Investigation Team (JIT) by means of action research at scientific level.

2.2 The Drugs JIT

2.2.1 *The establishment of the Drugs JIT*

There are two different versions concerning the origin of the idea to set up the Drugs JIT.
The first version asserts that it was the Head of the Central Unit of the Dutch National Crime Squad (*Dienst Nationale Recherche*) who came up with the idea of forming a JIT in addition to the initiative already taken on human trafficking from Bulgaria. He discussed the idea with his superior and subsequently with the project manager of the THB-JIT project. After they agreed, several investigations were taken into consideration for a JIT. The aim of establishing a JIT seemed to be decisive in this version.
The second version regarding the origin of the idea relates to an investigation in the United Kingdom, which had received information about a substantial amount of drugs being held in the Netherlands. Via the project manager of the THB-JIT project, the idea came up to start a JIT between the Netherlands and the United Kingdom. In conclusion, it can be said that, in this version, the factor of necessity played an important role in the decision to start a JIT. It is clear that the two aims of the THB-JIT project, namely, fighting crime and establishing a JIT were also present in the Drugs JIT.
In a second step, the public prosecution services of both countries liaised with the national representatives of Eurojust of both countries. After agreement on the drugs case investigated by the National Crime Squad of England and Wales (NCSEW) as a suitable target, the United Kingdom made an oral request to the Dutch for their assistance and support in investigating the Dutch side of this case while the remaining part of the investigation was not a subject for the JIT and remained under investigation in the United Kingdom.
On 24 November 2004 an Agreement on the Establishment of a Joint Investigation Team[7] was adopted between the Netherlands and the United Kingdom, explicitly referring to Article 13 of the EU Convention on Mutual Assistance and the Framework Decision on JITs (paragraph 8 of the agreement). In contrast to the THB-JIT project, the key players involved in the preparatory phase were largely identical to those of the JIT itself. The parties to the agreement were the public prosecution services and the National Crime Squads from both

---

[7] The agreement of 24 November 2004 was superseded by an amended version on 17 January 2005 (internal documents, not published).

states, and the two national members of Eurojust on the basis of their national law. Europol and Eurojust were not involved in the decision-making as such. Eurojust took up a facilitating role. They hosted meetings and chaired discussions in relation to the draft of the agreement. Europol representatives did not take part in the preliminary discussions on setting up a JIT. Before the JIT took up its duties, they had a week of preparatory training and team-building. They were informed of each other's legal system and legal cultures and the Dutch team members received language training. The team took up its task in the second half of January 2005.

The agreement of 24 November 2004 had to be amended following the obligation of JIT members to testify in Dutch courts according to Article 552qa, paragraph 3 of the Dutch Code of Criminal Procedure. In the amended version of 17 January 2005, a number of members of the NCSEW were taken off the list in order to only include those persons who were actually participating in the JIT and to free the other persons from the obligation to testify in a Dutch court. In doing so, it could be argued that they were no longer involved in the process and were, as a consequence, unable to testify in a Dutch court. The reason why the others could still sign the agreement involves the fact that they are not aware of any kind of information from the 'mother case' in the United Kingdom that could not be revealed in court.

Parallel to the JIT in the Netherlands, the NCSEW continued to investigate its drugs case. According to the JIT Agreement, in the course of both investigations the Netherlands and the United Kingdom are to provide evidence and intelligence to each other. In the Agreement, the reason for locating the JIT in the Netherlands is described with the aim of dismantling the Dutch branch of an ongoing criminal investigation (the 'mother case') by the NCSEW. Objections against the choice of transforming the British ongoing case into a JIT with part of the investigations situated in the Netherlands were twofold. First, the Netherlands was very motivated politically to start a JIT under its leadership during the EU Presidency. Secondly, the British authorities were afraid that, if the ongoing case were to be transformed into a JIT, this would potentially jeopardise the investigation.

2.2.2 The composition of the Drugs JIT

The Drugs JIT consists of the JIT team leader and the investigation team supervisor (responsible for the day-to-day work in the JIT), seven investigators and one administrative support person. There are three seconded British police officers; one holds the rank of detective sergeant and the other two are detective constables. The higher-ranking British officers are not mentioned in the agreement, although they do play a certain role in the JIT. Regarding the three British investigators, a rotation system applies: two seconded members are always in the Netherlands and one is in the United Kingdom. The close cooperation between the public prosecutor and the police in the Dutch criminal justice system is reflected in the JIT Agreement, in which two Dutch officials are named as JIT leaders: one public prosecutor and an officer from the Dutch National Crime Squad (*dienst nationale recherche*). The JIT can be subdivided into two sections, the 'inner' and 'outer' JIT.[8] The inner JIT consists of the Dutch police officers and seconded members working on the National Crime Squad premises in Driebergen. The outer JIT includes the higher police ranks[9] not located in Driebergen, the prosecution services of both countries, Eurojust members as well as the Europol liaison officers of both countries.[10]

3. GENERAL INTRODUCTION TO THE LEGAL FRAMEWORK OF JITS

3.1 International legal instruments providing a legal basis for operating JITs

Various treaties qualify as a potentially valid legal basis for setting up a JIT, provided they apply between the countries willing to set up a joint investigation and have not been excluded by the countries concerned as a valid JIT basis. The EU Convention on Mutual Assistance is the perfect maximized treaty basis for JIT constructs between the countries of the EU and will be discussed in detail below, together with the Framework Decision on JITs, which is a copy of Article 13 of the EU Convention on Mutual Assistance. Furthermore, the 1997 EU Naples II Convention (Article 24),[11] the UN Convention against Transnational

---

[8] In some respects, the distinction between inner and outer JIT reflects the terms of the meso and micro levels of police cooperation proposed by Benyon. See J. Benyon, et al., 'Understanding Police Cooperation in Europe Setting a Framework for Analysis', in: M. Anderson and M. den Boer; *Policing Across National Boundaries*, London, Pinter Publishers, 1994, p. 46-65.

[9] While the leading Dutch police officers are explicitly named in the Amended Agreement on the Establishment of a Joint Investigation Team, the higher ranking British police officers are not mentioned. Nevertheless, they play an important role in the JIT as superiors of the seconded members and are in regular contact with their Dutch counterparts. In the same way, the Europol liaison officers are not mentioned in the agreement.

[10] The Europol liaison officers are not mentioned as members of the JIT in the Amended Agreement on the Establishment of a Joint Investigation Team. Nevertheless, they play an important role concerning the exchange of information between the United Kingdom and the Netherlands.

[11] Convention of 18 December 1997 on Mutual Assistance and Cooperation between Customs Administrations, *OJ* C 24, 23.01.1998, p. 2-22.

Organised Crime (TOC) (Article 19)[12] and the 2001 Council of Europe (CoE) 2nd Additional Protocol to the European Mutual Assistance Convention (Article 20)[13] provide a legal basis for operating a JIT as well.

The so-called 1997 *Naples II Convention* (on mutual assistance and cooperation between customs administrations) may be used as a vehicle for mutual assistance by traditional judicial authorities conducting a criminal investigation into domestic or Community customs offences. Article 24 of the Convention provides an explicit basis for the setting up of JITs, albeit in different, less far-reaching wording than in Article 13 of the EU Convention on Mutual Assistance. Standard – i.e., non-anticipated – entry into force of the Naples II Convention depends solely on notification by Italy, being the only one of the Member States constituting the EU at the time the Convention was adopted by the Council that has failed, to date, to submit the required notification (being a pre-Amsterdam Treaty Convention, notification by all fifteen then Member States is required for non-anticipated entry into force). Various states have made a declaration accepting anticipated entry into force.

Article 20 of the *2001 CoE 2nd Additional Protocol to the European Mutual Assistance Convention* is an integral transposition of Article 13 of the EU Convention on Mutual Assistance. This potentially makes the 2001 Protocol an equally maximized treaty basis for the setting up of JITs as the EU Convention on Mutual Assistance, save that it can apply between an even much wider group of countries than the latter could allow for. Ironically, of the countries involved in the JIT initiative(s) under the Netherlands EU Presidency 2004, only Bulgaria has ratified the Protocol, which has already entered into force (only three ratifications being required to that effect).

Article 19 of the *2000 UN TOC Convention* allows for the setting up of JITs to prevent and combat transnational organised crime. The Article has been drafted in a very open, vague, and therefore flexible manner and its wording is rather general. The Convention has entered into force between ratifying state parties: including Belgium, Bulgaria, and the Netherlands. To date, Germany and the United Kingdom have only signed the instrument.

The table below outlines to what extent the four treaties contain (potentially) self-executing provisions for the respective components of maximized JIT co-

---

[12] United Nations Convention against Transnational Organised Crime, 12-15 December 2000, UN Doc. A/45/49.

[13] Second Additional Protocol of 8 November 2001 to the European Convention on mutual assistance in criminal matters, CETS No. 182.

operation that, from a law-enforcement perspective, create added value compared to traditional mutual assistance in the context of parallel investigations.

Table 1: Self-executing treaty provisions for JIT components adding law enforcement value

	EU Convention on Mutual Assistance	1997 Naples II Convention	2001 2nd Additional Protocol	2000 UN TOC Convention
seconded members:				
- Legal basis	Article 13	Article 24	Article 20	Article 19
- right to be present	Y (unless refused)	no provision	Y (unless refused)	no provision
- right to carry out investigative measures	non-self-executing	rule: no such right	non-self-executing	rule: for full respect sovereignty
representatives of third countries international bodies:				
- right to be present	non-self-executing	no provision	non-self-executing	no provision
- right to carry out investigative measures	non-self-executing	no provision	non-self-executing	no provision
right to directly request investigative measures in home country	Y	no provision	Y	no provision
right to provide the JIT with information which is available in home country	non-self-executing	Y: spontaneous info. possible (Article 17)	non-self-executing	no provision
right to use information lawfully obtained in home country	Y	Y (Articles 18 + 19.7)	Y	no provision
JIT-obtained evidence to be used as evidence in home country	no sufficiently clear self-executing provision	non-self-executing (Articles 18 + 19.7)	no sufficiently clear self-executing provision	no provision
criminal and civil liability regulated	Y (Articles 15-16)	Y (Articles 19.5-6-8)	Y (Articles 21-22)	no provision
right to carry and use service weapons regulated	no provision	no provision	no provision	no provision

In this context, it is assumed that the added value of a JIT, from a law-enforcement perspective, mainly depends on the operability of the following components of maximized JIT cooperation:

a. Legal basis for the establishment of a JIT;
b. regarding the status and mandate of seconded members:
   i. whether they have the right to be present during the execution of investigative measures;
   ii. whether they have the right to carry out investigative measures;
c. regarding the status and mandate of representatives of third countries or international bodies:
   i. whether they have the right to be present during the execution of investigative measures;
   ii. whether they have the right to carry out investigative measures;
d. whether seconded members have the right to directly request investigative measures in their home country;
e. whether seconded members have the right to provide the JIT with information available in their home country;
f. whether seconded members have the right to use information lawfully obtained within the JIT in their home country;
g. whether evidence obtained within the JIT may be used as evidence in the home country of the seconded members;
h. whether the criminal and civil liability regarding seconded members or foreign representatives has been regulated;
i. whether the right for seconded members or foreign representatives to carry and use service weapons has been regulated.

These components will equally constitute the grid for the country assessments later in this chapter (section 4).

3.2 The legal framework of the instrument of a JIT

Since the early 1990s, police and judicial cooperation in criminal matters is one of the areas within the European Union that has gained a constant flow of attention. After the introduction of the three pillar structure, when justice and home affairs was brought under the umbrella of the European Union, cautious steps were taken in the beginning to create a common EU policy in this field. Later on, a vast number of documents, both binding and non-binding, were produced in order to create a solid policy regulating police and judicial cooperation in criminal matters. In several of these documents, reference is made to joint investigation teams. Article 29 of the Treaty of Amsterdam states that the area of freedom, security, and justice within the EU must be achieved through preventing and combating crime, organised or otherwise. This treaty further states in Article 30 that, for the promotion of cooperation through Europol, Europol must be enabled to facilitate and support, among other things, operational actions of joint teams. The idea of joint teams was further elaborated during the European Council in Tampere, Finland, on 15 and 16 October 1999.

On that occasion, a first step towards the possibility to use the instrument of a JIT was taken. Conclusion No. 43 called for 'joint investigative teams to be set up without delay, as a first step, to combat trafficking in drugs and human beings as well as terrorism.' Finally, the instrument was worked out in more detail in a legally binding instrument namely in Article 13 of the EU Convention on Mutual Assistance in Criminal Matters (EU Convention on Mutual Assistance).

Only a few days after the attacks of 11 September 2001, a proposal for a draft Framework Decision on Joint Investigation Teams was presented. During the extraordinary Council Meeting on Justice, Home Affairs, and Civil Protection of 20 September 2001, it was stated that 'the seriousness of recent events has led the Union to speed up the process of creating an area of freedom, security and justice and to step up cooperation with its partners, especially the United States.'[14] To this end, the Council had to adopt various measures, including the Framework Decision on JITs.[15] The aim of this initiative was to provide an alternative for the use of the instrument of the JIT as the EU Convention on Mutual Assistance had not yet entered into force at that time owing to the delay in ratifying this convention. In the Preamble to the Framework Decision, it is clearly stated that JITs must be considered a welcome instrument to achieve a high level of safety within an area of freedom, security, and justice by combating crime through closer cooperation. The initial proposal limited the operation of joint investigation teams, in accordance with the Tampere conclusions, to three types of crimes, namely: trafficking in drugs, trafficking in human beings, and terrorism. Apart from that restraint, it reproduced Articles 13, 15, and 16 of the EU Convention on Mutual Assistance dealing with joint investigation teams. The only change made to the final text was a deletion of the limitation to the three crimes in the articles although it is still present in the Preamble under point 6. Because the Framework Decision is an exact copy of Article 13 (and Articles 15 and 16), the comments on this article below equally hold true for the provisions in the Framework Decision. The corresponding provisions in the Framework Decision will be placed between brackets.

According to paragraph 1 of Article 13 (Article 1 paragraph 1 Framework Decision), a JIT must be established by mutual agreement between two or more Member States of the EU. The aim of such a team must be the execution of

---

[14] Extraordinary Council Meeting, Justice, Home Affairs and Civil Protection, Brussels, 20 September 2001, 12019/01 (Press 327), p. 4.

[15] Framework Decision of 13 June 2002 on Joint Investigation Teams, *OJ* L 162, 20.06.2002, p. 1.

criminal investigations in one or more of the Member States setting up the team. The agreement is an important document because it must explicate the specific purpose of the team as well as the expected period and the composition thereof. A model agreement for a JIT was adopted as a Council Recommendation on 8 May 2003.[16]

Paragraph 1 further implies that the establishment of a JIT will be preceded by a request by one of the Member States. Although it does not indicate how and by whom such a request must be made, whether it can be done orally, and does not directly refer to a request for mutual assistance, paragraph 2 of Article 13 (Article 1 paragraph 2 Framework Decision) refers to Article 14 of the European Mutual Assistance Convention which deals with requests for mutual assistance. Therefore, the term 'request' in paragraph 1 must be considered as a request for mutual assistance and the general requirements from the European Mutual Assistance Convention for making such a request must be met. Furthermore, such a request must contain proposals for the composition of the team. The decision on the location of the team is important as the team will act in accordance with the law where it operates.[17] It is logical that the team is located in the state where the major part of the investigations will take place. Furthermore, the leader of the team must be a representative of the competent authority of the state where the team operates.[18] Because JITs will be mainly initiated in more complex cases in which more countries are involved, it is not clear from the onset from which country the team leader must be chosen when more states are involved. It is likely that more team leaders will be nominated and that each of them takes the lead for those operations taking place in their own country and that the coordination is done by the team leaders together. When, during the existence of the team, the focus of the investigations moves from one state to another, it must be possible to move the team to the other state and to nominate a team leader from that Member State. Members of the team who originate from other Member States than the state in which the team operates are referred to as seconded members.[19] However, this qualification seems superfluous as a person who is a seconded member for one operation can be a member in another operation, namely, when that operation takes place on the territory of his

---

[16] Recommendation of the Council of 8 May 2003 on a model agreement on the establishment of a JIT. This recommendation also includes an annex with a model agreement for the involvement of Europol, Eurojust, and/or OLAF, *OJ* C 121, 23.05.2003, p. 1.

[17] Article 13(3)b EU Convention on Mutual Assistance, Article 1(3)b Framework Decision on JITs.

[18] Article 13(3)a EU Convention on Mutual Assistance, Article 1(3)a Framework Decision on JITs.

[19] Article 13(4) EU Convention on Mutual Assistance, Article 1(4) Framework Decision on JITs.

home country. Following these implications, it is important that the instrument is used in a flexible way.

With regard to the operational powers of the seconded members, Article 13 states that they are entitled to be present when investigative measures are taken in the Member State of operation, unless decided otherwise by the team leader.[20] Any decision to exclude a seconded member from being present may not be based on the sole fact that the member is a foreigner. The team leader takes the decisions in accordance with the law of the Member State where the team operates. The team leader may also decide that seconded members will be entrusted with tasks of taking certain investigative measures.[21] Such an operation takes place in accordance with the law of the Member State where the team operates and must be approved by both the Member State of operation and the seconding Member State. Preferably such approval is included in the agreement establishing the team or it may be granted at a later stage. It may also apply in general terms or it may be restricted to specific cases or circumstances.[22] This will require an extensive knowledge of the law of the state in which the team operates. It is therefore important that seconded members are sufficiently educated in the law of the state of operation as well as the other states participating in the JIT as they are potential places of operation. Instead of executing the investigative measures themselves in their home countries, seconded members may ask their colleagues to take those measures. According to paragraph 7 of Article 13 (Article 1 paragraph 7 Framework Decision), '[t]hose measures shall be considered in that Member State under the conditions which would apply if they were requested in a national investigation'. The consequence of this provision is that information from such a measure will be directly available for the JIT and be used in further investigations by that team irrespective of the country where the investigation took place. The fact that, in this case, information can be shared without any formalities is based on the principle of mutual trust between the members of the JIT. Although it is often considered that this mutual trust is present between the Member States of the European Union, there is a need to strengthen this mutual trust.[23] When information or any other assis-

---

[20] Article 13(5) EU Convention on Mutual Assistance, Article 1(5) Framework Decision on JITs.

[21] Article 13(6) EU Convention on Mutual Assistance, Article 1(6) Framework Decision on JITs.

[22] Explanatory report on the Convention of 29 May 2000 on Mutual Assistance in Criminal Matters between the Member States of the EU, *OJ* C 379, 29.12.2000, p. 18.

[23] That mutual trust has to be strengthened especially with regard to further and closer cooperation within the EU follows from the Communication on the mutual recognition of judicial decisions in criminal matters and the strengthening of mutual trust between Member States, Brussels, 19.05.2005, COM(2005) 195 final.

tance is required from a EU Member State not participating in the JIT or from a third country, the general procedures on mutual assistance must be used. Such a request must be made by the competent authorities of the state of operation. Although paragraph 8 does not indicate that the assistance provided by the requested state will be used in the JIT, it seems obvious to explicate in the request that the information requested is to be used in a JIT and in which states participate in the JIT concerned. Then the requested state knows that the assistance provided may be shared with other states, and with which other states. If the number of participating states in the JIT is enlarged in the course of its duties, the providing state must again be requested for its approval to share the information with these new states. To avoid the procedure that the providing state's approval must be asked time and time again it would be easier to adopt a general clause in a request for mutual assistance indicating that the information can be used by the JIT regardless of its composition. When applying paragraph 9 (Article 1 paragraph 9 Framework Decision) this has to be taken into account as well. According to this paragraph, members of a JIT may, in accordance with their national law and within the limits of their competence, provide the team with information available in their country. This paragraph only refers to members of a JIT but, according to the explanatory report, this equally holds true for seconded members. Information obtained by the members and seconded members of the JIT may be used: a) for the purpose for which the team has been set up, b) for detecting, investigating, and prosecuting other criminal offences with the prior consent of the Member State where the information became available, c) for preventing an immediate and serious threat to public security, and d) for other purposes to the extent that this is agreed between the Member States setting up the team. This paragraph may also concern information which became available through a letter of request as explicated before. This means that this information may be used for detecting, investigating, and prosecuting other offences with the prior consent of that Member State (Article 13 paragraph 10(b) EU Convention on Mutual Assistance and Article 1 paragraph 10(b) Framework Decision). However, this paragraph limits the possibility for the providing state to object to further use. It states that consent may only be withheld in cases where such use would endanger criminal investigations in the Member State concerned (the providing state) or in respect of which that Member State could refuse mutual assistance. While paragraph 8 also concerns information obtained from a third state, paragraph 10(b) only covers the consent of the Member State where the information became available. Therefore, it is not clear whether this clause can be used against third states as well. It seems to be strange that states participating in a JIT may dictate to a third state what limitations it has to take into account, but this seems to be the consequence of the way this provision is drafted. Furthermore, if the information concerned was provided by a witness solely for the purposes for which the team was set up, the consent of the witness is required if the evidence is to be used for other purposes, except in the event of a situation referred to under c or d, i.e., preventing an immediate and serious threat to public security or previous agreement between the Member States setting up the team.

Although paragraph 11 (Article 1 paragraph 11 Framework Decision) indicates that this article is without prejudice to any other existing provision or arrangement on JITs, it does not exclude the possibility that this article can be used as a guidance for creating a JIT in relations between Member States.
Finally, paragraph 12 (Article 1 paragraph 12 Framework Decision) concerns the participation of persons other than representatives of the competent authorities of the Member States setting up the joint investigation team. When this participation has a legal basis, such arrangements can be agreed upon. The legal basis can either be sought in national legislation or other instruments. Examples of such persons may be appropriate persons from other states and representatives of, for instance, Europol and Eurojust. An example of an agreement between a JIT and such persons was provided by the Council.[24] These persons take a position which is different from the members and the seconded members and the rights conferred upon them by Article 13 do not apply to these persons unless the agreement expressly states otherwise.

The text of Article 13 and thus of the Framework Decision is rather informal as most important issues, such as, the competence of JIT members, can be arranged in an agreement. Depending on the implementation laws, this might leave great discretionary competence for the authorities involved in a JIT.

3.2.1 *The involvement of Europol*

Even where the domestic legislation of countries allows representatives of Europol and Eurojust to take part in JIT activities, it must be borne in mind that, at least for Europol officials (unlike Eurojust representatives, see below), formal and lawful participation in JITs is dependent on the entry into force of the November 2002 Protocol amending the Europol Convention.[25] The Protocol

---

[24] Recommendation of the Council of 8 May 2003 on a model agreement on the establishment of a JIT. This recommendation also includes an annex with a model agreement for the involvement of Europol, Eurojust and/or OLAF, *OJ* C 121, 23.05.2003, p. 1.

[25] Council Act of 28 November 2002 drawing up a Protocol amending the Convention on the establishment of a European Police Office (Europol Convention) and the Protocol on the privileges and immunities of Europol, the members of its organs, the deputy directors and the employees of Europol, *OJ* C 312, 16.12.2002.

requires notification by all Member States that had EU-membership status at the time it was adopted by the Council. So far, only four of the then fifteen Member States have done so. Ironically, nine out of the ten new Member States have already submitted the required notification. Upon its entry into force, the 2002 Protocol[26] (inserting an Article 3a on JIT participation in the Europol Convention) will enable Europol officials, albeit of course within the – most probably stricter – limits provided for by the law of the Member State where the JIT team operates, to assist in all JIT activities. However, it will not be allowed for Europol staff to take part in the taking of any coercive measures, not even where domestic legislation would allow them to do so. Further, the 2002 Protocol waives the traditional immunity of Europol officials taking part in a JIT (Article 2 Protocol) and properly regulates criminal and civil liability (Articles 3a, paragraph 6, and 39a Europol Convention) regarding possible JIT participation by Europol staff.

In particular as regards information exchange, the Protocol will enable Europol officials to liaise directly with JIT members and provide them (i.e., both members and seconded members) with information from any of the three components of the Europol computer system, in accordance with the Europol Convention. In the case of such direct information exchange, the Europol National Units (ENUs) of the Member States represented in the JIT as well as the Member State(s) having provided the information must be notified thereof by Europol. It must be noted that, until the Protocol takes effect, Europol officials may not directly exchange information with the JIT members. All Europol advice, strategic or technical advice, facilitation of information exchange or help with crime analysis must be channelled through the respective ENUs of the JIT states – in line with the Convention and the November 2000 Council Recommendation with respect to Europol's assistance to JITs. Unlike the retrieval of data from Analytical Work Files (AWFs), requiring the agreement of the analysis group, the retrieval of data from the general Europol information system may take place – again through the ENUs – without prior authorisation.

Still, several lawful indirect solutions may be found for a JIT to already liaise more or less directly with Europol, thus overcoming the mandatory detour via the ENUs. ENU officials may be appointed as JIT members themselves, making the JIT a direct recipient of Europol information. JIT countries may also decide to integrate (some of) their national liaison officers(s) at Europol – who are not Europol staff but remain national police staff – into the JIT. In doing so, a direct link with Europol can be secured: the liaison officers have direct access

---

[26] Protocol of 28 November 2002 amending the Convention on the establishment of a European Police Office (Europol Convention) and the Protocol on the privileges and immunities of Europol, the members of its organs, the deputy directors and the employees of Europol.

to the Europol information system and may also take part in analysis groups on behalf of their home countries. The latter is also possible for the national police experts of the various countries for whom it would be equally possible to take part in a JIT working on the basis of the AWF outcome. As concerns liaison officers or national experts being part of the analysis group, general agreement by the analysis group will remain necessary for them to be allowed to take AWF information directly to the JIT in which they take part. It should be stressed that each of the above scenarios for bypassing the otherwise mandatory ENU detour involves JIT participation only by representatives of the JIT countries' national police forces (Europol liaison officers, ENU representatives or national police experts) and not by actual Europol officials. The latter's genuine participation in JITs will only be possible, as was indicated before, following the entry info force of the 2002 Protocol.

3.2.2 Involvement of Eurojust

As regards Eurojust, the situation seems a little less complex. According to the February 2000 Eurojust decision, it is up to the Member States to define the right of their respective national members to act in relation to foreign judicial authorities (Article 9 paragraph 3). In cases where a state has chosen to allow its national member to fully retain its capacity of judicial (or equivalent) authority under domestic law, nothing prevents appointing that member to participate in a JIT as a judicial authority acting on the basis of its national law. Such a Eurojust JIT member clearly does not represent Eurojust as such in the team. He or she is to be seen as an ordinary JIT member or seconded JIT member, who happens to also have another capacity within Eurojust. JIT participation by Eurojust national members acting on the basis of their national law will therefore not be influenced by a possible lack of permission for or restrictions regarding Eurojust participation in the domestic legislation of one of the states constituting the JIT. Obviously, the latter will be the case when it comes to genuine participation by a Eurojust staff member officially representing Eurojust as a college.

3.2.3 Legal implications for the Member States

The EU Convention on Mutual Assistance entered into force on 23 August 2005 and is now in force for eighteen Member States.[27] This means that, in these countries, implementation law must be in force. For the states that have not yet

---

[27] It has entered into force for Austria, Belgium, Cyprus, Denmark, Estonia, Finland, France, Germany, Hungary, Lithuania, Latvia, the Netherlands, Poland, Portugal, Slovenia, Spain, Sweden, and the United Kingdom.

ratified the convention the establishment of a JIT might be based on the Framework Decision if they have implemented the Framework Decision properly. According to the Framework Decision on joint investigation teams (the core text of which has been literally copied from Articles 13, 15, and 16 of the EU Convention on Mutual Assistance), the EU Member States must transpose into national law the obligations imposed on them under the Framework Decision. Unlike treaties or conventions, the Framework Decision in itself cannot produce any direct effect. Therefore, strictly speaking, it cannot be used as an autonomous international legal basis for the establishment of JITs. This means that, in the absence of an applicable JIT treaty basis, the extent to which JITs can be operated entirely depends on the degree to which the countries have created a legal basis for the various components of maximized JIT cooperation (as meant in the EU Convention on Mutual Assistance or the Framework Decision) in their domestic legislation.

Although Members States were called upon to take the necessary measures to implement the provisions in the Framework Decision by 1 January 2003, and later by June 2004, many states have not yet adopted implementing legislation.[28] The legal obligations for states following the adoption of a Framework Decision in general and the consequences of not implementing a Framework Decision are explicated below. Afterwards it can be assessed to what extent the Member States participating in the THB-JIT project have fulfilled their implementation obligations as regards JITs under EU law.

As stated above, in general a Framework Decision cannot have direct effect. Consequently, the 2002 Framework Decision cannot be used as an autonomous international legal basis for the establishment of JITs. This means that, in the absence of an applicable JIT treaty basis, the extent to which JITs can be operated entirely depends on the degree to which the countries have created a legal basis for the various components of maximized JIT cooperation (as meant in the EU Convention on Mutual Assistance, the 2002 Framework Decision or the 2001 CoE 2nd Additional Protocol) in their domestic legislation.

In accordance with Article 34(2) Treaty on European Union (EU Treaty), a Framework Decision is similar to a directive of the first pillar, since it is binding as regards the result to be achieved for the Member States. The Member States are free to choose the form and measures used to achieve the result. The difference with the directive is that a Framework Decision does not have direct effect. This

---

[28] For an overview of the extent to which the Member States of the EU have implemented this Framework Decision, see the Report from the Commission on national measures taken to comply with the Council Framework Decision of 13 June 2002 on Joint Investigation Teams, Commission of the European Communities, 7.01.2005 COM(2004) 858.

means that individuals cannot directly invoke the provisions of a Framework Decision. The freedom to choose the form and measures is identical for directives and Framework Decisions and therefore the interpretation given to this freedom with regard to directives can be equally applied to the interpretation of Framework Decisions. With regard to this freedom to choose, it must be said that this only means that a Member State has a discretionary competence to decide on the kind of measures to be taken. To some extent, the content of the directive, and therefore of the Framework Decision, is already determined by the text of the instrument concerned.[29] The Member State may decide on the authority which is competent to adopt implementing measures, although it is determined that the implementing rules must be legally binding.[30] There are roughly two implementation techniques, namely, the adoption of national implementation rules and provisions which refer to an adopted directive.[31] Both the directive and the Framework Decision attribute the freedom to choose the form for implementation to the national authorities. Neither Article 249 EC Treaty nor Article 34(2) EU Treaty specify what authorities have to adopt implementing measures. It is dependent on the constitutional division of powers and this remains the autonomy of the Member State concerned as long as it implements the directive 'by means of national provisions of a binding nature'. Or, to use the words of Prechal, '[t]hus the choice of the measures, like the choice of the competent authority, is made within the framework of national constitutional law.'[32] The European Court of Justice (ECJ) has developed case law on several requirements that must be fulfilled in order to meet the implementation test. These requirements are: full effect, legal certainty, the binding nature of the measures, specificity, precision, and clarity.

A Member State may argue that it already fulfils its obligation of implementation by existing legislation. This is not rejected by the ECJ *per se* although the Court is rather reluctant to accept it. With regard to already existing legislation, Capotorti states the following:

> The content of national legislation in force is capable of achieving entirely the result laid down by a directive. It seems to us that in such cases the creation of new

---

[29] S. Prechal, *Directives in EC Law*, Second edition, Oxford, Oxford University Press, 2005, p. 73.

[30] S. Prechal, *Directives in EC Law*, Second edition, Oxford, Oxford University Press, 2005, p. 81-85.

[31] F. Capotorti, 'Legal Problems of Directives, Regulations and their Implementation', in H. Siedentopf and J. Ziller, *Making European Policies Work, The Implementation of Community Legislation in the Member States*, EIPA, Brussels, Bruylant – Sage Publications, 1988, p. 160-163.

[32] S. Prechal, *Directives in EC Law*, Second edition, Oxford, Oxford University Press, 1995, p. 88.

implementation provisions is not necessary. The remarkable phenomenon, which is then verified, is that the earlier provisions undergo a formal transformation: they become provisions 'bound' by the Community obligation to give effect to the directive (with subsequent consequences that can be imagined regarding the difficulty of changing its content).[33]

There seems to be less room for such implementation when the provisions of a directive or Framework Decision are detailed and precise, as it is not likely that existing legislation fully covers the content of the directive or the Framework Decision. If such an instrument contains more general wording, such implementation is accepted more easily.[34] If we apply these rules for the Framework Decision on joint investigation teams, it must be concluded that it cannot be categorised as a precise nor as a general instrument. The main aim of the Framework Decision, namely, the establishment of JITs, is very general and liable to multiple interpretations. This suggests that the way a JIT is executed leaves wide possibilities for national legislators and that the implementation of this part can be done in more general terms. On the other hand, as follows from the above, some items are elaborated upon in more detail which imposes an obligation on Member States to implement the Framework Decision in more detail.

If a Member State has not implemented a directive in time, the possibility for consistent interpretation exists. This means that a national rule on the same matter must be interpreted in conformity with the directive. This is a way to give effect to a directive which has not been transposed into national legislation in time. The ECJ has based the consistent interpretation in the first pillar on the binding force of the instrument in conformity with Article 249 EC Treaty, on the one hand, and the principle of community faith, on the other (Article 10 EC Treaty). Since the ECJ has applied the theory on the consistent interpretation in third pillar issues in the *Pupino* case,[35] the Court has concluded that the principle of loyal cooperation as a principle analogical to Community faith must be applied in third pillar issues as well, otherwise consistent interpretation cannot be established. In consideration 42, the Court states that the principle of Community faith must be equally applied in third pillar issues through the principle of loyal cooperation.

---

[33] F. Capotorti, 'Legal Problems of Directives, Regulations and their Implementation', in H. Siedentopf and J. Ziller, *Making European Policies Work, The Implementation of Community Legislation in the Member States*, EIPA, Brussels, Bruylant and Sage Publications, 1988, p. 161.
[34] S. Prechal, *Directives in EC Law*, Second edition, Oxford, Oxford University Press, 2005, p. 78.
[35] European Court of Justice, Case C-105/03, 16 June 2005.

It would be difficult for the Union to carry out its task effectively if the principle of loyal cooperation, requiring in particular that Member States take all appropriate measures, whether general or particular, to ensure fulfilment of their obligations under European Union law, were not also binding in the area of police and judicial cooperation in criminal matters, which is moreover entirely based on cooperation between the Member States and the institutions, as the Advocate General has rightly pointed out in paragraph 26 of her Opinion.

This means that, besides the obligation based on Article 34(2) to implement a Framework Decision, a more general obligation to comply with the content of the Framework Decision can be based on the principle of loyal cooperation.

Because the EU Convention on Mutual Assistance has now entered into force, it serves as the basis for countries party to the Convention and for those that have adopted minimal, partial, or limited transposition or implementation into national law, of the obligations imposed by the Framework Decision or of the related provisions of the EU Convention on Mutual Assistance. For the provisions in the Convention to be applied directly in these states, these components of JIT cooperation acquire direct effect as a result of the self-executing character of some of the provisions contained in the Convention providing a basis for setting up JITs. However, countries will only be able to operate the components of JIT cooperation for which they have created an explicit legal basis in their domestic legislation.

4. TO WHAT EXTENT HAS THE LEGAL FRAMEWORK ON JITS PROPERLY BEEN IMPLEMENTED IN THE PARTICIPATING MEMBER STATES?

Now that the obligations under the relevant EU law have been identified, we will take a closer look at the way the Member States participating in the THB-JIT project have implemented the applicable provision.

4.1 Belgium

In Belgium the new *Mutual Assistance Act* was adopted on 9 December 2004 and it entered into force on 3 January 2005, after having been published on 24 December 2004.[36] This Act contains the implementing legislation for the EU Convention on Mutual Assistance in criminal matters, including Article 13 on

---

[36] Wet van 9 december 2004 betreffende de wederzijdse internationale rechtshulp in strafzaken en tot wijziging van artikel 90ter van het Wetboek van Strafvordering, *B.S.* 24 December 2004.

joint investigation teams. Consequently, the Act has a wider scope than the mere implementation of the European instruments on joint investigation teams.

The Belgian law has limited the participants in a joint investigation team to those states that are party to an international instrument that is binding on Belgium and that provides for the establishment of joint investigation teams.[37]
In contrast to the Framework Decision, the law does not limit the cases in which a joint investigation team can be set up, nor does it contain any additional guidelines providing model cases in which a joint investigation team should be established.

a. Legal basis

According to Article 8(1), JITs may only be established to conduct criminal investigations in accordance with the provisions of the *international legal instruments* that apply, and may be composed only of members originating from state parties to an *international legal instrument* that is also binding on Belgium and provides the possibility of establishing such joint investigation teams. The explanatory memorandum to the bill makes it clear that *only a treaty or a bilateral agreement* that explicitly includes rules on the practice of joint investigation teams, the composition of the team, and the territory on which it operates *qualifies as an 'international legal instrument'*, which should be the basis of any joint investigation team.[38]

Notwithstanding such strict treaty requirements for the establishment of a JIT, there is considerable flexibility as to what treaty may legally underpin the setting up of a JIT. At present, apart from the EU Convention on Mutual Assistance, also the 1997 EU Naples II Convention, the 2000 UN TOC Convention,[39] and the 2001 CoE 2nd Additional Protocol to the European Mutual Assistance Convention qualify as valid legal bases, provided they apply between Belgium and the states that also have members in the JIT concerned.

This means that, according to the explanatory memorandum, strictly speaking, the Framework Decision on JITs cannot be a legal basis for establishing a JIT because the Framework Decision is neither a treaty nor a bilateral agreement.

---

[37] Article 8(1), Wet van 9 december 2004 betreffende de wederzijdse internationale rechtshulp in strafzaken en tot wijziging van artikel 90ter van het Wetboek van Strafvordering, *B.S.* 24 December 2004

[38] Kamer, 1278/001, Wetsontwerp betreffende internationale rechtshulp in strafzaken (Legislative proposal on international legal assistance in criminal matters), 19 November 2004.

[39] It entered into force for Belgium on 10 September, *B.S.*, 13 October 2004.

The wording of the Act, however, indicates the opposite, namely, that the Framework Decision is a suitable legal basis as it must be considered an international legal instrument.

b. Status and mandate of seconded members

i. The right to be present during the execution of investigative measures

In principle, seconded JIT members have the right to be present during the execution of investigative measures on Belgian territory. As an exception to this rule, the magistrate having the authority over the team while it is operating in Belgium, i.e., the team leader, may decide otherwise for particular investigative measures (Article 9(2) second sentence).

ii. The right to carry out investigative tasks

Further, when the team is operating on Belgian territory, seconded JIT members are allowed to carry out *any* judicial police task in conformity with Belgian law, provided they are accompanied by a Belgian official having the capacity of an *officer* of the judicial police and act under the leadership of the latter (Article 9(1) and (2) first sentence). The said 'judicial police tasks' encompass, *inter alia*, the detection and investigation of punishable acts, the gathering of evidence, the seizure of evidence or the proceeds of crime, the tracing and apprehension of suspects, all, of course, under the terms of Belgian law, as well as the drafting of official reports. Seconded JIT members are thus fully assimilated with Belgian police officials and may even perform actions reserved to officers of the judicial police. The sole – albeit important – precondition for the said full assimilation is that they may not act independently but must always be *accompanied* by a Belgian official with the capacity of an officer of the judicial police, the overall authority of the Belgian magistrate acting as the team leader being unaffected (Article 9(2)).

c. Status and mandate of representatives of third countries or international bodies

In the written agreement that must be concluded prior to the establishment of a JIT with the other participating countries (see Article 8(4)), it may be stipulated that representatives of non-participating countries and of Eurojust, Europol, or OLAF be joined to the JIT as *experts* (Article 9(3) first sentence).

i. The right to be present during the execution of investigative measures

Unlike that of seconded members, the right to be present during the execution of investigative measures on Belgian territory is dependent on the approval of the team leader (Article 9(3) second sentence).

ii. The right to carry out investigative tasks

They may not carry out any investigative task (Article 9(3) second sentence).

d. The right of seconded members to directly request investigative measures in the home country

Belgian seconded JIT members, when operating in another state, may request the competent Belgian authorities to perform investigative measures on Belgian territory. The Belgian authorities will deal with this request in the same manner as if it were made in the context of a domestic investigation (Article 10(1)).

e. The right of seconded members to provide the JIT with information that is available in the home country

For the purpose of the criminal investigations conducted by the JIT, Belgian seconded members may, in conformity with Belgian law, provide the JIT with information they can access in the context of a domestic investigation (Article 10(2)).

f. The right to use information lawfully obtained within the JIT in the home country

The information which a Belgian seconded member gathers in another state in the context of his participation in the JIT and in accordance with the law of that state, may be used for the same purposes as set out in paragraph 10 of Article 13 of the EU Convention on Mutual Assistance or Article 1 paragraph 10 of the 2002 Framework Decision on JITs (Article 10(3)).

g. The right to use evidence obtained within the JIT as evidence in the home country

In the final version of the new Mutual Assistance Act, the provision on evidence obtained abroad (Article 13) can make a real difference in practice, *including but not solely in the context of Belgian participation in a JIT*. In line with consistent Belgian jurisprudence the legislator has chosen to define criteria for the mandatory exclusion of evidence obtained abroad instead of spelling out under what conditions such evidence is acceptable. Evidence illegally obtained abroad may not be used in a Belgian court. Evidence the use of which would constitute a violation of the right to a fair trial is also excluded irrespective of whether it was obtained abroad or domestically. Summarising, the new provision mirrors the *forum regit actum* rule in the context of mutual assistance, embedded in Article 4 of the EU Convention on Mutual Assistance, in pointing out that evidence obtained abroad will generally not be tested for conformity with Belgian procedural criminal law. It suffices that it was obtained in conformity with the law of the state where it was gathered or, most probably, even in violation of a formality or procedural rule which, according to the law of the latter state, is not deemed sufficiently fundamental to result in nullity in case of non-observance. This seems to be quite a lenient rule and Belgian JIT members must surely bear it in mind.

Finally, as far as evidence lawfully obtained in Belgium by foreign JIT members is concerned, it should be recalled that foreign team members, as a result of their full assimilation with Belgian police officials, may draw up official reports and documents under Belgian law, which therefore will have the same evidential value as if drawn up by Belgian officials.

h. *Criminal and civil liability regarding seconded members or foreign representatives*

Article 12 of the new Mutual Assistance Act regulates, in full conformity with the provisions embedded in the EU Convention on Mutual Assistance (Articles 15-16) and the 2002 Framework Decision on JITs (Articles 2-3), criminal and civil liability regarding all foreign officials whose presence on Belgian territory is allowed, i.e., including seconded JIT members and other foreign representatives in such teams.

The provision applies even where potentially valid JIT treaty bases remain silent on the matter of liabilities regarding officials present abroad, such as the 2000 UN TOC Convention, as well as in any other situation of the legitimate presence of foreign officials on Belgian territory, e.g., as a liaison officer or in the context of the execution of traditional letters rogatory.

i. *The right of seconded members or foreign representatives to carry and use service weapons*

Belgium has chosen to regulate the right of seconded members or foreign representatives in a JIT to carry and use service weapons. Surprisingly, for example, the 1990 Schengen Implementation Convention, in the event of cross-border observation or hot pursuit (Article 40(3) under d, and 41(5) under e), and neither the EU Convention on Mutual Assistance nor the 2002 Framework Decision on joint investigation teams contain provisions on this matter. In this way, it is not necessary for each JIT to obtain *ad hoc* individual licences to possess and carry guns for seconded and/or other foreign officials in accordance with the normal domestic standards.

In its new Mutual Assistance Act, Belgium has chosen not only to regulate criminal and civil liability (*supra*) regarding all foreign officials whose presence on Belgian territory is allowed (including seconded JIT members and other foreign representatives in such teams), but also their right to carry and use service weapons (Article 11). Foreign officials may carry their official service weapons under the same conditions as Belgian police officials (assimilation). The actual use of these service weapons, however, has been limited to situations of legitimate defence of oneself or another, in line with Belgian legislation on the matter.

Again, as for liability matters, the related provision applies in any situation of the legitimate presence of foreign officials on Belgian territory, even where international legal instruments regulating such presence contain no provisions on the matter.

4.2 Germany

Germany has recently adopted legislation to implement the EU Convention on Mutual Assistance. This legislation led to the amendment of the *Gesetz über die Internationale Rechtshilfe in Strafsachen in der Fassung der Bekanntmachung vom 27. Juni 1994 (IRG)*.[40] Four new paragraphs were adopted, namely, on the transfer of data without request (§61a and §83j), audiovisual interrogation (§61b), and a section on 'other legal assistance', including a paragraph on joint investigation teams (§83k).

a. Legal basis

The text of paragraph 83k IRG does not contain any provisions on whether a treaty is required as a basis for operating a JIT. Indirectly, however, given the minimalistic character of Article 83k without providing a self-standing domestic legal basis for the establishment of a JIT, it is clear that it will not be possible to operate a JIT without an applicable treaty regulating this establishment. Support is also found in the explanatory memorandum to the bill,[41] mentioning – in a non-limitative fashion – both the EU Convention on Mutual Assistance and

---

[40] BGBl. I S. 1537.
[41] *Bundesrat*, Drucksache 723/04, 23.09.04, p. 11.

the 1997 Naples II Convention as potential JIT bases. Article 83k IRG appears to have been designed in a manner that will provide the required minimal domestic complement for Germany to be able to apply international treaties allowing for the setting up of JITs. In their turn, as the explanatory memorandum indirectly indicates,[42] the JIT provisions, provided they have been implemented and thus have become part of German national law, will supersede the provisions of the new Article 83k, wholly in line with Article 1, paragraph 3 IRG.

Given the fact that the explanatory memorandum does not limit the potentially valid treaty bases for setting up a JIT to the EU Convention on Mutual Assistance and the 1997 Naples II Convention only, it can be concluded that the 2000 UN TOC Convention and the 2001 CoE 2nd Additional Protocol to the 1959 European Mutual Assistance Convention may also qualify. Germany has submitted the required notification for the 1997 Naples II Convention under acceptance of its anticipated entry into force. It has not ratified the 2000 UN TOC Convention nor the 2001 CoE 2nd Additional Protocol. It cannot be anticipated whether ratification of the latter treaties is envisaged in the near future.

b. *Status and mandate of seconded members*

i. *The right to be present during the execution of investigative measures*

According to the explanatory memorandum to the implementation bill,[43] the right to be present for seconded members during the execution of investigative measures does not require new domestic provisions, the possibility to allow for the presence of foreign officials in the context of the execution of letters rogatory already being provided for under German criminal procedural law. When a JIT is based on a treaty other than either the EU Convention on Mutual Assistance or the 2001 CoE 2nd Additional Protocol (Article 13(5) and Article 20 respectively, being self-executing provisions, may have direct effect), a traditional request will still need to be received and granted by the German competent authorities, in accordance with Article 4 of the 1959 European Convention, in order for seconded members to be allowed to be present during the execution of investigative measures on German soil.

---

[42] *Idem*, stating that, as the 1997 Naples II Convention excludes the exercise of investigative powers by foreign JIT members, the provision of Article 83k, paragraph 1 IRG, providing the possibility to entrust the carrying out of investigative measures to seconded JIT members from other EU Member States, will remain a dead letter.

[43] *Bundesrat*, Drucksache 723/04, 23.09.04, p. 10.

ii. The right to carry out investigative tasks

Article 83k, paragraph 1, IRG restricts the possibility to entrust foreign JIT members with the carrying out of investigative measures to seconded officials from *EU Member States only*. The implementation legislation has clearly been drafted for primary use within the remit of the EU (aiming at allowing for ratification of the EU Convention on Mutual Assistance). However, nothing excludes participation in JITs by non-EU officials, albeit that they cannot be entrusted with the execution of investigative measures.

Unlike paragraph 5, paragraph 6 of Article 13 of the EU Convention on Mutual Assistance (mirrored in Article 20 of the 2001 CoE 2nd Additional Protocol) has been properly implemented in Article 83k(1) IRG. The provision is meant to introduce into German law the possibility to entrust the carrying out of investigative measures, under the leadership of the competent German officials, to JIT members that have been seconded by other EU Member States, provided the latter have permitted them to do so. No further limitations apply as to the type of measures they may be allowed to execute.

According to the explanatory memorandum, the provision will remain a dead letter for Germany where the underlying JIT treaty basis would be the Naples II Convention, which is said to exclude the possibility for foreign JIT members to carry out any investigative measures. It can be doubted, however, whether this is true. Article 24(3) of the Naples II Convention merely states that 'membership of the team shall not bestow on officers any powers of intervention in the territory of another state', which does prevent domestic law from bestowing such powers on them, as Article 83k(1) IRG seems to do.

The sole limitation is that the execution of investigative measures may not be entrusted to foreign team members seconded by non-EU Member States – which, in itself, does not exclude the participation of such members in a JIT operating in Germany.

c. Status and mandate of representatives of third countries or international bodies

Both Article 13 of the EU Convention on Mutual Assistance and Article 1 of the 2002 Framework Decision, in paragraph 12, make JIT participation by representatives of third countries or international bodies dependent on explicit permission, therefore in the laws of the Member States constituting the JIT or in a legal instrument applicable between them. The German legislation, in Article 83k(2), IRG, provides this possibility: persons other than those meant in paragraph 1 may be permitted to participate in a JIT, in accordance with the legal provisions of the JIT Member States or an agreement which is applicable between them. *A contrario*, given the fact that, on the basis of Article 83k(1), the execution of investigative measures may be entrusted to officials seconded by EU Member States, it must be concluded that *other persons* permitted to participate in JITs – being either officials from EU Member States not participating in the JIT or from non-EU Member States – cannot be entrusted therewith. Germany has explicitly chosen, it appears, not to make use of the possibility provided for in paragraph 12 of Article 13 of the EU Convention on Mutual Assistance (mirrored in Article 20 of the 2001 CoE 2nd Additional Protocol).[44] As for participation by officials from third states, no additional rules apply.

As for participation by Europol officials, the 2002 Protocol to the Europol Convention, upon entry into force, will constitute an agreement allowing Europol to participate. However, the newly proposed Article 83k(2) IRG must be seen to limit the powers of Europol officials foreseen in the future Article 3a of the Europol Convention. The possibility for Europol officials to assist in all JIT activities on German territory will not supersede the possibility for them *to be present* during all the team's activities. They will not be allowed to take part themselves in whatever investigative measures, even where these do not imply any degree of coercion. As stressed in the explanatory report, Europol officials will only be able to cooperate supportively with the JIT activities within the limits of Article 3, paragraph 1 of the current Europol Convention, i.e., in performing tasks of gathering, analysing, and exchanging information or intelligence only.

As for participation by Eurojust, finally, there seems to be no problem, as the 2002 Eurojust decision applies and has also been implemented in German national law.

d. The right of seconded members to directly request investigative measures in the home country

Article 83k IRG does not provide such a right. Thus, German seconded members participating in a JIT operating abroad will only be able to directly request investigative measures in Germany if the JIT is based on either the EU Convention on Mutual Assistance or the 2001 CoE 2nd Additional Protocol to the 1959 European Mutual Assistance Convention, Article 13(7) respectively Article 20(7).

---

[44] This is confirmed in the explanatory memorandum.

e. *The right of seconded members to provide the JIT with information that is available in the home country*

The requirements of paragraph 9 of Article 13 of the EU Convention on Mutual Assistance will be met by Article 83k(3) IRG. German JIT members will only be allowed to directly provide information to all other members or participants of the JIT, including personal data, if the functioning of the JIT will be improved by sharing this data.

In addition, as mentioned earlier, it remains possible in certain cases for the *Bundeskriminalamt* (BKA), on the basis of Article 14, paragraph 1, BKA Act and therefore also outside JIT contexts, to transmit personal data available to it to foreign police and judicial authorities.

f. *The right to use information lawfully obtained within the JIT in the home country*

The German implementing legislation, like the Dutch, has not transposed the provisions of Article 13(10) of the EU Convention on Mutual Assistance (literally mirrored in Article 20(10) of the 2001 CoE 2nd Additional Protocol).

In principle, the effect is that, unless the JIT basis is one of the above two treaties (in which case these may apply directly), it remains legally uncertain whether information that has been lawfully obtained within a JIT when operating abroad or by foreign JIT members can be used in Germany and, if so, for what purposes: for the JIT investigation only or also for other purposes?

Germany, however, in Article 83k(4) IRG, has regulated the reverse scenario, in which German JIT members have provided information to a JIT. Wholly in line with the possibilities offered by paragraph 10, under b and c of Article 13 of the EU Convention on Mutual Assistance (mirrored in Article 20 of the 2001 CoE 2nd Additional Protocol), the proposed provision makes the use of information by foreign JIT members for other purposes than for which the JIT has been established dependent on whether a request to use the information concerned for these other purposes could be granted.

g. *The right to use evidence obtained within the JIT as evidence in the home country*

The question of the domestic admissibility of evidence collected within the team when operating abroad is neither addressed in the German implementing legislation, nor in German law in general.

h. Criminal and civil liability regarding seconded members or foreign representatives

The German implementing legislation does not regulate liability questions regarding seconded members or foreign representatives. Thus, unless the JIT is based on either the EU Convention on Mutual Assistance or the 2001 CoE 2nd Additional Protocol to the 1959 European Mutual Assistance Convention of which Articles 15-16 and Articles 21-22 respectively provide adequate liability rules that may have direct effect, liability issues regarding foreign representatives in JITs operating in Germany will remain unregulated. This will be the case where the JIT basis is the 1997 Naples II Convention or the 2000 UN TOC Convention. It should be noted, though, that concerning liability regarding Europol officials, the 2002 Europol Protocol – following its entry into force – will serve as a safety net if national law does not contain provisions on liability issues. Adequate minimum criminal and civil liability rules are contained in the future Articles 3a, paragraph 6 and 39a of the Europol Convention.

i. The right for seconded members or foreign representatives to carry and use service weapons

The German authorities will have to arrange, for each JIT, the *ad hoc* issuing of individual weapons licences for seconded and/or other foreign officials in accordance with the normal domestic standards for the issuing of such licences to individual citizens.

4.3   The Netherlands

The Dutch Implementation Act for the EU Convention on Mutual Assistance, dated 18 March 2004,[45] entered into force on 1 July 2004.[46] Basically, the Act only introduced such legal changes as were deemed strictly necessary to comply with the Convention's requirements and is therefore quite minimalistic. However, this is not problematic because the Netherlands has adopted a monistic system and treaty provisions which are clearly formulated and self-executing can be applied without transposition. Most provisions in Article 13 of the EU Convention on Mutual Assistance are directly applicable. However, a new section on international joint investigation teams was inserted into the Code of

---

[45] *Staatsblad van het Koninkrijk der Nederlanden* (Dutch Bulletin of Acts and Decrees), 2004, 107.

[46] *Staatsblad van het Koninkrijk der Nederlanden* (Dutch Bulletin of Acts and Decrees), 2004, 181.

Criminal Procedure (CCP), to implement the EU Convention on Mutual Assistance, comprising the new Articles 552qa until qe, and a new 3rd paragraph was inserted into Article 13 of the 1990 Data Protection Police Files Act (*Wet Politieregisters*), creating the possibility to provide data from temporary police files for JIT purposes.[47] The complementary 1991 Police Files Decree (*Besluit Politieregisters*) was completed with a new Article 13a by a separate decision of 10 September 2002,[48] which came into force on 1 July 2004, giving more detail on providing data from police files to JITs.

Article 552(2)qa CCP requires a written agreement between the authorities of the countries setting up a JIT. In this document, at least, the following issues must be agreed upon:

1) The goal of the JIT, 2) the duration of the JIT, 3) the place of establishment of the JIT, 4) the composition of the JIT, 5) the investigative competences of the Dutch investigators on foreign territories, 6) the investigative competences of foreign investigators in the Netherlands, and 7) the duty of foreign investigators who are members of the JIT to act as a witness before the examining magistrate and to be present during the court proceeding in the Netherlands. This means that, in the event of a lacuna in the legislation, the written agreement can be used as a flexible instrument to organise a JIT.

The Board of Procurators General (*College van Procureurs Generaal*), on 10 June 2004, issued a circular letter on international JITs, giving the public prosecutors further instructions on the legal and practical operation and operability of JITs.
The circular letter is very clear, *inter alia*, about the underlying JIT philosophy, i.e., concentrating partial investigations in various countries in a single, joint investigation team, thus making sure that investigations in respect of a criminal group which is operating in several countries are not limited to just one branch, but that, on the contrary, the criminal group can be tackled in its entirety through coordinated investigations and actions by the various countries participating in the JIT.

---

[47] *Staatsblad van het Koninkrijk der Nederlanden* (Dutch Bulletin of Acts and Decrees), 1990, 414.
[48] *Staatsblad van het Koninkrijk der Nederlanden* (Dutch Bulletin of Acts and Decrees), 2002, 484.

a. Legal basis

According to Article 552qa CCP, the establishment of a JIT must be based on a treaty, meaning that any other country with which the Netherlands is willing to set up a JIT must be bound by a treaty providing for the possibility of establishing a JIT that is also[49] binding upon the Netherlands. The Procurators General's circular letter confirms the four valid treaty bases that were discussed before.

Now that the EU Convention on Mutual Assistance has entered into force, this instrument provides the most important legal basis. The required notification for the 1997 Naples II Convention has been submitted, and its possible anticipated entry into force has been accepted. Finally, the Netherlands has ratified the 2000 UN TOC Convention, but not the 2001 CoE 2nd Additional Protocol to the European Mutual Assistance Convention. It is unclear whether ratification of the latter is envisaged in the near future.

Strictly speaking, the Framework Decision on JITs cannot produce any direct effect and, therefore, does not qualify as an autonomous international legal basis for the establishment of JITs. However, this particular provision in Article 552qa has given rise to different interpretations.

The first interpretation indicates that because this article requires a conventional basis to set up a JIT, this limits the possibility for the Netherlands to establish a JIT with other Member States that are not a party to such a convention. As the United Kingdom had not yet ratified the EU Convention on Mutual Assistance at the moment the Drugs JIT between the United Kingdom and the Netherlands was established, the Convention could not be used as the basis on which to set up a JIT between the Netherlands and the United Kingdom, according to this narrow interpretation. In this view, it is believed that the fact that the United Kingdom has implemented the Framework Decision on JITs does not change this situation, as a Framework Decision cannot be seen as a convention. In the Report from the Commission of the EU on national measures taken to comply with the Council Framework Decision of 13 June 2002 on JITs of 7 January 2005, the Netherlands is criticized for the treaty requirement adopted in national legislation.[50]

The second interpretation is the adoption of the teleological and subjective interpretation methods for explaining this article. It is argued that, because the Framework Decision on JITs is an exact copy of Article 13 of the EU Conven-

---

[49] See also the Procurators General JIT circular, under paragraph 4.1, 1st point, explicitly stating that at least 'two treaty state parties' are required.

[50] Report from the Commission on national measures taken to comply with the Council Framework Decision of 13 June 2002 on Joint Investigation Teams, Commission of the European Communities, 7.01.2005, COM(2004) 858, p. 5.

tion on Mutual Assistance, the Framework Decision in this particular case can be seen as an indirect conventional basis on which to set up the JIT. Taking the intentions and aims of the Dutch and the United Kingdom legislators into consideration, it is clear that they wanted to make it possible to start a JIT in accordance with the text of Article 13 of the EU Convention on Mutual Assistance and the Framework Decision.

The third interpretation is that some will probably argue that a parallel can be drawn with the situation on the implementation of the Framework Decision on the European Arrest Warrant. On the basis of an opinion delivered on 19 October 2002 by the Dutch Council of State in the context of a parliamentary discussion on the June 2002 European Arrest Warrant (EAW), they can indeed conclude that the value of a Framework Decision equals that of a treaty. The question at stake was whether the Dutch Constitution, which in Article 2(3) requires a treaty basis for granting extradition, should be amended, given the fact that the June 2002 Framework Decision had imposed obligations upon the EU Member States to adopt national legislation allowing for mutual surrender on the basis of national arrest warrants issued in line with the standardized requirements embedded in the Framework Decision, as an alternative to former extradition based on treaty law. The Council of State took the standpoint that the cooperation of the Netherlands in the adoption of the Framework Decision required no prior amendment of the Constitution, for (a) the Framework Decision must be considered to be a set of rules of a binding supranational character for the Member States and (b) the adoption of the Framework Decision does not lead to a derogation from Article 2, paragraph 3 of the Dutch Constitution. The latter statement could be based on the fact that 'surrender' (as prompted by the Framework Decision) essentially differs in nature from 'extradition' as referred to in Article 2 of the Constitution, so that obviously the EAW and the *surrender* procedures between the EU Member States based on the EAW cannot imply a derogation from the traditional treaty requirement for *extradition*.

From this statement the conclusion cannot be drawn that the legal basis of a treaty equals the legal basis of a Framework Decision.

However, it is clear from Article 552qa CCP that the Dutch legislator did not implement the Framework Decision at all. In the parliamentary history of this article, attention was drawn to the Framework Decision that was being drafted at that time by the Dutch Council of State. But at that time the legislator did not see the necessity to mention the Framework Decision in the proposed law. If the legislator had wanted the Framework Decision to be a valid JIT basis as well, it would have been much easier if Article 552qa had been clear about this. This does not mean that the Framework Decision is superfluous, especially since its content is a duplication of Article 13, and a more liberal application of this instrument must be possible.

Strangely, it is stated in the Drugs JIT agreement that the competent authorities in the Netherlands can be a party to a JIT by virtue of Article 13 of the EU Convention on Mutual Assistance, and the Netherlands declaration dated 2 April 2004 in which anticipated entry force has been accepted. It is hard to see, however, how the 2000 Convention could be a basis for JIT cooperation in the relationship with the United Kingdom, the latter not having submitted the notification with acceptance of anticipated entry into force to the General Secretariat of the Council in order for the Convention to come into force in its relationship with other Member States that have done so, such as the Netherlands. The only possible legally valid basis for the Drugs JIT is adopting the second interpretation mentioned above, which is a reasonable option given the fact that both countries have adopted and implemented the same text.

b. Status and mandate of seconded members

i. The right to be present during the execution of investigative measures
The Dutch implementing legislation has not transposed the provisions of paragraph 5 of Article 13 of the EU Convention on Mutual Assistance (mirrored in paragraph 5 of Article 20 of the 2001 CoE 2nd Additional Protocol to the 1959 European Mutual Assistance Convention). Not having done so implies that, in the context of JITs based on another treaty than one of the above, seconded members do not automatically have the right to be present during the execution of investigative measures on Dutch territory. To that end, a traditional request must be received and granted by the Dutch competent authorities in accordance with either Article 4 of the 1959 European Mutual Assistance Convention or, in relation to the Benelux countries, Article 25 of the 1962 Benelux Treaty.

ii. The right to carry out investigative tasks
Article 552qb CCP concerns the competences of members seconded in a JIT. According to Article 552qb CCP – which in no way specifically concerns seconded members – investigative powers must be exercised in a JIT context in compliance with Dutch rules of criminal procedure laid down in or on the basis of the CCP, as well as with the applicable treaties between the JIT countries. Different interpretations of this provision can be defended and will be reflected upon below.
No discussion exists about the fact that the team needs to obey the law of the country in which it is active.

The first interpretation states that the JIT status of seconded members operating in the Netherlands does not bestow more investigative powers on them than the CCP and certain treaties already allow them to exercise in the current (pre-JIT) situation. This could mean that the seconded members have no more competencies than they already have on the basis of the Code of Criminal Procedure. Actually, this is a consolidation of the existing situation. The agreement setting up a JIT cannot change this; it can only limit the competencies of the seconded members. The team leader can give directions to the seconded members of the team.

As regards investigative powers provided for in applicable treaties, the only clear-cut examples seem to be the right to cross-border observation and hot pursuit under Articles 40-41 of the 1990 Schengen Convention (which, as indicated before, does not yet apply for the United Kingdom). In connection with Article 41 Schengen Convention, Article 54, paragraph 5 CCP must also be mentioned.[51] It provides a domestic legal basis for lawful apprehension of suspects on Dutch territory by foreign public officials in the context of cross-border hot pursuit in line with public international law (such as the Schengen Convention).

As regards Dutch rules of criminal procedure, the CCP provides the possibility for the competent Dutch prosecutor to also entrust the execution of a limited series[52] of special investigative techniques (which all require a preliminary order from the prosecutor, even where entrusted to a Dutch police official) to a foreign public official. Consequently, seconded JIT members would qualify for using these techniques, provided the Dutch prosecutor issues a specific order to that end.

The only special investigative techniques of which the use may, in accordance with the law of the Netherlands, in the sense of Article 13(6) of the EU Convention on Mutual Assistance (literally in Article 20(5) of the 2001 CoE 2nd Additional Protocol), be entrusted by the prosecutor to seconded members of a JIT operating in the Netherlands, are:[53]

– systematic observation, if necessary involving the entering of locked premises (Article 126g(9) and 126o(6) CCP);
– infiltration (Article 126h(4a) and 126p(4a) CCP);

---

[51] Article 41 of the Convention of 19 June 1990 applying the Schengen Agreement of 14 June 1985 between the governments of the states of the Benelux Economic Union, the Federal Republic of Germany and the French Republic, on the gradual abolition of checks at their common borders, Final Act, Protocol and Common Declaration, signed in Schengen 19 June 1990, the Schengen Convention.

[52] A. Klip and A. Smeulers, *Opsporing in de Euregio: gemeenschappelijke onderzoeksteams en parallelle opsporing* (Investigating in the Euregio; Joint Investigation Teams and parallel investigations), Maastricht 2004, Universiteit Maastricht, p. 14-15.

[53] See also the Board of Procurators General's JIT circular, under paragraph 6.2, which even only mentions the possibility of systematic observation in Article 126g(9) CCP.

- pseudo-purchase or pseudo-services (Article 126i(a) and 26q(4) CCP), and
- systematic information gathering (Articles 126j(4a) and 126qa(4) CCP).

A second interpretation is that Article 552qb CCP only concerns the execution of competences and not the attribution of competences.[54] In this view, the attribution of competences can be based on Article 552qa(3) which states that, among other things, the competences of seconded members must be fixed in the agreement underlying the Convention. This means a very flexible system, although it is unlikely that the granting of competences must be based on an agreement which has to be negotiated each time.

A foreign investigator is also obliged to testify, if the Dutch authorities request him to do so, and he has a reporting duty concerning his activities on the basis of Article 552qa(3) CCP. Finally, he is not allowed to perform any coercive measure or investigative methods other than those mentioned in the order.[55]

In the first approach regarding the competencies of seconded members, it is questionable whether these competencies are sufficient to meet the aim of the JIT. Looking at the overall picture, we are inclined to conclude that it is not. The seconded members actually have no more competencies than they have under the current situation. If the aim of a joint investigation team is to act more efficiently when dealing with a case of a transnational nature, this will hardly be accomplished with the competencies of the seconded members provided for in the legislation.
However, if the basis for the attribution of competences must be found in Article 552qa(3), there is more flexibility.
An interpretation before the court on this issue could bring a welcome clarification on this matter.

When adopting the first interpretation, the agreement for the Drugs JIT seems erroneous when it comes to its paragraphs 9.2 and 9.3. Under paragraph 9.2, it is stated that 'the seconded members of the JIT are allowed to apply the same investigative measures as the Dutch members, except when the seconded members are limited by *their* national law in the application of these measures (552qb CCP).' On the contrary, according to this first interpretation, seconded members are not able to exercise any investigative powers at all unless this is provided for in and in compliance with applicable treaties or Dutch national criminal

---

[54] This view is not shared by Vermeulen.
[55] Article 6 Cooperation Decision on special investigative powers of 15 December 1999, *Staatsblad van het Koninkrijk der Nederlanden* (Dutch Bulletin of Acts and Decrees), 1999, 549, also cited in A. Klip and A. Smeulers, *o.c.,* 14.

procedural law, on the basis of Article 552qb. In other words, the law governing the powers of seconded JIT members is not that of their home state, but that of the Netherlands, which appears to be very restrictive, giving no new powers at all to foreign officials operating in a JIT context.

However, when taking the second interpretation the members of the Drugs JIT have acted correctly in accordance with the legislation, as Article 552qa(3) requires that the competences of seconded members are clearly indicated in the agreement. By naming explicitly the investigative measures that seconded members may undertake on Dutch territory in paragraphs 9.2 and 9.3 of the agreement, they have acted fully in compliance with Dutch law.

c. *Status and mandate of representatives of third countries or international bodies*

Both Article 13 of the EU Convention on Mutual Assistance and Article 1 of the 2002 Framework Decision on JITs, in paragraph 12, make JIT participation by representatives of third countries or international bodies dependent on explicit permission to that effect in the laws of the Member States constituting the JIT or in a legal instrument applicable between them. With the entry into force of the EU Convention on Mutual Assistance their participation became possible for JITs based on this Convention. As the Dutch implementing legislation itself does not provide such a possibility, participation by third country representatives or representatives of bodies such as Europol and Eurojust not based on the EU Convention on Mutual Assistance must find its legal basis in another instrument.

It seems that only upon the entry into force of the 2002 Protocol, which will insert a new Article 3a of the Europol Convention regarding JIT participation by Europol officials, will genuine Europol participation in JITs (in the sense of the future Article 3a in the Europol Convention) in which the Netherlands participates become legally possible. Only then will there be an applicable legal instrument between EU JIT members explicitly permitting such Europol JIT participation.

The 2002 Eurojust decision does not autonomously permit JIT participation by representatives of Eurojust as a college. Formal Eurojust participation in JITs therefore appears to be impossible.

d. *The right for seconded members to directly request investigative measures in the home country*

The Dutch implementing legislation does not provide such a right. Thus, Dutch seconded members (i.e., participating in a JIT operating abroad) will only be able to directly request investigative measures in the Netherlands if the JIT is based on either the EU Convention on Mutual Assistance or if the 2001 CoE 2nd Additional Protocol to the 1959 European Mutual Assistance Convention, Article 13(7) or Article 20(7) respectively, allows this. If the JIT has another treaty basis, which does not provide such a derogation from the normal rule that investigative measures in other states will be requested through a mutual assistance request (such as the 1997 Naples II Convention or the 2000 UN TOC Convention), Dutch seconded members will not have the right to directly request investigative measures in the Netherlands unless a provision to this end is adopted in the agreement establishing that JIT.

e. The right for seconded members to provide the JIT with information that is available in the home country

In order to meet the requirements of paragraph 9 of Article 13 of the EU Convention on Mutual Assistance, a new third paragraph was inserted in Article 13 of the 1990 Data Protection Police Files Act, creating the possibility for Dutch JIT members to provide data from temporary police files for JIT purposes. The complementary 1991 Police Files Decree was also completed with an Article 13a. According to the new provision, seconded members of a JIT established in the Netherlands may be provided with information on the same footing as Dutch Police officials, even where it concerns information from temporary police files, and information can also be provided to Dutch police officials in a JIT operating abroad.

Further, according to Article 552qd CCP, documents that could contribute to a conviction and data carriers located in the Netherlands may immediately be put at the disposal of a JIT operating abroad, but remain subject to Dutch law. The use of these documents and data carriers abroad as evidence will be dependent on prior court authorization.

f. The right to use information lawfully obtained within the JIT in the home country

The Dutch implementing legislation has not transposed the provisions of Article 13(10) of the EU Convention on Mutual Assistance (mirrored in Article 20(10) of the 2001 CoE 2nd Additional Protocol to the 1959 European Mutual Assistance Convention).

In principle, the effect is that, unless the JIT basis is one of the above two treaties (in which case these treaty provisions may apply directly), it remains legally uncertain whether information that has been lawfully obtained within a JIT when operating abroad or by foreign JIT members can be used in the Netherlands, and, if so, for what purposes – for the JIT investigation only or also for other purposes.

This effect, though, is mitigated by the new Article 552qc CCP. According to this provision, the evidential value of documents drawn up abroad by foreign JIT members in the course of their investigative and prosecutorial JIT activities will equal that of documents regarding corresponding activities by Dutch officials in the Netherlands, whereby the value attached to the documents concerned may not exceed their evidential value according to the state of origin of the foreign JIT members. This means that information lawfully obtained abroad by foreign JIT members in their home country, if embedded in official documents or reports and even where the JIT basis would be the 1997 Naples II Convention or the 2000 UN TOC Convention, may be used in the Netherlands. Such documents or reports even potentially have the same evidential value as documents and reports containing information resulting from similar activities in the Netherlands by Dutch authorities.

Article 552qc CCP does not provide any solution whatsoever regarding information lawfully gathered abroad by foreign JIT members in the territory of a JIT state other than their home country, not even if the latter country is the Netherlands. Moreover, it may even be assumed that foreign JIT members operating in the Netherlands do not even have the competence to draw up documents or reports in the Netherlands, given the fact that, by virtue of Article 552qb CCP, their JIT status does not bestow on them any more powers than they could have on the basis of the CCP or applicable treaties,

g. *The right to use evidence obtained within the JIT as evidence in the home country*

Apart from what has been indicated in the previous paragraph regarding *documents or reports* providing *information* resulting from investigative or prosecutorial JIT activities abroad, the question of the domestic admissibility of evidence collected within the team when operating abroad is not addressed in the Dutch implementing legislation, nor in Dutch law in general. The Board of Procurators General's circular letter only recalls the general duty for the prosecution to see to it that evidence collected in flagrant violation of Dutch criminal procedural rules does not enter Dutch criminal proceedings (paragraph 7.3).

h. Criminal and civil liability regarding seconded members or foreign representatives

The Dutch implementing legislation does not regulate liability questions regarding seconded members or foreign representatives. Thus, liability issues regarding foreign representatives in JITs operating in the Netherlands will remain unregulated, unless the JIT is based on either the EU Convention on Mutual Assistance or the 2001 CoE 2nd Additional Protocol to the 1959 European Mutual Assistance Convention, Articles 15-16 and 21-22, respectively, providing adequate liability rules that have direct effect. This will be the case where the JIT basis is the 1997 Naples II Convention or the 2000 UN TOC Convention. It should be noted, though, that in the case of liability regarding Europol officials the 2002 Europol Protocol – following its entry into force – will serve as a safetynet if national law remains silent on liability issues. As indicated before, adequate minimum criminal and civil liability rules are contained in the future Articles 3a, paragraph 6 and 39a of the Europol Convention.

i. The right for seconded members or foreign representatives to carry and use service weapons

For each JIT, the Dutch authorities will have to arrange the *ad hoc* issuing of individual weapons licences for seconded and/or other foreign officials in accordance with the normal domestic standards for the issuing of such licences to individual citizens. This cumbersome procedure could have been avoided by adopting generic legal provisions on the matter, for example, in Belgium.

4.4 The United Kingdom

As a common-law country, the United Kingdom takes a special position when it comes to the implementation of EU legislation. In the United Kingdom, the executive has very broad implementing powers based on the European Community Act of 1972. Section 2(2) can be used as a basis for the implementation of 'any Community obligation'. Parliamentary control is very limited and often restricted to a so-called negative resolution procedure, which means that the statutory instrument enters into force if neither of the Houses rejects the proposal.[56] According to Vandamme, 'the separation of powers does not appear to be a very well developed feature of the (unwritten) British Constitution.'[57] Ac-

---

[56] Th. Vandamme, The Invalid Directive, The Legal Authority of a Union Act Requiring Domestic Law Making, Groningen, Europa Law Publishing, 2005, pp. 239-247.

[57] Th. Vandamme, The Invalid Directive, The Legal Authority of a Union Act Requiring Domestic Law Making, Groningen, Europa Law Publishing, 2005, p. 239.

cording to United Kingdom practitioners involved in the Drugs JIT, the consequence of this position is that the United Kingdom does not need to implement the Framework Decision on JITs in Acts of Parliament, but that it is allowed to take the measures required and thus to establish a JIT as it belongs to the ordinary competences of the United Kingdom authorities unless they are forbidden by law.[58] This power is said to be a leftover of the Royal Prerogative. They therefore strongly disagree with the Commission that the United Kingdom did not fulfil its obligations under the Framework Decision because most of the rules on JITs are adopted in non-binding circulars.[59]

a. Legal basis

Various cooperation concepts may be considered a joint investigation team, as far as the United Kingdom is concerned. Unlike in the other countries covered in this chapter, the use of the term is not restricted to JITs within the meaning of Article 13 of the EU Convention on Mutual Assistance (mirrored in Article 1 of the 2002 Framework Decision) or Article 20 of the 2001 CoE 2nd Additional Protocol. Even cross-border observation and hot pursuit under Articles 40-41 of the 1990 Schengen Convention qualify as JITs,[60] as well as basically any other form of intensified cooperation with foreign law enforcement officials, even when it is informal (most probably on the basis of a Memorandum of Understanding) and even where investigations in the various countries involved remain fully parallel to one another and not 'joint' in the strict sense of the word, as seems to be the case, for example, in the Drugs JIT. Home Office Circular 53/2002 on the 2002 EU Framework Decision on JITs sufficiently demonstrates the extremely flexible interpretation which the United Kingdom attaches to the term 'joint investigation team'. The Circular states that 'joint teams have for many years been a feature of international cooperation in investigating cross-border crime' (paragraph 2), albeit only that 'until now, there has not been an internationally agreed framework for establishing and operating the teams', that they 'have instead been established on the basis of understandings between the competent authorities setting up the teams' and that 'these arrangements have worked well' (paragraph 3). Further, in Annex A to the Circular, it is reiterated that the 'Framework Decision does not mean that JITs may only be established

---

[58] Statement made by the United Kingdom representative at Eurojust and the prosecutor involved in the Drugs case.

[59] Report from the Commission on national measures taken to comply with the Council Framework Decision of 13 June 2002 on Joint Investigation Teams, Commission of the European Communities, 7.01.2005, COM(2004) 858.

[60] The International Joint Investigation Teams (International Agreement) Order 2004 (Statutory instrument 2004 No. 1127).

under the formal arrangements which it elaborates' (paragraph 2) and that there 'is no obligation to set up a JIT if less formal ways of working are more appropriate' (paragraph 7).
Consequently, the United Kingdom has hardly come up with implementing legislation for JITs because, according to its system, this is unnecessary.
Further, only two Home Office Circulars on the issue of JITs have been produced: the above-mentioned Circular 53/2002 and the later Circular 26/2004, both providing information on the 2002 EU Framework Decision on JITs.
As a consequence of the apparent United Kingdom leniency in setting up JITs, the United Kingdom considers a treaty basis unnecessary.

This could have the consequence that, each time a JIT is established, all issues must be regulated in an agreement or Memorandum of Understanding (MoU). However, Circular 53/2002 under point 5 states: 'With the coming into effect of the relevant provisions of the Police Reform Act, on the first of October 2002, competent authorities in the UK are now able to establish Joint Investigation Teams under the Framework Decision with competent authorities of any of the other Member States which are similarly in the position to operate the Framework Decision.'

As stated above, the adoption of non-binding measures such as circulars are generally not sufficient to implement Framework Decisions. Strictly speaking, Framework Decisions themselves cannot have any direct effect nor create obligations *between* states (being only binding *upon* states). Surely, none of their provisions produce any effect, unless adopted in domestic legislation, which has hardly been the case as far as the United Kingdom is concerned. According to the United Kingdom authorities, however, implementation in binding legislation is not required as their competence to establish JITs is based on the Royal Prerogative.

b. Status and mandate of seconded members

i. The right to be present during the execution of investigative measures
The United Kingdom has not transposed the provisions of Article 13(5) of the EU Convention on Mutual Assistance (mirrored in Article 20(5) of the 2001 CoE 2nd Additional Protocol to the 1959 Convention). Not having done so implies that in the context of JITs based on ar treaty other than one of the above (provided these already apply), seconded members will not automatically have the right to be present during the execution of investigative measures on United Kingdom territory. To that end, strictly speaking, a traditional request will need to be granted by the United Kingdom competent authorities in accordance with

Article 4 of the 1959 European Mutual Assistance Convention.

On the basis of Home Office Circular 53/2002, however, it may be assumed that the United Kingdom will, in principle, grant seconded members the right to be present, stating so in the JIT agreement, as if it were a Memorandum of Understanding (MoU).

ii. The right to carry out investigative tasks

The United Kingdom has not transposed the provisions of paragraph 6 of Article 13 of the EU Convention on Mutual Assistance (Article 20(6) of the 2001 CoE 2nd Additional Protocol), either. Not having done so implies that seconded members cannot be entrusted with the tasks of taking investigative measures, whatever treaty is the basis underlying the JIT. Neither paragraph 6 of Article 13 of the EU Convention on Mutual Assistance or paragraph 6 of Article 20 of the 2001 CoE 2nd Additional Protocol can be considered to be self-executing, not even in monistic systems.

Home Office Circular 53/2002 seems to confirm this, indicating that it will not in general be possible under United Kingdom law for seconded JIT members to exercise coercive powers such as search and seizure, nor to question witnesses.

c. Status and mandate of representatives of third countries or international bodies

Mutatis mutandis, reference can be made to what has been said in this respect for the Netherlands.

Home Office Circular 53/2002 seems to confirm this, stressing, however, that, in anticipation of the entry into force of the 2002 Europol Protocol, Europol may still play an important and valuable role in advising on organised crime threats and can add value to Member States' own operational information. As indicated earlier, the Circular also addresses such pre-Protocol assistance by Europol through the ENU (at the National Criminal Intelligence Service/NCIS). The importance of informing and consulting Europol through the NCIS at the early planning stages of a JIT is stressed. As for Eurojust, the Circular suggests making early contact with the United Kingdom representative. About participation in a JIT by the United Kingdom national Eurojust member, acting on the basis of United Kingdom law, or of a representative of Eurojust as such, the Circular remains silent.

d. The right for seconded members to directly request investigative measures in the home country

According to Section 16, paragraph 2, under (b) of the Crime (International Cooperation) Act 2003, a search warrant or a production order may be applied for and executed without a traditional mutual legal assistance request to that effect, provided it is applied for by a United Kingdom member (being a police or customs officer) of a JIT in relation to the JIT's investigations overseas. The seconded United Kingdom officer is deemed to have personal knowledge of the joint investigation just as he would in making such an application in a domestic investigation.

This waiver of the traditional requirement to apply for investigative measures by means of letters rogatory will remain a dead letter if a JIT is established on the basis of either the Naples II Convention, the UN TOC Convention, or the CoE 2nd Additional Protocol, as none of these treaties have, to date, been specified for the purposes of the statutory provisions relating to JITs.

e. The right for seconded members to provide the JIT with information that is available in the home country

The United Kingdom has not transposed the provisions of paragraph 9 of Article 13 of the EU Convention on Mutual Assistance (Article 20 of the 2001 CoE 2nd Additional Protocol). Cooperation in a JIT context, therefore, will not have any added value compared to traditional cooperation in criminal matters. Home Office Circular 53/2002 confirms that the sharing of information by seconded United Kingdom members must be in accordance with United Kingdom law – which has not been amended in this respect – and within the limits of their own competence.

f. The right to use information lawfully obtained within the JIT in the home country

The United Kingdom has not transposed the provisions of Article 13(10) of the EU Convention on Mutual Assistance (Article 20 of the 2001 CoE 2nd Additional Protocol), either. The effect is that, unless the JIT basis is one of the above two treaties (in which case the provisions may apply directly), it remains legally uncertain whether information that has been lawfully obtained within a JIT when operating abroad or by foreign JIT members can be used in the United Kingdom and, if so, for what purposes – for the JIT investigation only or also for other purposes.

g. *The right to use evidence obtained within the JIT as evidence in the home country*

Further, the question of the domestic admissibility of evidence collected within the team when operating abroad is not addressed in United Kingdom law. Section 9 of the Crime (International Cooperation) Act 2003, regarding the 'use of evidence obtained', has not been amended. It appears, therefore, that it will not be possible to use evidence obtained within a JIT as evidence in the United Kingdom. Section 9 only shows the possible use of evidence obtained pursuant to a traditional request for assistance issued by a competent United Kingdom authority. It can be argued that the original request of the United Kingdom that was used by the Netherlands to establish a JIT serves as the basis for such use of evidence.

h. *Criminal and civil liability regarding seconded members or foreign representatives*

Section 103 of the Police Reform Act 2002 provides a legal basis for civil liabilities arising from JIT operations involving police officers from United Kingdom forces and law enforcement officers from abroad. The section extends the liabilities of chief officers of police and the Directors General of the NCIS and the NCS by providing that they are liable for any unlawful conduct by members of JITs formed in accordance with specified international agreements to which the United Kingdom is a party. As regards criminal liability, Section 104 of the same Act provides that, just as it is already an offence to assault or obstruct a person assisting a constable in the execution of his duty, it is also an offence to assault or obstruct foreign JIT members.

Both Sections 103 and 104, however, will remain a dead letter if a JIT is based on either the Naples II Convention, the UN TOC Convention, or the CoE 2nd Additional Protocol, as none of these treaties have, to date, been specified for the purposes of the statutory provisions concerned.

i. *The right for seconded members or foreign representatives to carry and use service weapons*

Like the Dutch and the German authorities, the United Kingdom authorities will need to have recourse for each JIT to the *ad hoc* issuing of individual weapons licences for seconded and/or other foreign officials in accordance with the normal domestic standards for the issuing of such licences to individual citizens.

5. WHAT CAN BE THE ADDED VALUE OF A JIT AND HOW CAN IT BE ACHIEVED?

When a certain country is investigating a criminal offence with an international dimension, information from and cooperation with law enforcement officers and judicial authorities from other states is often needed. In those cases, the investigation can benefit from the participation of law enforcement and other relevant personnel from another state in which there are links to the offences in question. Until recently, this type of cooperation at the operational law enforcement level lacked the possibility of (full) participation of foreign officers, and common decisions on strategies, working methods and leadership. From a formal point of view, these investigations were separately executed at 'different sides of the border' (mirror investigations). International exchange of intelligence required formal requests for legal assistance between the parties involved. Many hurdles had to be cleared in the process of cooperation, such as the identification of the competent authority and person abroad, the checking of a request by several authorities in both the sending and the receiving country and the time-consuming procedure for the submission of requests and materials In terms of efficiency and effectiveness, a strong need was felt to improve the formal structure. For this purpose, a JIT was thought to have added value.

As the THB-JIT project and the Drugs JIT showed there is not one single way a JIT can be established; on the contrary, there are many ways to set up a JIT.

The advantages of a JIT must be seen in the direct cooperation of police officers and judicial authorities from different countries in one operational investigation. A JIT may provide the most direct form of cooperation in which the organisation of the investigation in more countries is conducted by one team. This speeds up the exchange of information and the procedures used for mutual assistance in transnational investigations. The possibilities for the direct exchange of information not only exist for the police but also, and in particular, for the prosecution. This will speed up the process of mutual assistance.

Another advantage of a JIT is the central coordination of investigations in different countries by the team leader of a JIT. The overall picture of the activities in the different countries is obtained more easily and one person is responsible for coordination, which minimises the risk of duplication.

Another advantage of a JIT is that it creates the possibility for the execution of investigative measures by officers from abroad on foreign territory. It depends on the implementation legislation of the countries concerned whether this possibility is fully applied or not and under what conditions.

Although a JIT brings great advantages for the prosecution, the main effort to run a JIT must be made by the police. It is a different way of working for the police. They have to organise the secondment or accommodation of police officers, probably execute their daily work in a foreign language, explain the details of their own system, etc. Because mutual assistance is mainly the domain of the judiciary, it will benefit most from the effects of a JIT. However, the police themselves will benefit from more speedy procedures for mutual assistance as it might enable them to choose the right steps in the investigation on the basis of the information shared in the JIT.

Another advantage for the police and the prosecution is the closer and intensified contacts with colleagues abroad. Because, until recently, the prosecution did not have so many contacts abroad, the increase of such contacts must be seen as an advantage. Furthermore, it is expected that practitioners will gain a better knowledge of each other's legal system and organisational structure.

Because the seconded members themselves participate in the collection of evidence a JIT is an extra guarantee that information is collected in accordance with basic (human rights) standards. The seconded members have a possibility to check the collection of information directly instead of relying on the collection of evidence in good faith by the other country. Thus, it seems that a JIT provides an extra opportunity to check whether information and evidence is gathered in accordance with the internationally accepted human rights standards.

6. CONCLUSION

It was made clear in this chapter that various international instruments can provide a legal basis for the establishment of a JIT. Now that the EU Convention on Mutual Assistance has entered into force, the relevance of the Framework Decision on JITs has diminished. However, the fact that these two EU instruments have the same content but a different legal basis raises some interesting fundamental questions that were addressed in this chapter.

As was explained in this chapter, self-executing provisions of a treaty can be applied directly in a state that is party to this Convention. A Framework Decision is said to lack this effect as it is shown, in Article 34(2) EU Treaty, that Framework Decisions in general lack direct effect. This means that the rule from the *Van Gend and Loos* case, namely, that Community law is an autonomic legal order directly binding upon the Member States, does not apply to police and judicial cooperation in criminal matters. However, the European Court of Justice of the EC has recently weakened this strong legalistic standpoint. In the *Pupino* case, it applied the theory of consistent interpretation, which was originally developed for directives, also to Framework Decisions, without elaborate argumentation. The Court also explicitly adopted the principle of loyal cooperation for police and judicial cooperation in criminal matters. In ruling 38, it

stated that the Court's jurisdiction to give preliminary rulings would be deprived of most of its useful effect if individuals were not entitled to invoke Framework Decisions in order to obtain a conforming interpretation. This means that the Court has implicitly accepted that, under certain conditions, Framework Decisions can have direct effect as well. This could mean that also with a minimalistic implementation of the provisions in either the Framework Decision or the treaty, the full regime applies when the provisions are self-executing. As we have seen above, most provisions of Article 13 of the EU Convention on Mutual Assistance and thus the Framework Decision on JITs, are self-executing.
However, this is still not a stable ground for establishing a JIT on the Framework Decision on JITs unless it is fully implemented in national legislation. The Framework Decision on JITs remains an a-typical instrument in that it is a duplication of Article 13 and was consequently meant as a temporary instrument.

As we have seen before, the United Kingdom as a common-law country does have an exceptional approach towards its obligations on the basis of the Framework Decision which is based on its different constitutional division of powers. It was said that the law enforcement officers derive their power to establish a JIT from a legacy of the Royal Prerogative. Consequently, it does not require a written legal basis in formal law to be granted this power but it is competent to operate JITs unless it is forbidden by law. EU law normally requires legally binding provisions to implement directives. It remains to be seen whether the position of the United Kingdom will still stand if a case is brought before the European Court of Justice and thus whether legally binding provisions are required to implement Framework Decisions. Looking at the Court's reputation in this regard, we are inclined to say that the Court will do so at some point in the future.

Then what does this mean for the legal basis on which the Drugs JIT was established? It seems that formally and with a strict interpretation of the treaty requirement in Dutch legislation, the Framework Decision on JITs does not provide a legal basis for the JIT. However, in this particular case, in which the Framework Decision is an exact copy of Article 13 and with the aim of the Framework Decision to speed up the entry into force of this article by adopting the teleological interpretation method, both the Framework Decision and Article 13 could serve as a legal basis.
However, it would have been more consistent if the Dutch legislator had not adopted the treaty requirement in such strict terms.

CHAPTER II
LAW ENFORCEMENT INFORMATION EXCHANGE IN THE PRE-OPERATIONAL PHASE OF A JIT

Eveline De Wree*

A Joint Investigation Team cannot be established out of nothing. Some initiatives have to be taken before two or more EU Member States can engage in a THB-JIT project. We could refer to this preparatory stage as 'the pre-operational phase'. In this phase, some questions have to be answered, the two most important ones referring to the *possibility* and *desirability* of setting up a JIT. In the scientific research concerning a JIT – in which the progress of two JIT projects was followed – it became clear that quite a few questions arose concerning the pre-operational phase. In this chapter the question of how information exchange could and should take place in the pre-operational phase of a JIT will be dealt with.

In the first instance, the sharing of intelligence and information between EU Member States will be discussed. After all, in the pre-operational phase a JIT-worthy case has to be identified, and possible JIT partners have to find each other. The information exchange in this phase should therefore enable the achievement of these two objectives. Recommendations will be made on the practical organisation of the information exchange, and the scope and type of the intelligence/data to be shared.
In the second instance, the necessity of a separate intelligence phase – called a JIG (Joint Intelligence Group) – will be examined. This new instrument has been tested during the THB-JIT project. In this chapter the functions given to the JIG, and its added value will be evaluated. Also the problems and concerns related to the use of this instrument will be elaborated upon.
Finally, in conclusive comments recommendations will be made for best practices in the pre-operational phase of a JIT. Recommendable characteristics of

---

* Eveline De Wree is a researcher at the Institute for International Research on Criminal Policy (IRCP), Ghent University (Belgium).

C. Rijken and G. Vermeulen (Eds.), *Joint Investigation Teams in the European Union*
© 2006, T·M·C·ASSER PRESS, The Hague, The Netherlands and the Authors

this phase will be summed up, so that brief but action-oriented guidelines are available to those who may be interested.

1. SHARING OF INTELLIGENCE AND INFORMATION

The desire to start a JIT must always be accompanied by the sharing of information. After all, a key characteristic of a JIT is the fact that at least two Member States are involved. One of the most urging concerns in the pre-operational phase is the ways in which a case can be identified that allows for the setting up of a JIT. Consequently, first a link between two or more Member States has to be established.

1.1   The identification of a JIT-worthy case

There are two ways of establishing a JIT: it could be started in a bottom-up initiative, or implemented as a top-down project. National law enforcement authorities will naturally have to be aware of the existence of a JIT worthy case, in which important information is shared by two or more parties. This knowledge could stem from their own investigations (bottom-up), or from intelligence gathered by Europol (top-down). The choice for one or both scenarios has an important impact on the course of the initiative/project, not in the least on the way intelligence could be shared in the pre-operational phase.
From the JIT Project and the Drugs JIT lessons could be drawn regarding both approaches. While the Drugs JIT was characterised by a strong bottom-up nature, more top-down elements could be found in the THB-JIT project, although a strong national case already existed.

1.1.1   *In a bottom-up initiative*

If the identification of a JIT-worthy *case stems from national investigations*, the national authorities concerned could handle information exchange in the pre-operational phase with their own means and on the basis of available information. In the Drugs JIT, for example, the United Kingdom law enforcement agencies carried out an investigation into cocaine trafficking. In this investigation, a considerable amount of intelligence had already been gathered, and it pointed towards a link with the Netherlands, as some suspects lived there, and their identity was known. The available English intelligence was subsequently shared with their Dutch counterparts. Finally, on the basis of this information, the Netherlands and the United Kingdom decided to set up a JIT. The intelligence available in the ongoing United Kingdom case was used as a basis to start

the JIT. A prolonged pre-operational phase was thus technically redundant.
These (very specific and concrete) data which had already been gathered in national investigations could serve as searching criteria for other national law enforcement authorities and in this way facilitate the identification of linked cases.

If national authorities take the lead in the establishment of a JIT, it is recommendable that these authorities have already gathered substantial data concerning a case and have reasons to suppose that links exist to other Member States. After all, law enforcement agencies that dispose of intelligence and data stemming from national investigations can identify possible operational points of linkage, and requests to other states (in which the receiving party is asked if linked cases could be identified) can therefore be as detailed as possible. National authorities which do not dispose of sufficient action-oriented operational data which allow for a linkage to be made should be discouraged from dispersing requests to establish a JIT.
In the two THB-JIT projects that have been followed in the action research, the United Kingdom and the Netherlands tried to set up the JIT on both occasions. In their first attempt, namely the THB-JIT project, the initiative failed as the United Kingdom and the Netherlands were not the countries who could play a central role, as they did not dispose of sufficient case information to be a JIT initiator. In the second attempt, they succeeded as their national law enforcement authorities had already advanced sufficiently in their national investigations to make the identification of linked cases a much easier task.

1.1.2 *In a top-down project*

The identification of a JIT-worthy case could also stem from *intelligence gathered by Europol*. Europol receives a great deal of valuable information in, e.g., organised crime reports, which allow for common trends to be detected.[1] In the initiative aimed at starting a THB-JIT, Europol had learned from the organised crime reports that several Member States experienced problems with regard to Trafficking in Human Beings involving Bulgarian nationals. Here, they also found important indications that several Member States were directly confronted with the trafficking (e.g., because they were situated on one of the main routes for trafficking) and should be able to gather data regarding the phenomenon.

---

[1] T. Schalken and M. Pronk, 'On Joint Investigation Teams, Europol and Supervision of their Joint Actions', *European Journal on Crime, Criminal Law and Criminal Justice*, 2002, Vol. 10/1, p. 70-79.

Also, Germany had already built up a strong national case, in which knowledge existed on the identity of some offenders, the type of relations they had, their regions of origin, the reasons why there had been an increase in their criminal activities, and the (il)legal means they used. On the basis thereof, other countries involved in the project could verify if a case existed with links to this 'mother-case'. The THB-JIT project as a whole, however, could not be characterised as a bottom-up initiative, since a strong top-down dynamic had developed quite early in the project.

Here, Europol is the facilitating authority. From the knowledge drawn from the organised crime reports, requests could be directed to the countries which mentioned these common problems in their reports. Information should therefore not be exchanged between the countries directly, but may be gathered at Europol. As Europol has its own information analysis tools, these could be used for the pre-operational phase of a possible JIT. It can use all of the infrastructure present to gather information – especially the Analysis Work File (AWF). The aim of an AWF is to obtain information on certain criminal activities, which relate to a case, person or organisation, and in order to commence, assist or conclude, bilateral or multilateral investigations.[2] This instrument is thus already oriented towards cooperation between two or more EU Member States. In this sense, it is a very suitable instrument to be used in the preamble to a JIT. Also, countries that are not a party to the AWF could provide the file with information (such as EU Member States, third countries, and other supranational organisations).

Sometimes, these existing pre-operational instruments of bodies such as Europol should however be (slightly) adjusted for this specific use. For the setting up of an AWF, for example, feasibility studies were made by the police services of Belgium, Germany, the Netherlands and the United Kingdom. All countries involved agreed on the feasibility, and different elements were taken into account. Most elements of feasibility related to the support existing for the initiative or the commitment of the participants. A basic factor in the assessment of the feasibility was the national support for the initiative which existed (on a political, administrative and operational level). The willingness to cooperate existing among national police officers and the existence of a legal framework were explicitly mentioned as factors contributing to the feasibility of the AWF. Next to this, a substantial amount of data (and intelligence) on Bulgarian perpetrators and victims was judged to be available. The latter was however not substantiated with concrete results. This clarifies that a feasibility study is not

---

[2] Article 10, Council Act of 3 November 1998 adopting rules applicable to Europol analysis files, *OJ* C 026, 23.01.1999.

sufficient for the setting up of a JIT, and should always be complemented with the mutual exchange of operational data, allowing for an immediate check on the existence of linked cases. An operational hit/no-hit check should always be integrated in feasibility studies when the AWF is meant to serve as a pre-operational phase of a JIT.[3]

In this second scenario, involving bodies such as Europol, increased risks exist, however, that the duration of the pre-operational phase will increase. In the run-up to the THB-JIT the AWF was opened, but soon it was soon considered by its participants to be an operational phase in itself. The operational needs were especially considered 'pressing' as law enforcement should move quickly to reduce the number of potential victims[4] – the overall goal being a response within a short period of time. However, considering the fact that many problems emerged in negotiating the scope of the AWF, it took a long time to establish it. Hence we see that the 'operationalisation' of the pre-operational phase slowed proceedings down, instead of speeding them up – although the AWF had initially been opened under the 'urgency procedure'.

Also, political motivations had interfered in the normal course of the THB-JIT project. The first attempt to set up a JIT – concerning THB – was linked to several other initiatives, such as an Action Plan of the EPCTF and to the Dutch EU Presidency. There were two projects which tried to allow the AWF to work to their advantage, one being the Action Plan Bulgaria and the other being the JIG/JIT-initiative. Both were thus trying to pull the AWF towards their objectives. And although both initiatives did not strive for completely opposing goals, their objectives were also not identical. This strongly overcomplicated the progress in the THB-JIT project.[5] After all, one must not forget that a JIT mainly

---

[3] The scientific research also made clear that a feasibility study needs to focus on legislative aspects as well, so as to avoid suprises at a later stage.

[4] EUROPOL, 'Order opening Analysis Work File', 19 November 2003.

[5] The project had been the result of two initiatives; the Action Plan Bulgaria (APB) initiated by the European Police Chiefs Task Force (EPCTF), on the one hand, and the JIT initiative promoted by the Dutch EU Presidency. Thereafter the two objectives of these initiatives – fighting Trafficking in Human Beings related to Bulgaria and establishing the first JIT – were merged in one project. This combination alone would not have been critical as such, but it enabled cooperation between countries that – as it turned out in hindsight – prioritised one of the two objectives. As long as it was not obvious that there was no legal basis for a common JIT, all of the countries strived for the same goal. But as soon as it turned out that a JIT was only possible for two of the countries involved the project fell apart. The Netherlands and the United Kingdom established a bilateral JIT while Germany started investigations on Trafficking in Human Beings supported by Belgium and Bulgaria using conventional instruments of transnational police cooperation. The differences in the prioritisation of the two objectives were obviously not identified or

has operational objectives. The successful investigation and prosecution of the crime concerned is thus the main objective of every JIT initiative. Therefore, one should avoid the situation where the JIT would have to serve double agendas, and thus become part of a complicating political project. It is clear that this situation is not encouraging for the course of the initiative. The pre-operational phase should thus be uniquely coupled with the start of a JIT initiative. Working in a JIT will already be a new and undiscovered area for most of the law enforcement agencies who will work within the framework of a JIT during the first following years. Confusion concerning objectives and tasks should therefore be avoided at all costs, restricting the JIT's role to obtaining of an operational goal.

1.2   Finding possible partners for a JIT

A JIT should be started on a *need* basis. This means that the establishment of a JIT is only useful when the parties concerned all feel that the JIT is necessary to facilitate or unblock investigations. This factor of necessity plays an important role. A JIT may only be set up when this instrument is necessary for the success of the proceedings. It is important that a case is identified in which the use of a JIT can have a real added value for the investigation and prosecution of a crime. Other reasons (e.g., political) can never be a good basis to start with such an instrument. A JIT needs to be used at all times as an instrument facilitating mutual cooperation in criminal matters and can never be used as a goal in itself.

The initiating authority, being a body such as Europol or a Member State which has identified a 'mother case', should thus issue a request to law enforcement authorities in which they are asked to verify if they are working on cases that are linked to a certain topic or a concrete case.

Therefore, a (once only) request should be made to the parties concerned to gather information linked to this specific topic or case. In order for the successful identification of linked cases to be possible, a thorough inquiry should be carried out by the requested party. This request should pass through a central authority which, in its turn, and if necessary, could pass the question on to the different local/decentralised authorities. On the basis of possible points of linkage, which may have arisen from national investigations, for example, different

---

were at least underestimated by the management of the project. Since even the initiators favoured one particular objective – the establishment of a JIT – a concerted action against Trafficking in Human Beings using the instruments in place could not be perceived as an alternative to the plan initially foreseen.

law enforcement agencies could provide the national/central authority with cases that match the requirements. If a transparent and up-to-date operational database exists, the consultation of this database suffices as an inquiry. Often, however, data collection processes on the national level suffer from infancy problems, or they lack transparency, and the consultation thereof may therefore not provide an adequate result. Also, the risk exists that information concerning ongoing investigations is not up to date. After the national inquiry has been carried out, the central/national authority should provide the requesting party with the cases that could be relevant. If no case is identified as having a clear link with the case which has given rise to the request, the initiation of a JIT should not be started.

In a JIT the only countries that should be included are those that have concrete cases linked to cases in other EU Member States. After all, these are the countries with a direct concern in the establishment of a JIT. They are the ones which can have the greatest input, and the greatest output if a JIT is established. Involving other countries which do not share this direct concern only brings an extra burden to the JIT. In the case of the attempted THB-JIT, the opening order of the AWF already made clear that the method chosen was not the most efficient. The steering group of the JIT initiative had reached an agreement concerning the fact that the AWF should cover 'THB with regard to Bulgaria as a source and transit country' (although the steering group did not have this formal competence). The choice for this particular scope was mainly determined by the concern for the participation of the United Kingdom: the term 'transit country' was included in order to allow the United Kingdom to join the AWF, as at that time the sexual exploitation of Bulgarian women via criminal groups of Bulgarian origin was not a problem in the United Kingdom. Here we see that the pre-operational phase becomes less focused on reaching an operational goal in a concrete case. This is what should be avoided at all costs.

1.3   The scope of shared intelligence

The first and main objectives of the sharing of information in the pre-operational phase is to obtain a 'yes' or 'no' response, to the question of whether the establishment of a JIT would be possible and desirable.

1.3.1   *In a bottom-up initiative*

When national investigations detect a 'mother case' for which they want to know if linked cases can be identified, the scope of the initial information exchange should be rather narrow, as the main objective here is to share information on linked cases. The first question one must answer in the pre-operational phase, is whether the commencement of a JIT is possible (because of the existence of linked cases). When a first narrow sounding finds that linked cases do exist, with, for example, the same offenders or the same victims, the basic condition for the establishment of a JIT is fulfilled.

The pre-operational phase should however also bring an answer to the question of whether a JIT is desirable in the cases concerned. After all, the facilitation of investigations in all countries involved has to create a surplus value, allowing for more efficient and more effective investigation and prosecution. The presence of *common grounds* could create a basis on which a JIT could create this added value.

The operational phase should enable the possible JIT partners to determine whether *enough intelligence* is present in the partner countries involved to allow for the continuous progress of the THB-JIT project. One of the advantages of a JIT is that members seconded to a JIT could be present during investigative tasks. Their presence allows for them to provide input – an input that stems from the national investigations in which they have been implicated. The presence of seconded members during interrogations and the carrying out of telephone taps allows for the necessary quality of the information which can be drawn from these measures to be improved. The different partners in the JIT should thus allow for an extra input in the case on the basis of the intelligence of their own national investigations.[6]

In the pre-operational phase an answer should also be sought to the question of whether evidence can be found in one or more partners to the JIT. One of the objectives of the JIT is that the members of the team could work together on the investigative tasks and the gathering of evidence. A JIT could have the greatest added value if *evidence is to be gathered in more than one country*, and will thus not be restricted to one partner. After all, the purpose of the JIT is the facilitation of investigation and prosecution, because partners to the JIT can avoid the continuous sending of rogatory commissions.[7] This goal can be optimally achieved when one country functions as the operation site, and evidence

---

[6] T. van Noord, 'Joint teams: een stappenplan voor de oprichting', *Algemeen Politieblad*, 2003, No. 10, p. 21.

[7] In the THB-JIT project it was found, however, that some national law enforcement agencies did not think that the actual setting up of a JIT was necessary, because they thought it possible to work with rogatory commissions in a 'pragmatic way', meaning that they do not send a rogatory commission for every investigative task, but only subsequently for the information and objects they want to use as evidence.

gathering in the other JIT partners can progress via the seconded members. They can ask for investigative tasks to be carried out in their own country as if they would be a national investigation.

For the linked cases which are identified, information exchange should be able to determine whether enough intelligence is available, and if evidence is expected to be gathered in more than one partner to the JIT. For this, the existing channels of information exchange can be used.

1.3.2 *In a top-down project*

The other path is the identification of a JIT-worthy case via Europol. Again there are two options for the sharing of information at the start of a JIT initiative.

The sharing of information could take place on a large scale, or with a narrow scope. Both ways have advantages and disadvantages.

The most important disadvantage of the wide scope is that so much information could be gathered that it becomes very difficult to detect the really useful information, and to discern it from less action-oriented data. An information overload is created.

A narrow scope creates the problem that a great deal of energy has to be invested in ensuring that the data provided actually has a link to the case concerned. Moreover, it is very likely that this type of intelligence sharing rules out information that becomes relevant at a later stage (e.g., for prosecution purposes). For the establishment of the JIT concerning trafficking in human beings, the narrow scope of the AWF turned out to be an impediment to the intelligence gathering.

It has to be taken into account that no 'mother case' exists in this scenario, and links have to be sought in a 'pool' of cases. The only basis which to start is to have a certain 'topic'. In the attempted THB JIT the topic in question was *trafficking in human beings, from and through Bulgaria*. The different EU Member States therefore had to look for cases matching this model. This led to some discussion, as the different participants had diverging opinions concerning which scope they should to work with.

This discussion was renewed because Europol had amended the text of the opening order of the AWF by adding the sentence 'and any associated criminal activities within Europol's mandate uncovered in the course of the investigation into these networks' without the prior notification of the parties involved. The addition of this sentence was considered to be a legal safeguard, which is standard for all opening orders, allowing for the storage of all information relating to the criminal network. The criteria for the data collection of the AWF are laid down in the opening order of the AWF. In general opening orders tend to have quite a wide scope, enabling the flow of information to be as extensive as possible in order to be sufficiently flexible to respond to changes due to the investigation results. It enables the collection of data concerning connected crimes (e.g., arms trafficking, drugs), and not only the crime for which the AWF has been established.

Several countries involved objected to this new formulation, because they feared that the focus on THB would be abandoned and the scope would be too broad, allowing the use of the AWF to gather as much information as possible, whether connected to THB or not. Finally, a show of hands led to the deletion on the amendment.[8]

Considering the fact that the identification of linked cases is surely not an easy task when no concrete searching variables are available, a wide scope should be considered. The recommendation could therefore be made to start the sharing of intelligence in a top-down scenario based upon a wide scope, especially when it can fit within the framework of data protection. It is however strongly recommended to organise information from the very start and to label it with codes (Highly relevant; Relevant; Context information) so that a rapid filtering of information – when sufficient links have been established – is possible.

Following this example, those cases found where the offence is human trafficking and the offender is a Bulgarian national, would be labelled 'highly relevant'; suspicions concerning the exploitation of a Bulgarian prostitute would be 'relevant'; and false documents or suspicious residence permits could be 'context information'.

Also in this scenario, the pre-operational phase should bring an answer to the question of whether a JIT is desirable in the cases concerned. In this case, the Europol analyst will initially be responsible for answering this question, on the basis of the intelligence which the different partners have brought to the AWF. Europol analysts should recommend JITs – if linked cases are identified – when *enough intelligence* is available in more than one Member State, and when the expectation exists that under normal circumstances *evidence can be gathered in more than one Member State.*

---

[8] C. Rijken, 'Scientific research JIT – First report', 3 October 2004, p. 27.

1.4 Type of data shared

Two types of data could be provided to possible JIT partners, being historical and live data. The sharing of historical data is valuable as it provides background knowledge. This should however be reserved for the operational phase. After all, the expected outcome in the pre-operational phase is a 'yes' or 'no' response to the questions whether the establishment of a JIT would be possible and desirable. Only information on ongoing criminal acts that might be suitable for the establishment of a JIT should therefore be shared among the possible JIT-partners.

The most common problem found when intelligence sharing initiatives are started (e.g., in an AWF) is that the provision of live date is not satisfactory. One of the most important difficulties is the identification of key variables which can be used in the exploration process. After all, it is not an easy task to find a relevant case among the thousands of cases police and judicial authorities are working on. Therefore it is very important that the requesting party identifies searching criteria in its first request, such as the names of the perpetrators, the names of the victims, the means used (registration number of a car, weapons, etc.). These criteria provide hit/no-hit information. If no such criteria are available, a combination of criteria could be considered, e.g., the nationality of the offender/victim, the possible location of the crime, the type of offence, etc. A standard form could be drafted, mentioning all the criteria.

1.5 Practical organisation

The practical organisation of information exchange differs according to the actors involved. If possible JIT partners choose to make use of the existing channels for information exchange and not to involve supranational bodies, the possibilities will vary according to differences in the regulations. If Europol is involved, the procedures for the AWF can be applied.

1.5.1 *Sharing intelligence through national law enforcement agencies*

In the pre-operational phase Member States can exchange information bilaterally, using the different channels allowed. National legislation on information exchange will in this case be the basis for the exchange. Differences exist between national regulations, concerning.[9]

---

[9] Some examples of national regulations are given so as to make it possible to illustrate the different aspects. The examples do not pretend to be exhaustive.

▪ *Authorities who can share information*

According to different national regulations both police and judicial authorities are involved in information exchange. Some types of information can be distributed independently by the police authorities, for other types of information the authorisation of a magistrate is necessary.

Often the use of coercive measures for information exchange is a decisive criterion, as this was stipulated in the Schengen Convention.[10] But also the type of information could determine whether the police or justice authorities can decide on its dissemination. Some countries choose to work with a restrictive list, others use category names to refer to types of information.

- *Belgium*: Only information that is mentioned in the Annex A to the guideline by the Board of Procurators General of 14 February 2000 can be independently supplied by police authorities. Also, it has to concern information that was gathered without the use of any coercive measure.[11]
  If the foreign police service wants to use the information as evidence, authorisation is necessary from the National Magistrate or from the Magistrate of the Local Public Prosecutor's Office. In fact, all the information not mentioned in Annex A of the guideline needs authorisation before police forces can disseminate it. An important remark has to be made regarding the first category of information. The competency of the police services to exchange information independently is still restricted when the intelligence requested forms part of a judicial investigation. In that case, authorisation by the competent magistrate will be necessary.[12] The basis for this can be found in Article 125 Royal Decree of 28 December 1950.[13]
  For Belgium the conclusion can therefore be drawn that in order for most information to be shared the authorisation of a magistrate is necessary.
- *The Netherlands*: Article 552i CCP refers to the exchange of information between police officers. This provision states that the police may ex-

---

[10] M.G.W. den Boer, 'Internationale politiesamenwerking' in C. Fijnaut, E.R. Muller and U.R. Rosenthal, eds., *Politie: studies over haar werking en organisatie,* Alphen aan den Rijn, Samsom, 1999, p. 577.

[11] This article is similar to the Dutch provisions, as it was introduced in pursuance of Articles 39 and 46 of the Schengen Convention.

[12] D. van Daele, *Openbaar Ministerie en strafrechtelijk beleid*, Antwerp, Intersentia, 2002, p. 378

[13] K.B. van 28 december 1950 houdende algemeen reglement op de gerechtskosten in strafzaken, *B.S.* 30 januari 1950.

change information as long as no coercive measures are involved.[14] The Public Prosecutor does not have to be involved when information that was gathered without the use of coercive measures is exchanged. No involvement is needed either when it concerns the exchange of strategic information, information on the policy or open source information. Even information that is part of ongoing investigations can be disseminated.[15]

Judicial authorities may also share information without police involvement.

- *Belgium*: The new law on mutual legal assistance[16] stipulates that the Minister of Justice can provide other states, without a request from another state (thus, on its own initiative), with information that is useful for proceedings falling under the competency of the receiving state. The competent magistrate in this case could also provide the information, subject to the condition that the information has been sent to the Minister of Justice beforehand. A refusal can be issued within 24 hours.[17]
- *The United Kingdom*: Information is often exchanged on an informal basis by United Kingdom police officers. More formal rules do exist, however, when it comes to the exchange of 'evidence'.[18] The Mutual Provision of Evidence has been regulated in the Crime (International Cooperation) Act 2003. Section 7 of the Act[19] sets out the authorities which may make requests for assistance in obtaining evidence from abroad in relation to a prosecution or investigation taking place in the United Kingdom. These requests can only be made by a prosecuting authority when (a suspicion exists that) an offence has been committed. Then, the evidence may not be used without the consent of the appropriate overseas authority. Section 13 deals with the handling of incoming requests for assistance in obtaining evidence located in the United Kingdom. This is possible when a territorial authority for a part of the United Kingdom receives a request in relation to criminal proceedings or a criminal from a court exercising criminal jurisdiction or a prosecuting authority or another authority which appears

---

[14] The authorisation of the Prosecutor is nevertheless necessary in cases prescribed by Articles 552k, 552l and 552m of the Code on Criminal Procedure.

[15] C.J.C.F. Fijnaut, E.R. Muller and U. Rosenthal, *Politie. Studies over haar werking en organisatie,* Alphen aan den Rijn, Samson, 1999, p. 606.

[16] G. Vermeulen, T. Vander Beken, E. De Busser, C. Van den Wyngaert, G. Stessens, A. Masset and C. Meunier, *Een nieuwe Belgische wetgeving inzake internationale rechtshulp in strafzaken,* Antwerp–Apeldoorn, Maklu, 2002, p. 155-163.

[17] Wet betreffende de wederzijdse internationale rechtshulp in strafzaken en tot wijziging van Artikel 90ter van het Wetboek van strafvordering, *B.S.* 24 December 2004.

[18] Article 103(7), Police Reform Act 2002.

[19] Crime (International Cooperation) Act 2003.

to have the function of making such requests for assistance or an international authority. The evidence will be obtained if in the requesting country the proceedings have been instituted or if an investigation into the offence is being carried out. The Secretary of State nominates the court which is appropriate for the purpose of giving effect to the request.[20]

What is clear, however, is that for most information that should be shared in the pre-operational phase of a JIT, the involvement of judicial authorities is necessary or recommendable, because in most EU countries the public prosecution service is responsible for criminal investigations and it decides on the transfer of (sensitive) data. An early involvement by the judiciary is also recommended so as to counterbalance the (natural) tendency of police domination.

It is also important, however, to inform judicial actors on the use of the JIT, so that they understand its functioning and needs. In this way they can better understand and assess the requests for information exchange in the (pre)operational phase.

– *The United Kingdom*: The sharing of information from ongoing investigations could be a rather sensitive matter. In the Drugs JIT, United Kingdom law enforcement agencies were often afraid to share information, fearing that their investigation would be jeopardised.
– *Germany*: Information exchange, to an important extent is often mediated by the dependency on decisions of the public prosecutor.[21] In Germany, law enforcement authorities had been sensitised to the THB-JIT project. As a result, the respective public prosecutors did not object to the transfer of data from ongoing investigations to Europol.

The national organisation of the authorities that can share information may also differ between the different Member States. One of the most important factors here – especially for the identification of JIT-worthy cases – is the structure of the police force. The way in which the police are organised in EU Member States is often quite similar, consisting of local/regional forces and a national force. In this structure (a department of) the national force is responsible for the investigation of more serious forms of crime, or those with an international character. The existence of such a national department with a continuous interest in different types of crime, such as trafficking in human beings and drug trafficking, could facilitate intelligence gathering. After all, this could mean

---

[20] Mutual Provision of Evidence under the Crime (International Cooperation) Act 2003.
[21] *Gesetz über die internationale Rechtshilfe in Strafsachen* (IRG-Gesetz)

that collection routes already exist, and it is much easier to find matching or linked cases. Some examples of police organisation are given below.

- *The Netherlands*: The country is divided into 25 police regions. Besides the regional police forces, a national police force exists (Korps Landelijke Politiediensten, KLPD). The department responsible for national criminal investigations (Divisie Recherche) is equally responsible for international police cooperation as well as for the international exchange of police information and maintaining contact with Dutch liaison officers abroad and foreign liaison officers in the Netherlands. The Dutch National Crime Squad (Landelijk Recherche Team, LRT) forms part of this department. It is responsible for investigating international crimes such as human trafficking, drug trafficking, terrorism, money laundering, and fraud. Recently, a new working group was set up, aimed at improving the information flow from the local forces to the national level on the topic of THB. Before this, no such organised information flow existed, and it seems that it took some time to get it off the ground.
- *Germany*: In Germany, the police force is made up of the Bundeskriminalamt, and the Länder Kriminal Amter. At the local level THB will mostly be dealt with by specialised police units; the same applies to public prosecutors. As the responsibility for investigating THB cases is largely that of the local police forces, situation reports are used as a mechanism to collect and summarise relevant information and to disseminate information about recent developments and trends. Additionally, a two-day conference is held every year to discuss the situation reports. Apart from this 'transparent' data collection, information is routinely exchanged informally between the local police forces, the LKA as the heads of the local police forces, and the BKA. Within the BKA a special unit exists which is responsible for serious crime such as THB. Another unit uses the results of analysis reports produced by the former unit to assess the suitability of the data for the initiation of investigations and to contact the respective public prosecutor. In relation to THB and Bulgaria the BKA had established a special analysis project even before the start of the THB-JIT project. The analysis project was supplemented by a special data base.[22]
- *The United Kingdom*: There are 53 different regional police forces in the United Kingdom (England 40, Scotland 8, Wales 4, and Northern Ireland 1). These police forces all conduct their own investigations autonomously

---

[22] *Gesetz über das Bundeskriminalamt und die Zusammenarbeit des Bundes und der Länder in kriminalpolizeilichen Angelegenheiten (Bundeskriminalamtgesetz – BKAG) – Bundes Kriminal Amt Gezetz 1997* [Law on the Bundes Kriminal Amt].

and run separate databases. During the operational investigative phase the NCS can access information.[23] A national intelligence model is in place, whose purpose it is to identify cross-overs and to facilitate the sharing of relevant intelligence. In the United Kingdom cases on THB, for example, are routinely dealt with by local and regional police forces but since THB is considered a crime of a serious nature the cases can be transferred to the NCS upon request. Besides that it is the task of the NCIS to gather and assess all relevant intelligence on THB. However, the different police forces, being the original owners of the intelligence, can apply a handling code which prevents the NCIS or the NCSEW from sharing the information with each other or with third parties. In practice, information is routinely classified as sensitive and will not be passed on in order not to jeopardise ongoing investigations.

– *Belgium*: In Belgium, the police organisation can be described as integrated, and structured on two levels, being the local and the national level. Within the national police, for example, one unit is designated to focus on THB and on people smuggling. Within the local police forces the number of officers specifically designated to THB depends on the importance of the region. In Belgium no special database on THB exists, however. Instead, the information is fed into a general database for police investigations. The police are under an obligation to file reports on THB cases, the context of which is automatically distributed to the police service in general.

The description of the police organisation points to the conclusion that it is possible in several EU countries to carry out the necessary information exchange – especially regarding the identification of a JIT-worthy case – through the central/national level. After all, police forces are organised in such a way that a central contact point could be identified, which passes on information requests to local police forces. Sometimes, transparent data collection on a certain topic has even been put in place, which facilitates the identification of linked cases even more so.

The same holds true for the judicial actors. In the THB-JIT project under review the start of the project (a top-down approach instead of bottom-up) meant that without a specific case at hand the case prosecutors in the different countries could not yet be ascertained. Judicial actors must be involved from the very beginning, however, if the judicial organisation comprises national prosecutors.

---

[23] The National Crime Squad (Secretary of State's Objectives) Order 2002, Statutory Instrument 2002, No. 779.

The appointment of national prosecutors, next to prosecutors with local competence, is a common trend in EU countries, so the involvement of these actors should not be problematic.

- *Contact points for information exchange*

Considering the fact that specialised services exist at a national level in the police organisation, contact points for information exchange should be sought at this level. They often deal with different types of international information exchange within the police.

- *Belgium*: The contact point for information exchange on the police level is the Directorate for Operational International Police cooperation which falls under the police force's General Directorate for Operational Support.
- *The Netherlands*: The distribution of information occurs through the KLPD. More specifically, the International Network Service (DIN) of the KLPD manages five information channels: Interpol, Europol, the Schengen Information System and the SIS on the national level: through the SIRENE office. Furthermore, the DIN is the coordination point for liaison officers who are stationed abroad by the KLPD and for foreign liaison officers in the Netherlands. The National International Coordination Centre registers all messages and international requests for mutual assistance that enter the service. Finally, the National Criminal Investigation Department also plays an important role in the information gathering and exchange and more specifically concerning requests for mutual assistance.

- *The purpose of exchanging information*

The purposes of information exchange that are defined in national legislation are mostly broadly defined so that it does not hamper information exchange from taking place.

- *The Netherlands*: Article 18 of the Data Protection Police Files Act determines that the rules set out in Article 13[24] of the Police Files Decree apply

---

[24] The rules determined in Article 13 of the Police Files Decree have to be considered as special provisions with regard to Articles 552h-552q CCP. According to Article552h paragraph 1 CCP, Articles 552h-552q CCP are only applicable when no other laws contain provisions on the handling of a request for mutual assistance. This means that for the purpose of supplying information from police files to foreign police authorities, the rules laid down in Article 13 of the Police Files Decree are applicable. Articles 552h-552q are in this respect only of a complementary nature.

to the supply of information from police files to police authorities in other countries. Data from police files can be disseminated to police authorities in another country if this is necessary for the effective execution of police tasks in the Netherlands or for performing tasks resulting from information from the Dutch authorities. Furthermore, the data can be provided so as to prevent a serious and threatening danger or for the investigation of a crime that has affected the legal system of a country or for the effective execution of the police tasks in that country.

– *Germany*: The legal basis for the exchange of information in Germany is the BKA law of 1997. The BKA can transfer person-related data to police and justice authorities that are competent for the prevention and prosecution of criminal acts, insofar as this is necessary (1) for the fulfilment of their tasks; (2) for the prosecution of criminal acts or the execution of sentences according to the regulations which apply to international legal assistance; (3) for the prevention of a threat to public security, or when there are indications that a serious offence is to be committed. The responsibility for the admissibility of the transfer lies with the BKA. The receiver can only use the data for the purpose for which they have been sent.[25]

1.5.2   *Sharing intelligence through Europol*

EU Member States that want to set up a JIT also have the possibility to make use of the instruments available at the EU level. The most useful EU instrument for the exchange and analysis of information is the 'Analytical Work File' which exists at Europol.

The working methods of the AWF can be described as follows: the national police headquarters serve as Europol contact agencies, collecting information gathered at the local and regional police level. The information is pre-analysed by the national police headquarters and forwarded to Europol. At Europol a direct information exchange between the countries involved in the AWF takes place through the liaison officers based at Europol. At the same time, the data are fed into a database in which historical as well as live data are compared.
As soon as an AWF has been commenced, and the necessary arrangements have been made with regard to the organisation and data protection (cf., Article 12 Europol Convention), analysis may begin and results may also be transmitted – though only after the approval of the Management Board (with regard to com-

---

[25] *Gesetz über das Bundeskriminalamt und die Zusammenarbeit des Bundes und der Länder in kriminalpolizeilichen Angelegenheiten (Bundeskriminalamtgesetz – BKAG) – Bundes Kriminal Amt Gezetz 1997* [Law on the Bundes Kriminal Amt], § 14.

pliance with Article 12 Europol Convention). The transmission of data will be recorded in the file concerned. If any cross-links (that could serve as the basis for joint investigations) are found by the Analysis Group, the AWF Member States are informed. This implies that the national police headquarters of the Member States will be informed via the liaison officers. If further information is needed from the Member States the liaison officers of the respective countries at Europol are called upon to contact the persons responsible in the Member States so that the necessary requests may be transmitted.

Any country (or institution), irrespective of being a EU member or a member of the AWF, is free to supply data to the work file. However, non-members are not entitled to receive information from the work files, as long as the AWF members do not decide otherwise.

The transmission and analysis of information is thus the basis on which the AWF works, and the results can be subsequently used by all the parties involved. The AWF thus merely makes the necessary hits, and then the results can be used by the participants.

When information exchange occurs through an AWF, the legal framework of Europol applies. This implies that information gathered in the AWF remains subject to the ownership and responsibility of the Member State that disseminated it. The Member State itself decides what will happen to the information. Article 10 paragraph 8 of the Europol Convention of 26 July 1995[26] states that the Member State is *'the sole judge of the degree of the sensitivity of an item and variations thereof.'* The article further mentions: *'Any dissemination or operational use of analysis data shall be decided on in consultation with the participants in the analysis.'* This means that, in principle, it is not self-evident that information is automatically passed from the AWF to the JIT. Each Member State can decide that certain information cannot be disseminated or that certain conditions will be attached to any dissemination. But if authorisation is obtained from the Member State that owns the information and the other partners in the AWF agree as well, there should not be a problem in the information from the AWF to the JIT. Whenever data will be disseminated or used, the participants in the analysis will decide on the basis of consensus. When a Member State joins an analysis in progress, it may not disseminate or use the data without the prior agreement of the Member States initially involved. The information flowing from an AWF can be used by a Member State as information and

---

[26] Convention of 26 July 1995 on the establishment of a European Police Office, Europol Convention.

even as evidence in a criminal investigation as long as the Member State where the data originated thereby from agrees.[27]

This agreement is of the utmost importance. In the THB-JIT project the dissemination of information was at first allowed, but was refused at a later stage, because one of the members objected thereto.

2. THE USE OF A JIG

During the project to start a THB-JIT, the participants invented a new instrument, called a 'Joint Intelligence Group'. Because no pre-investigative phase was provided in the Framework Decision on JIT, or in the EU Convention on Mutual Legal Assistance of 2000, the countries involved decided to set up a Joint Intelligence Group (JIG).

2.1 **A new instrument**

As mentioned above, no regulations have been provided for the pre-operational phase of the JIT. The participants in the THB-JIT project therefore set up the JIG of their own initiative. They thought that this instrument could help them in the run-up to the operational phase.

This Joint Intelligence Group operated within the boundaries of its specific nature:

No legal framework was created for the JIG, which means that the national rules on information gathering and exchange applied to the functioning of this concept.

The JIG was set up alongside, and in relation to, the AWF. The members of the JIG were to be the country representatives in the AWF.[28] The only 'new' member would therefore be the JIG team leader, whose task it was to facilitate the rapid transfer of data to the AWF. The intelligence gathering of the AWF and the JIG could – in theory – work differently in so far as Europol is bound by a

---

[27] T. Schalken and M. Pronk, 'On Joint Investigation Teams, Europol and Supervision of their Joint Actions', *European Journal on Crime, Criminal Law and Criminal Justice,* 2002, Vol. 10/1, p. 70-82.

[28] In practice however, the members of the JIG were not always the same persons as the representatives in the AWF. Some countries were represented in the JIG by their national specialists in trafficking in human beings, and not by their representatives at Europol.

formal procedure (the scope of the AWF, transmission, analysis, storage of data). The JIG itself was not bound by the opening order or the data protection rules of Europol.

2.2 What is a JIG? Two perspectives

The JIG was a completely new instrument. It had come to exist as a part of work in progress. The working methods as well as the purpose of the JIG were not formally established, but were developed in successive discussions.

Different visions on the role of the JIG seem to have grown among the participants to the initiative. Two main perspectives were proposed by the partners to the THB-JIT initiative concerning the role that the JIG should/could fulfil.[29] The JIG could either function as the facilitator for the AWF between the Member States and Europol on the one hand, or act as a receiver of data from the AWF and from other countries, on the other. In the first perspective the JIG was considered to be a group of proactive investigators who bring data to the AWF.[30] Here, the JIG would be an enforcement of the AWF. In the second perspective, emphasis was placed on the analysis role which the JIG should/could fulfil. In the letter of intent of 03/12/2003 the JIG was described as an intelligence phase, necessary in order to analyse the available data. The JIG would therefore start its work after the information had been gathered, and act as a target group within the framework of the AWF.[31]

In both models, the AWF is responsible for the actual analysis, and the JIG could thus not be detached from the AWF.

2.2.1 The JIG as an enforcement of the AWF

In the first view, the JIG is not a structure or an instrument. It is perceived as a function to support and stimulate the intelligence process of gathering, collecting and exchanging information. The JIG members could be the same persons as the ones in the analytical working group. However, being a JIG member, they would have an extra role: responsibility for stimulating collection process. The main differences in the competences of the two leaders would then be that the head of the Analysis Group works on the information available, while the

---

[29] These are, of course, ideal types, and the uncontaminated existence of both next to each other should be looked upon with the necessary amount of scepticism. Moreover, the two models for the JIG could also succeed one another, meaning that the role of the JIG is dependent on the current stage of the project.

[30] Report of the meeting of the Joint Investigation Team steering group, 15 October 2003.

[31] C. Rijken, 'Scientific research JIT – First report', 3 October 2004, p. 32.

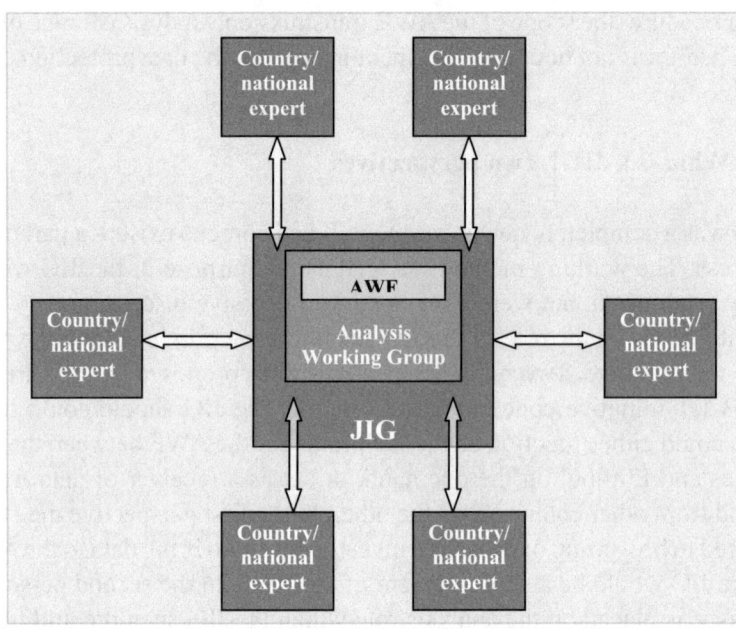

JIG team leader organises the continuous flow of information towards the AWF. The JIG is thus considered to be a necessary link between the AWF and the Analysis Working Group on the one hand, and the different countries on the other. In this sense, the JIG is not an institution or a structure; it is a function which provides emphasis to the analysis group and enforces its functioning. The JIG is based on the same idea (inviting people to send information) and therefore duplicates the efforts of the AWF. The establishment of a JIG in this perspective serves to make up for the difficulties in the functioning of the AWF. If the AWF works as it should, this type of JIG would not be necessary. An amelioration of the AWF is in this case preferable to the creation of a JIG.

2.2.2 *The JIG as an addition to the AWF*

In this perspective the JIG should not intervene in the work carried out in the AWF. The JIG would only start to be active after a target group has been identified in the AWF – if no such group is found, then the JIG exists only formally. This means that, if the AWF would come up with a JIT-worthy offender group, this should be passed on to the JIG/JIT initiative, which would then take over the investigation and collect as much data as possible concerning the target group. Here the JIG is a phase that follows the AWF, after a target group has been identified.

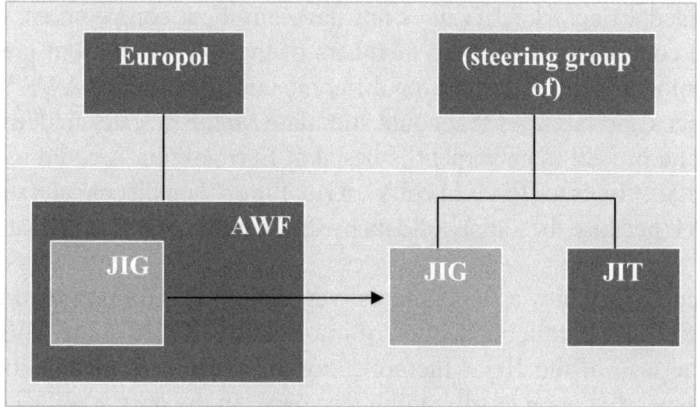

Once a target group is identified, however, there are no longer any reasons to postpone the actual start of the JIT. The countries in the AWF that have found linked cases can set up a JIT and draft the JIT agreement that could serve as a legal basis for the information exchange and the investigative tasks that will be carried out from that moment onwards.

An additional added value of the JIG was seen in the fact that it provided an opportunity to engage in bilateral relationships with other contributors, such as third countries and non-governmental organisations.[32] The JIG partners should then invite more partners – countries that are not members of the AWF – to send information on the target group: the members of the JIG would not limit their contacts to those with their national authorities, but would also engage in contacts with other countries. In this way, intelligence on the target group could be enlarged with information from other countries. Following this perspective, the JIG should thus gather intelligence other than that of the AWF. It would not be a problem, however, to postpone the interaction with third countries and bodies to the operational phase of the JIT. A further elaboration of the possibilities for information exchange will follow in the next chapter.

2.3 Problems and concerns relating to the use of a JIG

The JIG was a dry run for a new instrument. Its use seemed to be accompanied by certain problems and concerns.

2.3.1 *A JIG existing next to an AWF*

The AWF was the already existing instrument for the pre-operational phase. An additional instrument should only have been created if it would have allowed

---

[32] F. Francis, 'Project initiation document', 1 December 2003, p. 2.

for an added value. The JIG does not have any new competences, however. Quite the contrary: whereas the members of the JIG can not put pressure on other members to deliver more or different information, the AWF has some competences and facilities that could stimulate Member States to deliver information. The project management is based at Europol, but it could use the national contact points to 'force an entry'. Also, Europol could consider the closing of the AWF because the supply of data by the Member States is not satisfactory.

It is difficult to see how a JIG could deliver additional information to the AWF. In the THB-JIT a parallel collection of information existed at the AWF and the JIG.[33] One task of the JIG – the collection of additional information for the AWF – is clearly meant to fill intelligence gaps. In the past, AWF's have often lacked efficiency due to Member States' reluctance to (rapidly) provide data of any value. Accordingly the concept of a JIG was created in order to actively help stimulate the information flow, to improve the quality of data and to close identified information gaps. These functions could all be taken by the AWF, and do not require the instrument of a JIG.
Also, the filling of intelligence gaps is in any case a task which should be executed once a case suitable for a JIT has been chosen. It transpired that no suitable case had been selected and the JIG was unable to perform this task. The THB-JIG has not gathered any information outside the AWF. The JIG was meant to make up for the shortcomings of the AWF, but it did not succeed in this. If the functioning of the AWF would be improved, however, then a JIG would be technically redundant.

Filling intelligence gaps that have remained after the collection of intelligence in the AWF could thus better be done after a suitable case for a JIT has been chosen. Then, however, a separate JIG phase would not be necessary and the filling of intelligence gaps could take place within the operational JIT. Considering that a distinction needs to be made between the AWF and the JIG, no other solution exists than to conclude a JIT agreement after obtaining the results from the AWF and before starting the JIT with the JIG included in this phase as an intelligence function/instrument. At this point, a distinction can no longer be made between the JIG and the JIT. This had the additional advantage that in this case a subsequent legal framework existed, being that of the JIT. Moreover, the

---

[33] The limits of what could be done in the JIG were also set by the conditions of the AWF. For example, in the beginning the AWF information was exchanged with that of the JIG. At a later stage however, Belgium – one of the members of the AWF – objected to this practice. From that point onwards, the AWF information could no longer be dealt with in the JIG. This led to rather difficult situations, e.g., because of the fact that a part of the steering group received AWF reports, while the other members, including the president, were not allowed to know their content.

accelerated start of the operational phase would allow for the members to set up the JIT in one country and work there as a team. Through this intensified cooperation, it is easier to find a common approach and to gather knowledge on the participating countries' expectations, which in its turn will improve cooperation.

2.3.2 What about a JIG in a bottom-up procedure?

The JIG was established in relation to the AWF. Every function it was granted had to do with the identification of a JIT-worthy case. This was thus the main problem which the JIG had to solve. In a bottom-up procedure, a 'mother case' would already have been identified, and an instrument like a JIG would not have any use, as it had been perceived in the THB-JIT project. After all, when a first link has been established, this already enables the setting up of a JIT and the pre-operational phase should not be prolonged. A further analysis of the information of the partners to the JIT could then take place within the operational phase, after the agreement has been established, and within the legal framework of the JIT. Thus, the need for a JIG does not occur when a request for a JIT follows a bottom-up procedure and not a top-down procedure.

The only real issue here is who will be responsible for analysing of the information gathered if no supranational structure is involved.[34] In the bottom-up scenario, this question is especially relevant for the operational phase of the JIT (cf., the next chapter). One remark that can already be made here, however, is that the operational JIT would benefit from the presence of members with different profiles in the JIT, so that different functions can be fulfilled within the JIT, being investigation and analysis. Also, it is recommendable to involve Europol as often as possible in the JITs that are set up. Europol through the instrument of an AWF could fulfil functions which are not within the scope of the JIT, but which could be useful for its functioning. After all, an operating JIT is still in need of updated data. The AWF could add to the continued supply of new data to the operational JIT, from Member States that are not a party to the JIT. Also, when several JITs are set up at the same time, Europol could be responsible for any overview of the existing JITs, and possibly identify links between existing joint investigation teams or cases.

2.3.3 Efficiency of a JIG

The construction of a JIG in preparation for the JIT added to the bureaucratic and formal character of the THB-JIT project.

---

[34] Analysis was not a function attributed to the JIG as it was set up in relation to the AWF, which could then carry out this task.

Meetings were organised in which members were to discuss the information exchanged and the progress made in the project. This formal way of functioning had the disadvantage, however, that a great deal of investment already had to be made in the pre-operational phase, an investment that the participants were not all willing or able to make. The different partners involved always had to be represented at the meetings. This representative thus had to put his normal tasks aside, and reserve time for the new project – without being sure that a return on his investment would be assured. This and other factors contributed to the fact that the Member States did not always assign the same representatives.

Consequently an additional burden was created, taking the form of recurrent and repeated discussions on the original ideas, the distribution of responsibilities, the role of the JIG, the formalities stemming from the establishment of a JIG and a steering group, etc. As a consequence, time and energy was lost and had to be recovered at a later stage (see also in more detail Chapter VI).

3. TOWARDS CONCLUSIONS: HOW SHOULD INFORMATION EXCHANGE TAKE PLACE IN THIS PHASE?

In this chapter we have looked at the different possibilities for information exchange in the pre-operational phase of a JIT, and discussed their most important advantages and disadvantages.

3.1 Recommendable characteristics

Therefore, in these conclusions an overview of some recommendable characteristics can be presented. On the basis of the previous discussions, we can conclude that information exchange in the pre-operational phase should take place.

3.1.1 *Rapidly and efficiently*

It is to the advantage of every partner in the JIT that the pre-operational phase is as short as possible. After all, if a JIT can be established, the operational phase has many advantages allowing for an acceleration of the ongoing investigations. In a JIT means can be used which no national investigation, or mirror investigation, could resort to.

Rapidity and efficiency can best be achieved in simple structures, which do not burden the project unnecessarily. This means that no new structures should be set up if it is possible to use the existing ones. In the THB-JIT project both a steering group and a JIG were set up to guide the pre-operational phase of the JIT. Afterwards, most of the participants in the project declared that (one of or both) these structures were dispensable. They all preferred a pre-operational phase with a simple structure, in reaction to the experiences gained as a result of the complexity of the THB-JIT project.[35] It was commonly agreed that the more countries are involved, the more complex the (pre-operational) structures will be.

3.1.2   *Using available information and instruments*

In the THB-JIT project a top-down approach was adopted, meaning that the project started out with a general process of intelligence gathering, the aim of which was to select a suitable case for realising an operational JIT. This approach can be distinguished from a so-called bottom-up approach – used in the Drugs JIT – in which a concrete investigation/a common target is already present at the outset and further intelligence gathering is built upon it.

The top-down approach has proved to be very difficult and time-consuming. An extensive intelligence phase has been required to identify common interests and strategies and to single out suitable target groups. In interviews participants in the THB-JIT project stated that they favoured a bottom-up approach for commencing a JIT. Also, practitioners tend to be much more motivated to apply a new tool if the need to apply it stems from ongoing investigations and pressing common problems. The '*need*' basis could therefore be identified as one of the success factors in starting a JIT. The establishment of a JIT relying on ongoing investigations in one or more countries helps to avoid a complex and time-consuming 'JIG phase' and ensures that the persons involved have a great motivation to support the JIT.

For the Drugs JIT, it cannot really be argued that there was a specific pre-operational phase in which intelligence was gathered in order to assess whether it was possible/desirable to set up a joint team. Instead, the fruits of national investigations were sufficient to start a JIT. This makes clear that a separate pre-operational phase is not always necessary. This seems to be especially the case when a JIT is commenced by a bottom-up initiative.

When an analysis instrument does prove to be necessary, however, the AWF instrument at Europol should be used to assess whether a JIT is possible and desirable. At this moment in time the AWFs are not yet being applied as they should.[36] A great deal of criticism can still be heard concerning the input to the AWF as well as its output.[37] The problems concerning the input to the AWF

---

[35] This aspect also refers to the distinction between the bottom-up and top-down approach.
[36] P. Vermaas., 'Europol verre van optimaal benut', *Algemeen Politieblad,* 1999, 17, 12-16.
[37] L. Groffils, N. Van Eeckhout and J. Vanermen, 'Europol en gemeenschappelijke onderzoeksteams', in G. Vermeulen, ed., *Aspecten van Europees formeel strafrecht,* Antwerp, Maklu, 2002, 9 en W. Bruggeman, 'De toekomst van Europol. Gewild of gedoogd?', *Panopticon,* 2004.

could be partly resolved by creating a standardised format for data supply to AWFs. On the other hand, data supply could also be stimulated by the functioning of the AWF itself.[38] If AWFs prove their right of existence by supplying their members with excellent operational results that could never have been created without the AWF, this will stimulate Member States to use the instrument more often. Now, Member States sometimes find that the AWFs are more utilized for gathering and storing data, rather than the production of operational results with an added value.

Furthermore, an agreement [39] has been signed between Europol and Eurojust on the basis of which Europol shall supply analysis data and analysis results to Eurojust. The intelligence from the AWFs also enables the latter to decide whether the establishment of a JIT is necessary. Eurojust can subsequently ask the competent authorities of the Member States involved to consider setting up a Joint team.[40]

3.1.3 Aimed at identifying links

In the pre-operational phase, one should thus not be occupied with, e.g., 'the identification of illegal structures of trafficking in human beings'[41] – treating the pre-operational phase as an operational phase in itself, but the identification of possible links between ongoing investigations in two or more countries. This 'identification of illegal structures' could then be done much more rapidly and efficiently in the operational phase, as additional means would be available within the framework of a better coordination between countries. In the Belgian feasibility study for the AWF it was even clearer that the objective strived for had an operational nature, as its goals were to: 'dismantle and/or destabilize the criminal groups in the short term (six months), with coordinated investigations/ operations in the participating countries.'[42] The lingering during the pre-operational phase, however, slowed operations down, instead of speeding them up.

---

[38] C. Fijnaut, 'Europol en Eurojust, politiële en justitiële samenwerking in strafzaken', *Justitiële Verkenningen*, 2001, jrg. 27, nr. 2, (11) 11-12.

[39] Agreement of 9 June 2004 between Eurojust and Europol, URL: <http://www.europol.eu.int/legal/agreements/Agreements/17374.pdf>.

[40] Article 6, a, iv of the decision of 28 February 2002 setting up Eurojust with a view to reinforcing the fight against serious crime, *OJ* L 63, 6.03.2002, p. 1.

[41] This is however what happened in the attempt to establish the THB-JIT project. This goal by the AWF was described by the steering group of the JIT-initiative.

[42] Federale Politie – Centrale Cel Mensenhandel, 'Feasibility study – AWF Maritsa', 7 November 2003.

3.1.4 *With the involvement of judicial actors*

A joint investigation team is a form of judicial cooperation in criminal matters. Serious indications exist, however, that the participants in this project perceived a joint investigation team as a form of police cooperation. Most importantly, in the examples seen in the scientific research the pre-operational phase mainly consisted of interactions between police actors. The national judicial authorities were occasionally involved, but not on a structural basis. Eurojust participated in the THB-JIT project from the beginning as an observer.

The involvement of judicial actors is very important, however. Considering the importance of the role of the prosecutor in the civil law system, and his role in the proceedings, the non-involvement of the national prosecutors in the preparatory phase of the JIT creates the risk that efforts and time are lost. After all, police forces operate under the authority of the judicial actors. Due to the minimal representation of the judicial authorities in the THB project, for example, the steering group was often not able to take *ad hoc* decisions at its meetings because authorisation had to be obtained in the home country.

3.2 Challenges and questions to be answered

The scientific research concerning both JITs also showed, however, that the machinery to be used to set up a JIT was also in need of lubrication so that it could run more smoothly. The greatest challenges seem to lie in the involvement of Europol in the pre-operational phase of a JIT, and the ways in which the supply of information from national investigations could be stimulated.

3.2.1 *Bilateral or centralised?*

If information exchange takes a bilateral form, the question arises how information flows should be organised if more than two countries set up a JIT. If information is exchanged directly between two Member States, and information is not fed into a central platform such as the AWF, the danger exists that the other Member States involved in the initiative are not necessarily informed. Therefore, the central collection of information by Europol is favoured due to its standardised information collection procedure.

Also no instrument allows for better data protection and the handling of sensitive information. Each Member State that provides information to Europol can decide whether the information can be disseminated or if certain conditions apply to dissemination. According to Article 10, paragraph 8 Europol Convention, the Member State that communicates the data to Europol is the one which determines the degree of its sensitivity. If a Member State informs Europol that the dissemination of information provided by that Member State is subject to prior authorisation, the dissemination of analysis containing the data equally requires prior authorisation. Any dissemination or operational use of analysis data shall be decided upon in consultation with the participants in the analysis. A Member State joining an analysis in progress may not disseminate or use the data without the prior agreement of the Member States initially concerned therewith. The information coming from an analytic work file/AWF (Articles 10 ff. Europol Convention) can be used by a Member State as information and even as evidence in a criminal investigation as long as the Member State supplying the data thereby agrees.[43]

There are, however, also some disadvantages to be found in the use of an AWF. In normal circumstances, an AWF is opened on the initiative of Europol, or at the request of the Member States,[44] after which a project description is made. The countries involved all carry out feasibility studies. (Cf., Common Process for National Feasibility study and Collection Plan – Pre-opening of the AWF).[45] Only then can a formal approval by the Management Board follow, after consultation by the Joint Supervisory Body.[46] Then an Opening Order has to be agreed upon, which elaborates the type of information that can be stored in the AWF. First, however, agreement on this matter has to be reached between the Member States. It is therefore crystal clear that many investments have to be made before an AWF can be opened, especially considering the fact that the pre-operational phase should be as short as possible.

Considering that the AWF combines advantages in its structure that cannot be found in any other international instrument, all efforts should be made to turn it in to an instrument that is also characterised by efficiency and rapidity, so as to remove the final obstacles to its widespread use.

3.2.2 *Stimulating information flows*

One of the main difficulties in the THB-JIT project was that the supply of information from the Member States to the AWF was not sufficient. For this reason, one even tried to grant a stimulating function to the JIG so as to increase the

---

[43] 'Scientific research JIT – Second report', 16 January 2005, p. 56.
[44] Article 12, Council Act of 3 November 1998 Adopting Rules Applicable to Europol Analysis Files, *OJ* C 026, 23.01.1999.
[45] EUROPOL, 'Order opening Analysis Work File', 19 November 2003.
[46] Article 5, Council Act of 3 November 1998 Adopting Rules Applicable to Europol Analysis Files, *OJ* C 026, 23.01.1999.

flow of information. The idea was that – in order for the JIG to be more effective than the AWF – the JIG could act with authority in order to bring information from the countries in question to the AWF. The authority of the members of the JIG to put pressure on the authorities of the Member States to deliver information would then be based on the steering group. This means that the information collection process would not depend on asking and convincing, but on the issuing of binding requests by the JIG to national police services (of the participating countries). In this way an official expectation that information should be shared would be created, meaning that a reluctance to share information would imply repercussions from the law enforcement top.

The idea behind this JIG model is not without interest, as the information flow to the AWF was clearly found to be problematic. A solution could be to give the request for information a binding character, in the sense that the receiving authority is obliged to answer the request within a reasonable time. Thus, if a (national) contact point receives a request, this actor should in his turn issue binding requests to the other (regional) departments to answer affirmatively or negatively the question whether they have knowledge about related cases. An answer should thus be provided anyway, whether it is positive or negative, and within a reasonable time.

3.3   A stepping- stone to the operational phase

If in the pre-operational phase information exchange has succeeded in reaching its objectives, the actual setting up of the operational phase can take place: the case is identified, the partners are known and they know that the setting up of a JIT is both possible and desirable. Then, however there are new problems to be tackled. These will be discussed in the next chapter.

CHAPTER III
LAW ENFORCEMENT INFORMATION EXCHANGE IN THE OPERATIONAL PHASE OF A JIT

Annelies Balcaen[*]

This chapter will discuss the law enforcement information exchange in the operational phase of a JIT. The Drugs JIT between the Netherlands and the United Kingdom is the only JIT that has thus far been operational. Therefore, this case will be the central focus of examination. An ongoing investigation in the United Kingdom on cocaine trafficking identified a link to the Netherlands, with some suspects living there. Available British intelligence was shared with the Dutch counterparts and consequently it was decided to set up a JIT between the Netherlands and the United Kingdom.

The THB-JIT project under review did not enter the operational phase. Therefore, the research focussed on the extent to which the stated differences in criminal proceedings in the participating countries were discussed and expected to constitute problems at a later stage and whether they affected the preliminary discussions on establishing a JIT. Consequently, this THB-JIT project will only be examined from a theoretical point of view.

Law enforcement information exchange in the operational phase of a JIT comprises different possibilities. Firstly, there is the information exchange that can take place between the members of the JIT. Secondly, information can be exchanged between EU Member States which are not party to the JIT and the JIT itself. The third form of information exchange concerns the exchange of information with third countries.

---

[*] Annelies Balcaen is researcher at the Institute for International Research on Criminal Policy (IRCP), Ghent University (Belgium).

C. Rijken and G. Vermeulen (Eds.), Joint Investigation Teams in the European Union
© 2006, T·M·C·ASSER PRESS, *The Hague, The Netherlands and the Authors*

1. INFORMATION EXCHANGE BETWEEN THE MEMBERS OF A JIT

The information exchange between the members of a JIT implies that persons from different countries share information, which originates from their countries, with each other during the operational phase of a joint investigation team. Ideally, this information exchange should take place as if the investigation was a common national investigation. No traditional requests for mutual assistance should be issued in order to receive information from a seconded member of the team.

In the Drugs JIT, this resulted in the following situation: since the JIT was established in the Netherlands, the English police officers were the seconded members of the team and information could be exchanged between the Dutch police officers and their English colleagues.

The information exchange within the operational phase of a JIT is of crucial importance for the success of the concept of a joint investigation team, in the absence of which the aim of a joint investigation team (enhancing mutual cooperation in criminal matters) cannot be obtained.

Several questions can be asked in relation to this information exchange.

Firstly, questions emerge about the legal basis of this information exchange and, more specifically, about the conditions for this information exchange, the kind of information that can be exchanged and the formalities which have to be fulfilled.

Furthermore, questions concerning the obstacles or problems encountered when exchanging information can be raised.

Finally, it can be questioned whether the information lawfully obtained within a JIT may be used in the home country.

These questions will be addressed in the following sections.

1.1 **Legal basis of the right for seconded members to provide the JIT with information which is available in the home country**

The legal basis for the information exchange between the members of the JIT can be found in Article 1 paragraph 9 of the Framework Decision on JITs[1] and Article 13 paragraph 9 of the EU Convention on Mutual Assistance:[2]

---

[1] Council Framework Decision of 13 June 2002 on Joint Investigation Teams, *OJ* L 162, 20.06 2002, p. 1-3.

[2] Convention of 29 May 2000 on Mutual Assistance in Criminal Matters between the Member States of the EU, *OJ* C 197, 12.07.2000, p. 1.

A member of the joint investigation team may, in accordance with his or her national law and within the limits of his or her capacity, provide the team with information available in the Member State which has seconded him or her for the purpose of the criminal investigations conducted by the team.

According to this paragraph, the national legislation of the home state still plays an important role in determining whether it is possible for a member of the JIT to provide the team with information originating from his/her home country.

1.1.1 Implementation legislation

A member of the team can only share information as long as this is possible according to the national legislation of his/her country and within the boundaries set by this legislation.
This may however cause some problems when the Member State has not enacted sufficient legislation to allow this information exchange to take place.

This problem was clearly present in the operational JIT. The legislative measures taken in the Netherlands and the United Kingdom will therefore be the subject of the following sections.

1.1.2 The Netherlands

As already mentioned in chapter I, the Netherlands has inserted a new third paragraph in Article 13 of the Data Protection Police Files Act of 1990[3] in order to meet the requirements of Article 13 paragraph 9 of the EU Convention on Mutual Assistance. This created the possibility for Dutch JIT members to provide data from temporary police files for JIT purposes. Complementary to this, the Police Files Decree was completed with an Article 13a. According to this article, seconded members of a joint team established in the Netherlands may be provided with information on the same footing as the Dutch police officers and information can also be provided to Dutch police officers in a foreign team.

Furthermore, Dutch officials who participate in a JIT established in one of the participating countries, may place the results of the investigations at the disposal of the team subject to certain conditions. These conditions involve the fact that Dutch legislation is still applicable to the information gathered and these documents can only be used as evidence when they are placed at the disposal of the team (Article 552qe CCP).

---

[3] Data Protection Police Files Acts (*Wet Politieregisters*), Wet van 21 juni 1990, *Staatsblad van het Koninkrijk der Nederlanden* (Dutch Bulletin of Acts and Decrees) 1990, 414.

Applying this legislation to the Drugs JIT, it can be argued that the English seconded members had the right to receive information on the same footing as Dutch police officers. And if the team would have been replaced by one another country, the Dutch police officers could also receive information.

The data analysis in the Drugs JIT does not differ from any other national investigation: one police officer functions as the analyst; the other investigators are not involved in the analysis of data as such. Once a new investigation is commenced, a computerised data system is used to fill in the data (MRO: Meldingen Recherche Onderzoeken). As a starting point, the goals of the investigation have to be stated (in this case tackling drug illegal imports as part of the drug trafficking) as well as information available on the suspects. All information gathered in the course of the investigation has to be put on record and is subsequently fed into the database. The system will indicate any links to another investigation running in the Netherlands in order to avoid duplications. The database is not only administered by the police, but also by customs, the military police as well as other special investigating services.

1.1.3   *The United Kingdom*

The United Kingdom has not transposed the provision of Article 13(9) of the EU Convention on Mutual Assistance and therefore cooperation in a JIT context will not have any added value compared to traditional cooperation in criminal matters. The Home Office Circular of 1 October 2002 on the EU Framework Decision on joint investigation teams[4] confirms that the sharing of information by seconded members must be in accordance with the law of their Member State and within the limits of his/her own competence.
This means that in the Drugs JIT, the seconded English police officers were still dependent on national legislation to provide the team with information.
The THB-JIT project did not enter the operational phase. However, the legislative measures taken to transpose the provisions on the right for seconded members to provide the JIT with information which is available in the home country were studied and consequently the situation in Belgium and Germany will be explained.

1.1.4   *Belgium*

Article 10 paragraph 2 of the Mutual Assistance Act of 9 December 2004 states that Belgian seconded members may, for the purpose of the criminal investiga-

---

[4] Home Office Circular of 1 October 2002 on the EU Framework Decision on Joint Investigation Teams.

tion conducted by the JIT and in conformity with Belgian law, provide the JIT with information which they could access in the context of a domestic investigation.[5]

1.1.5 *Germany*

Two relevant bills, one for the implementation of and another for the approval of the EU Mutual Assistance Convention entered into force in August 2005. The first bill was aimed at inserting a chapter regarding 'remaining legal assistance' in the IRG (The Gesetz über die internationale Rechtshilfe in Strafsachen) including a new Article 83k, which must allow for cooperation in genuine JITs. The requirements of paragraph 9 of Article 13 of the EU Convention on Mutual Assistance have been fully met by Article 83k, paragraph 3 of the IRG act. Where necessary for JIT action, German JIT members will be allowed to provide information directly to all other members or participants in the JIT, including personal data.

1.1.6 *Information available to seconded members*

A second condition mentioned in Article 10(9) of the Framework Decision on JITs and Article 13(9) of the EU Convention on Mutual Assistance concerns the availability of information to the seconded members. The information from the home country can only be exchanged with other JIT members as long as it is available to the seconded members.

In general, law enforcement authorities in the EU have access nationally to information from different sources, public or private, whenever this is necessary for the fulfilment of their tasks. Such access is specifically provided for by law or is incorporated in the general rule of the duty to collaborate with the authorities. In some cases, access is only possible with a judicial warrant.

1.1.7 *The Netherlands*

In the Netherlands, the central authority having access to operational information is the KLPD (Korps Landelijke Politiediensten or the National Police Services Agency, in other words the National Police Force). Together with the 25 regional police forces, it forms the Dutch Police. The management of the KLPD

---

[5] *Article 10 § 2 of the wet van 9 december 2004 betreffende de wederzijdse rechtshulp in strafzaken en tot wijziging van artikel 90ter van het wetboek van strafvordering* (the law on mutual assistance in criminal matters), *B.S.*, 24 December 2004.

lies in the hands of the Minister of Internal Affairs (Minister van Binnenlandse Zaken en Koninkrijkrelaties).

Article 38 of the Police Act of 1993[6] states that the KLPD is in charge of the national and specialist execution of police tasks, in cooperation with the regional police forces, the royal 'Marechaussee' (Military Constabulary) and the prosecuting authorities. More specifically, the KLPD is responsible for the gathering, registering, processing, managing, analysing and the provision of information on behalf of the regional police forces, the prosecuting authorities and the royal 'Marechaussee' (police force). Furthermore, the National Police Force is also competent to exchange information on the international level.[7]

Services within the KLPD
The KLPD is composed of twelve executive services performing the core activities of the police force. The International Network Service (DIN) and the National Criminal Investigation Information Service (DNRI) are the services of the force which are responsible for the supply of information. The former is the office to which Dutch and foreign investigative authorities can request for information and the latter is the office that provides information to the Dutch police forces.

Another Service that was put under the management of the KLPD as of 1 January 2004, and was integrated in the latter on 1 January 2005, is the National Criminal Investigation Department (*Dienst Nationale Recherche*). This Service is responsible for combating serious or organised crime with a national or international character. Furthermore, the service functions as an expert in certain areas, including trafficking in drugs and trafficking in human beings. Within these areas, the service focuses on information gathering, investigations and the giving of advice on preventive measures.[8] The National Criminal Investigation Department is internationally minded and is also an important partner for the execution of international requests for mutual assistance.

---

[6] *Wet van 9 December 1993 tot vaststelling van een nieuwe politiewet* (Law on the establishment of a new law on Police), *Staatsblad van het Koninkrijk der Nederlanden (*Dutch Bulletin of Acts and Decrees*)* 1993, 724.

[7] *Korps Landelijke Politiediensten* (National Crime Squad), URL: <http://www.politie.nl/KLPD/>.

[8] *Organisatie van de Dienst Nationale recherche* (National Intelligence Service), URL: <http://www.politie.nl/klpd/klpddiensten/dienst_nationale_recherche/info/organisatie.asp>.

1.1.8 The United Kingdom

National Crime Squad
The National Crime Squad is engaged in the investigation of serious and organised crime. Their activities require the creation, storage, retrieval, archiving and disposal of operational and non-operational records. Records are created and maintained for strategic, policy and performance issues, as well as personnel and operational matters. These records are kept in accordance with the requirements of Data Protection, Codes of Practice on Access to Government Information, Freedom of Information and Public Records Acts.[9] The National Crime Squad is the only authority that can access information belonging to local police forces during the operational investigative phase.

NCIS
The National Crime Intelligence Service is a non-departmental public body responsible for the gathering, storage and analysis of information in order to generate criminal intelligence. The NCIS provides intelligence to the different local police forces and the National Crime Squad, and acts in support of these police services carrying out their criminal intelligence activities.[10] The working arrangements between NCIS and its partners are contained within partnership agreements, working protocols and memoranda of understanding. NCIS will become part of the new Serious Organised Crime Agency (SOCA), planned to start work in 2006.[11]

The National Strategy for Police Information Systems
The Home Office and ACPO[12] set up a long term programme with the aim of providing common police IT applications for England and Wales: the National Strategy for Police Information Systems. As the different local police forces often make use of the same sort of information, the development of national IT systems was deemed necessary in order to make a better communication of information possible. The introduction of the IT system should do away with the paper-based case files, which means that efforts are often duplicated and

---

[9] <http://www.nationalcrimesquad.police.uk/downloads/R13.pdf>.
[10] Section 2, Police Act 1997.
[11] <http://www.ncis.co.uk/ncis.asp>.
[12] To overcome differences in policies in the different local police forces, the Association of Chief Police Officers (ACPO) was set up. In this way the different forces are encouraged to work together, to employ common policies, strategies and methods. ACPO's members are police officers who hold the rank of Chief Constable, Deputy Chief Constable or Assistant Chief Constable, or their equivalents, in the 45 forces of England, Wales and Northern Ireland, the national police agencies and certain other forces in the United Kingdom.

that the sharing of information is rather difficult. Also, the IT programme should make it possible for police forces and criminal justice organisations to share information and work in partnerships.[13] The National Strategy for Police Information Systems was conceived as a method to improve information sharing by the integration of IT systems within and between the different police forces.[14] The most important objectives of this Strategy relate to the provision of national information technology and communications systems and to create an interface between the police and criminal justice organisations.[15] The Case Preparation application enables the sharing of information with other criminal justice organisations like the CPS. Case files will also have a unique reference number, making it easier to track their progress through the criminal justice system. The full capacity of the NSPIS Custody and Case Preparation is due for completion by March 2006. At this point it has been implemented in ten forces.[16] A body called PITO is in charge of the NSPIS. PITO includes representatives from ACPO, local authorities and the Home Office. PITO is in charge of the management of the Police National Network and the provision of information from the Police National Computer, which is a source of police intelligence available to all forces nationwide.[17]

Since Belgium and Germany were not involved in the Drugs JIT, but were participants in the THB-JIT project, the availability of information to the seconded members was studied mainly in the field of human trafficking, the central phenomenon in the THB-JIT project.

1.1.9 *Belgium*

Central Unit on Human Trafficking
The most important basis for the gathering and processing of police information are Articles 44/1 to 44/11 of the Law on the Office of the Police of 5 August 1992.[18]

---

[13] Metropolitan Police – The National Strategy for Police Information Systems, URL: <http://www.met.police.uk/doi/nspis.htm>.
[14] Home Office, consultation documents, URL: <http://www.consult-me.co.uk/csc-case-studies-home%20office.htm>.
[15] PITO, URL: <http://www.pito.org.u;/aboutPITO/vision/index.htm>.
[16] PITO, criminal justice integration, URL: <http://www.pito.org.uk/what_we_do/criminal_justice_integration/custody_case.htm>.
[17] Metropolitan Police – The National Strategy for Police Information Systems, URL: <http://www.met.police.uk/doi/nspis.htm>.
[18] *Wet 5 augustus 1992 op het politieambt* (Law 5 August 1995 on the Office of the Police), *B.S.*, 22 December 1992.

Regarding the phenomenon of trafficking in human beings, the access to operational information is based on Ministry Guideline 10/2004 on the policy for the investigation and prosecution of human trafficking.[19] This directive came into force on 1 May 2004 and it is an amended version of the initial Ministry Guideline 12/1999.[20]

The central authority having access to the operational information is the Central Unit on Human Trafficking, which is part of the General Directorate of the judicial services and falls under the Crime against Persons Directorate. The Central Unit centralises the information on persons or companies, suspected of being involved in human trafficking. This information was gathered by the police services and the administrative control agencies of different levels. The Central Unit is involved in strategic and operational analysis concerning the seriousness, the extent, the nature and the evolution of the phenomenon and informs the magistrates about their results.

General National Database
Police Services and administrative services carry out controls with the aim being to obtain data that could lead to the prosecutions of perpetrator of human trafficking. Ministry Guideline 10/2004 further refers to Directive MFO-3 of the Ministers of Justice and Internal Affairs on the information management for the judicial and administrative police of 14 June 2002 which states that the data obtained need to be sent to the information crossing points at district level. These data will then be placed in a general national database.[21] Directive MFO-3[22] is the executive instrument of Article 44/4 of the Law on the Office of the Police of 1992 which deals with the processing of information gathered by the police services.

---

[19] *Omzendbrief nr. COL 10/2004 van het College van Procureurs-generaal bij de Hoven van Beroep betreffende de aanpassing van de richtlijn van de minister van justitie houdende het opsporings- en vervolgingsbeleid betreffende mensenhandel*, (Circular COL 10/2004 of the Board of Procurators General of the Appeal Courts on the Amendment of the Guideline of the Minister of Justice on the Investigation and Prosecution of trafficking in Human Beings) URL: <http://www.poldoc.be/dailydoc/document/col/2004/col0410RichtlijnMJ.pdf>.

[20] *Omzendbrief nr. COL 12/1999 van het College van Procureurs-generaal bij de Hoven van beroep betreffende de richtlijnen van de Minister van Justitie houdende het opsporings- en vervolgingsbeleid betreffende mensenhandel en kinderpornografie*, (Circular COL 12.1999 of the Board of Procurators General of the Appeal Courts on the Guidelines of the Minister of Justice on the Investigation and Prosecution of Trafficking in Human Beings and Child Pornography) URL: <http://www.poldoc.be/dailydoc/document/col/1999/col9912n.pdf>.

[21] ANG = *Algemene Nationale Gegevensbank, (General National Database)*.

[22] *Gemeenschappelijke richtlijn MFO-3 van 14 juni 2002 van de Ministers van Justitie en van Binnenlandse Zaken betreffende het informatiebeheer inzake gerechtelijke en bestuurlijke politie* (Joint Directive of the Ministers of Justice and Internal Affairs on Information Management with regard to the Judicial and the Administrative Police), *B.S.*, 18 June 2002.

The operational information stored in the General National Database can be accessed by every police officer in the country. However, certain conditions are attached to this access. Firstly, police services can only access personal data and intelligence on certain events, groups and persons insofar as there is a 'concrete interest' in relation to the exercise of their tasks. This means concretely that a police officer asking information on an annoying neighbour will not obtain the information unless he can prove that he needs this in the light of his specific assignment.[23]

Furthermore, the Law of 8 December 1992 on the protection of privacy needs to be respected in a very strict manner.

Finally, there has to be a supervising authority that oversees the process of gathering and processing data. Information gathered by the judicial police falls under the authority of the Minister of Justice, while information gathered by the administrative police falls under the supervision of the Minister of Internal Affairs.[24]

In Belgium, there is only one police database, which makes it possible to monitor the information flow. Central police authorities can use the system to ask for all police reports on a certain type of crime, which would provide them with information on the amount of police reports and their location. So, if central authorities would want to check the input to in AWF, they can see whether the units working on the subject are sending their information to the AWF.

1.1.10 Germany

The BKA

The Bundeskriminalamt (BKA) can store, change and use person-related data, as far as this is necessary for its task as a central authority. The BKA can collect data from the national and regional police services for the completion of a specific task or for the purpose of analysis. The BKA can also collect data from other (public) authorities, from authorities and institutions of other states, and from international organisations which are competent for the prevention or prosecution of criminal acts, when the national and regional police departments do not dispose thereof.[25]

---

[23] 'Politie moet informatie correct verwerken', *POL nr. 8*, URL: <http://www.fedpol.be/police/fedpol/pol/8/pol8_9.htm>.

[24] Gemeenschappelijke richtlijn MFO-3 van 14 juni 2002 van de Ministers van Justitie en van Binnenlandse Zaken betreffende het informatiebeheer inzake gerechtelijke en bestuurlijke politie (Joint Directive of the Ministers of Justice and Internal Affairs on Information Management with regard to the Judicial and the Administrative Police), B.S., 18 June 2002.

[25] § 7 *of the Gesetz über das Bundeskriminalamt und die Zusammenarbeit des Bundes und der Länder in kriminalpolozeilichen Angelegenheiten (Bundeskriminalamtgesetz-BKAG), Bundesgesetzblatt 1997, Teil I nr. 46.*

Police Information System

It is the responsibility of the BKA to gather and analyse all the necessary information, and to inform the prosecution services immediately of the data gathered and the links which have been found. For this purpose the BKA possesses an electronic police information system – in between the national and regional level. The BKA should ensure compliance with the regulations and the administration of the system. If requested, the BKA can also support the Länder in the processing of data – following the regulations of the Länder. [26]

The Ministry of Home Affairs stipulates – in consultation with the home ministries and the senate administration of the Länder – which data should be inserted in the system. Participants to the information system are the BKA, the LKA, and other police institutions of the Länder and the Bundesgrenzschutz and customs services insofar as they are responsible for border police tasks. Only the service which has brought certain data in is competent to make changes to those data. The sender is responsible for the correctness of the data he has submitted, and the receiver has the responsibility for the admissibility of such data.[27]

National Data Transfer

The BKA can transfer person-related data to Länder and Bundes police departments, insofar as this is necessary for the fulfilling of its task or those of the receiver. The BKA can also send person-related data to other public authorities, if this is provided for in certain regulations, e.g., for the purpose of prosecution or execution of sentences, or for the prevention of any threat. The receiver can only use the information for the purpose for which they have been transferred. An alteration purpose is allowed if the data could also have been transferred for this purpose.[28]

Institutions and other public authorities can send person-related data to the BKA on their own initiative when factual bases exist to consider that the transfer is necessary for the fulfilment of the tasks of the BKA. A duty to transfer data only exists when this is necessary for the prevention of a danger to life, integrity or freedom. When the transfer follows from a request of the BKA, the latter bears the final responsibility – while normally the responsibility for the admissibility of the transfer lies with the sending authority.[29]

In conclusion, it can be argued that if national legislation allows the exchange of information and the necessary information is available to the members of the

---

[26] BKAG, §§ 1 and 2.
[27] BKAG, § 11.
[28] BKAG, § 10.
[29] BKAG, § 24.

JIT, the instrument of the JIT can provide a useful tool in enhancing mutual cooperation in criminal matters by speeding up the information flow which is necessary in an environment of increasing international crime.

However, there are other obstacles that could also hinder the fluid information exchange between JIT members. Some of them were experienced in the course of the operational Drugs JIT.
Differences in national legislation, a reluctance to share information, differences in the categorisation of information, the lack of availability of information to the JIT members are problems that will be the subject of the following sections.

1.2 Obstacles in the information exchange between the members of a JIT

1.2.1 *Differences in national legislation*

Since national legislation plays an important role in the information exchange within a JIT, this national legal framework may cause serious problems for the information exchange within a JIT.

Within the Drugs JIT, the disclosure principle and the difference in its application in the Netherlands and the United Kingdom have caused some problems relating to the exchange of information from telephone interceptions.

Disclosure describes the extent to which the prosecution and the defence have to disclose to each other, before trial, certain information pertinent to the case.[30] In the United Kingdom, the duty of disclosure is regulated by Part I, ss 1 to 21 of the Criminal Procedure and Investigations Act of 1996 (CPIA),[31] supplemented by a Code of Practice issued under that Act and which is regulated by ss 32 to 39 of the Criminal Justice Act (CJA) of 2003. The Code of Practice makes the investigator (the police) responsible for ensuring that any information relevant to the investigation is recorded and retained.[32]

---

[30] S. Seabrooke and J. Sprack, *Criminal Evidence and Procedure,* London, Blackstone 1999, p. 226.

[31] Criminal Procedure and Investigations Act 1996, URL: <http://www.hmso.gov.uk/acts/acts1996/1996025.htm#aofs>.

[32] For an overview of the material to be retained see J. Sprack, *A Practical Approach to Criminal Procedure*, Oxford, University Press 2004, p. 139.

As a general rule, the prosecution has the duty to disclose evidence which is at their disposal to the defence. This duty has two aspects: The obligation to notify the defence of the evidence upon which the prosecution intend to rely and, secondly, the duty to make available to the defence any material of relevance to the case upon which they do not intend to rely – 'unused material'.[33] Unused material has to be disclosed if it is relevant and assists the defence and which may undermine the prosecution case, unless a judge decides that this need not be disclosed in the interest of public interest immunity (PII). This means that unused material must not automatically be given to the defence. Normally a PII will be granted to protect the source of sensitive information.

Section 3 of the CPIA requires the prosecutor to disclose previously undisclosed material to the accused if, in the prosecutor's opinion, 'it might undermine the case for the prosecution against the accused'. Once CJA 2003 ss 32 to 39 come into force, this subjective test is replaced by a new objective test for the disclosure of material by the prosecution.[34]

There is no duty to disclose either under Common Law or under CPIA:

- material for which a claim of public interest immunity is upheld by the court (public interest immunity);
- material which falls under statutory exceptions: section 2 of the Interception of Communication Act of 1985, section 17 of the Regulation of Investigatory Powers Act of 2000[35]

Material must not be disclosed if a court has concluded that it is not in the public interest to do so (s 3(6) CPIA). Material should be withheld, for example, if it is so sensitive that it is subject to public interest immunity. The Code of Practice gives examples of such sensitive material (paragraph 6.12):

- Relating to national security;
- given in confidence;
- relating to the identity or activities of informants or undercover police officers;
- revealing the location of premises used for police surveillance;
- revealing surveillance techniques and other methods of detecting crime.

---

[33] J. Sprack, *A Practical Approach to Criminal Procedure*, Oxford, University Press 2004, p. 137.
[34] J. Sprack, *A Practical Approach to Criminal Procedure*, Oxford, University Press 2004, p. 155.
[35] <http://www.cps.gov.uk/legal/section 20/index.html>.

Thus, the public interests that might justify an objection to disclosure in a criminal case include those that fall into three broad categories: Protecting police operations (e.g., informant immunity and analogous cases), protecting national security and the proper functioning of the government and its services and protecting confidences (e.g., social service reports).[36]

Following from these examples, evidence may be excluded under the broad heading on public police in situations in which the disclosure of evidence would be damaging in some way to *public interests,* including the effective operation of the public service and the administration of justice.[37] Ultimately, it is the responsibility of the court to decide on the extent of disclosure. The prosecutor may make an application to the court that material should not be disclosed on the basis that it is not in the public interest to disclose it.

Public interest immunity does not mean that material cannot, or must never, be disclosed in legal proceedings or otherwise. What it means is that special care must be taken to decide where the balance lies between the two competing public interests before any question of disclosure is decided.
For example, in case there is sensitive information which, if revealed, seriously jeopardises the anonymity of a police informant and thus the life of this person, the court can decide that the public interest immunity principle applies and the information cannot be disclosed. A police officer could be prosecuted on the basis of an offence that is called misconduct in public office when he discloses information he should not have disclosed. However, this is a common criminal law offence and not a specific one related to the disclosure principle and the public immunity interest principle.

In the Netherlands, there is no such disclosure procedure. Any information used as a basis for investigative powers must be disclosed in court and may well become known by the defence. The Dutch criminal justice procedure is governed by the principle that in a criminal prosecution, full disclosure will be made of the way in which the investigation was carried out. This principle applies equally to special powers of investigation.[38] Investigative measures carried out by the police must be recorded in a police file. The written records are prepared by the police under oath, and may be used as evidence in court.[39]

---

[36] S. Seabrooke and J. Sprack, *Criminal Evidence and Procedure,* London, Blackstone 1999, p. 191
[37] M. Redmayne, 'Criminal Justice Act 2003, (1) Disclosure and its Discontents', *Criminal Law Review,* 2004, p. 441.
[38] National Public Prosecutor's Office, *Dutch Special Powers of Investigation Act 2000,* 2.6.
[39] P.J.P. Tak, *The Dutch criminal justice system.* The Hague, Ministry of Justice, WODC, 2003 p. 49.

A report by the Parliamentary Inquiry Committee on Police Investigation of 1996 revealed that the police extensively used illegitimate undercover policing methods. The main reasons for this were the following: the lack of legislation and clear rules, the lack of authority and supervision by the prosecution service, and the lack of organisation within the police force, fostered by the relative independence of the Criminal Intelligence Units, whose investigation was either sealed off – only to be disclosed by the public prosecutor in court – or remained secret.[40] Due to the conclusion of the Committee Report and the ensuing Parliamentary debate, the Dutch Special Powers of Investigation Act was enacted, entering into force on 1 February 2000. One of the main goals of the Act was that investigations must be transparent and must offer scope for monitoring the methods used. It must thus be possible to publicly account for the powers used in the investigation during a court hearing.[41] For the court to be able to assess usability and reliability for the purposes of criminal proceedings, the deployment of any special powers of investigation must be accounted for in a written report known as a 'proces-verbaal' (PV).[42]

However, both national law and precedent recognise that certain information may be protected for reasons of safeguarding individuals or on the basis of serious investigative interests. Thus, serious socio-civic interests, the effectiveness and the efficiency of the investigation, other serious investigative interests and the security of persons such as informers, victims and investigating officers can be taken into account. Ultimately, it is the judge hearing the case who will decide what information remains concealed. Some documents may even be withheld from the knowledge of the court and the defence.[43]

According to Article 13, paragraph 3(b) of the EU Convention on Mutual Assistance (Article 1 of the Framework Decision on JITs), the joint investigation team shall carry out its operations in accordance with the law of the Member State in which it operates. Correspondingly, since the Drugs JIT operated mainly in the Netherlands, the disclosure rules of the Netherlands applied in this investigation. As a consequence, all information on the investigation is put on paper in an official report as part of the police file.

---

[40] P.J.P. Tak, *The Dutch criminal justice system*. The Hague, Ministry of Justice, WODC, 2003 p. 27.
[41] National Public Prosecutor's Office, *Dutch Special Powers of Investigation Act 2000*, Introduction.
[42] National Public Prosecutor's Office, *Dutch Special Powers of Investigation Act 2000*, 2.4.
[43] Examples of such documents include information on witnesses who have been threatened, information from files relating to a witness protection programme, internal reports of an infiltration coordination team, etc. (National Public Prosecutor's Office, *Dutch Special Powers of Investigation Act 2000*, 2.6).

Due to this contrast in regulations, British investigators were very reluctant to provide information to the JIT. As the United Kingdom investigators have to comply with British law and policy when supplying information to the JIT, they have to safeguard sensitive information from being disclosed. In some cases, disclosure even amounts to a criminal offence (e.g., disclosure of the results of telephone interceptions). The investigators in the JIT, by contrast, are obliged to record every piece of information supplied to them in the police files and used as a basis for investigation. The British participants in the JIT feared that the disclosure principles of the Netherlands could possibly jeopardise the ongoing British investigation because the information could become known to the defence in the course of the ongoing investigation in the United Kingdom.

The differences in disclosure have seriously affected the flow of information between the United Kingdom 'mother case' and the JIT.

Another measure taken by the United Kingdom in the light of the disclosure principle, and thus to protect the sensitive information from their ongoing investigation in the United Kingdom, was the appointing of seconded English police officers who had limited knowledge of the ongoing drugs case in the United Kingdom. Consequently, the seconded English officers were never fully involved in the United Kingdom investigation. Commissioned with operational tasks such as surveillance, they were never briefed on issues of intelligence and the sources of sensitive information. The disclosure issue was also the reason for the United Kingdom to restrict the number of seconded officers so that the information exchange was easier to safeguard.
Article 552qa paragraph 3 of the Dutch CCP prescribes that the seconded members of a joint team must be willing and able to testify in court. If the seconded members would know about the sources of sensitive information from the ongoing investigation in the United Kingdom, this could jeopardise the case.

The advantage of choosing seconded members based on their limited prior involvement in the drug investigation in the United Kingdom is described as allowing the seconded members to take part in the JIT without the risk of compromising intelligence if asked to testify as a witness in a Dutch court. The disadvantage is that their limited knowledge affects the speed of inquiries between the JIT and NCSEW. If the seconded members had more insight into the United Kingdom investigation, they would be in a better position to help the JIT gain an overview of the criminal activities of the Dutch suspects and their involvement with British suspects, and to help in the coordination of both investigations.

1.2.2 Lack of availability of information to the members of the JIT

The above-mentioned problem relates to the problem of availability of information to the members of the JIT.
This problem was also experienced in the Drugs JIT. The ongoing investigation in the United Kingdom on cocaine trafficking had already gathered a lot of intelligence. On the basis of this intelligence, a link was identified to the Netherlands and it was decided to set up a JIT.

In the light of the aforementioned, it is self-evident that the exchange of information between the JIT and the ongoing investigation in the United Kingdom is undoubtedly an important one, because a great deal of useful information concerning the case originates from the United Kingdom and is essential information for the Drugs JIT located in the Netherlands.

The agreement on the establishment of a joint investigation team of 24 November 2004 mentioned in its Article 9.7 that evidence and intelligence from the investigation in England and Wales will be shared with the Dutch authorities unless contrary to law or policy.

The prosecutors in both countries reached an agreement on the need for close consultation and respective coaching as a precondition for direct information exchange. The agreement implied that the United Kingdom investigators, when submitting information directly to the investigation team supervisor, would not mention the source of the information but only the operational information stemming from the source. The JIT in turn could use this information as tactical information, as long as the NCSEW stated that the information was obtained legally.[44] The tactical information could be used as a basis to conduct a new telephone interception or surveillance or any other investigative measure performed within the framework of the JIT. It was equally agreed that the JIT would refrain from using information submitted by the United Kingdom investigation without prior authorisation from the United Kingdom. The JIT would inform the United Kingdom investigators in detail of the purposes for which the information supplied would be used, the way in which the information would be used as well as the possible consequences for the United Kingdom resulting

---

[44] The Netherlands, bound by legal and judicial assistance treaties with another country, generally follows the principle of legitimate expectations, which entails confidence in the other country's judicial system and the obtainment of information and evidence even if obtained with the aid of investigative powers which are not subject to the same safeguards as provided under national law in the Netherlands (National Public Prosecutor's Office, *Dutch Special Powers of Investigation Act 2000*, 3.1.).

from the use of this information. Following this agreement, the investigation team supervisor consulted the Dutch case prosecutor daily to discuss these issues from the prosecutor's perspective.

However, the information provided to the English investigation originates from different institutions in the United Kingdom who are the owners of that information. This implies that the authorities responsible for the United Kingdom investigation are not at liberty to decide what happens with the information and, consequently, the information cannot be disseminated without the consent of these institutions.
One (or more) of the institutions providing the United Kingdom case with information did not want their sensitive information to be forwarded directly to the JIT case in the Netherlands, even not through the team supervisor. Consequently, Europol was asked to act as an intermediary for the sensitive information between the United Kingdom case and the Dutch JIT.

Sensitive information received by the Branch Intelligence Unit of the police force dealing with the case in the United Kingdom would be forwarded to the central National Criminal Intelligence Service. They would forward the sensitive information to Europol, after which it would be sent to the Dutch desk and the International Network Service DIN, who would pass it on to the Drugs JIT.

The justification for this decision can be found in the fact that the institution(s) in the United Kingdom was/were afraid that if the information was disseminated directly to the team leader, the source of the information would at a certain point be revealed and this would jeopardise the ongoing investigation in the United Kingdom. Europol thus acts as a fire wall. This offers an insurance for the British authorities that the source of the information is properly protected. Furthermore, Europol officials are protected by their diplomatic immunity in case they would be asked questions in court, something which the English police officers involved in the JIT cannot resort to.

This lack of availability of information to the seconded members is a serious impediment to the functioning of a JIT. The aim of a JIT is to facilitate mutual cooperation by avoiding letters of request every time a country needs information from another Member State. If Europol is again involved in this process of information exchange, the added value of a joint team might be jeopardised, since the flow of information will be delayed by the intermediate stations the information has to pass. This delay would not necessarily be caused by Europol itself, but if they act as another chain through which the information needs to pass, the possibility increases that an organisation where the information passes keeps the information a little too long. This would not be an intentional act, but just the result of a normal human error.

This time-consuming procedure might jeopardise the effectiveness of a joint investigation team, since necessary information is received at a much slower pace which means that the JIT loses valuable time necessary to act quickly to certain events taking place. It can furthermore be questioned whether such an investigation is not just a mere traditional parallel investigation carried out in the United Kingdom and the Netherlands.

In contrast to the sensitive information, non-sensitive information could be exchanged between police officers involved in the United Kingdom case and the ones involved in the Drugs JIT through a mere telephone call or e-mail. Telephone contacts were made on a daily basis and the English police officers in the Netherlands were provided with a laptop so that they could send and receive e-mails from their British colleagues.

The problem of the availability of information for seconded members of the JIT could of course have been solved by transforming the United Kingdom investigation into a JIT with a part of the investigation to be executed in the Netherlands. In that way, information from the United Kingdom ongoing case would become information from the JIT and thus an exchange of information is no longer needed.

1.2.3 *Differences in the categorisation of information*

In relation to information, it is possible that the classification protection regimes applied in the police forces of the different Members States are different. These differences may constitute a significant obstacle to the exchange of essential information within a JIT.

In the Drugs JIT, the United Kingdom made a strict division between intelligence and tactical/operational information. Due to the already described disclosure rules in the United Kingdom, there is a strict division between the sources of information (intelligence) and the information that is gathered in the course of relying on intelligence sources, e.g., informers, telephone interception (tactical or operational information). Whereas intelligence sources are protected, tactical or operational information can be shared without restrictions. Thus, information of a non-sensitive nature (e.g., car number-plates, locations, identification of suspects, previous convictions) can be exchanged directly between the members of the JIT.

Since this strict division is not present in the Netherlands, information could be exchanged more easily.

1.2.4   Reluctance to share information

The aforementioned disclosure rules caused some reluctance to share information in the Drugs JIT.

The NCSEW was described as being very careful in exchanging information within the Drugs JIT so as not to jeopardise its ongoing parallel investigation in the United Kingdom.

The tool of the JIT can be effective and functional, not only when states adopt the necessary legal framework, at both domestic and international levels, but also when the right atmosphere exists. The latter element entails trust between law enforcement authorities and their field officers across borders.[45]
Cooperation in the form of information exchange requires a basic trust in each other, which is not always present in daily practice.

This is especially true when information has to be exchanged with colleagues who do not know each other. Despite the reluctance on the part of the ongoing United Kingdom investigation to exchange information with the Drugs JIT, this project has nevertheless shown that police officers working together in one country on the same case have the potential to strengthen working relationships and increase the level of trust and might lead to an easier information exchange in the future.

1.3   Right to use information lawfully obtained within the JIT in the home country

Article 1 paragraph 10 of the Framework Decision on JITs and Article 13 paragraph 10 of the EU Convention on Mutual Assistance states:

> Information lawfully obtained by a member or seconded member while part of a joint investigation team which is not otherwise available to the competent authorities of the Member States concerned may be used for the following purposes:
>
> a) For the purposes for which the team has been set up;

---

[45] M. Plachta, 'Joint Investigation Teams. A New Form of International Cooperation in Criminal Matters', *European journal of crime, criminal law and criminal justice,* Vol. 13/2, 2005, p. 284-302.

b) subject to prior consent of the Member State where the information became available, for detecting, investigating and prosecuting other criminal offences. Such consent may be withheld only in cases where such use would endanger criminal investigations in the Member State concerned or in respect of which that Member State could refuse mutual assistance;
c) for preventing an immediate and serious threat to public security;
d) for other purposes to the extent that this is agreed between the members states setting up the team.

It clearly follows from this provision that it is self-executing. The explanatory report on the EU Convention on Mutual Assistance remarks that the Irish delegation pointed out that where the information in question relates to a voluntary statement provided by a witness solely for the purposes for which the team was set up, the consent of the witness should be required for its use for other purposes unless the requirements involving an immediate and serious threat to public security are satisfied.

The report mentions further that although the text does not provide direct guidance on this point, it would be in keeping with the spirit of the article that such matters should be the subject of consultation between the Member States establishing the team and that, as appropriate, the consent of the witness should be sought.[46]

In relation to the Drugs JIT, it will be examined whether information lawfully obtained within the JIT can be used in the Netherlands or the United Kingdom. Furthermore, in the context of the THB-JIT project, the legal provisions on the subject in Belgium and Germany will be discussed as well.

1.3.1 *The Netherlands*

The question of the domestic admissibility of evidence collected within the team when operating abroad is not addressed in the Dutch implementing legislation, nor in Dutch law in general, which need not be problematic because of the self-executing character of this provision in the EU Convention on Mutual Assistance.[47]

---

[46] Explanatory report on the Convention of 29 May 2000 on Mutual Assistance in Criminal Matters between the Member States of the European Union, *OJ* C 379, 29.12.2000 p. 7.

[47] G. Vermeulen, *Advisory Opinion, JIT and pre-JIT cooperation possibilities in the relationship between the Netherlands and other countries involved in the JIT-initiative(s) initiated under the Netherlands EU Presidency 2004, in particular Belgium and Germany*, 16 January 2005, p. 17 (not published).

The guideline on the international joint investigation teams of the Board of Prosecutors General only declares that the officers of justice have to see to it that no evidence is brought into the Dutch criminal proceedings if it has been gathered in a way that violates the Dutch rules on criminal proceedings.[48]

1.3.2 *The United Kingdom*

The United Kingdom has not transposed the related provision of Article 13 of the EU Mutual Assistance Convention (mirrored in Article 20 of the 2001 CoE 2nd Additional Protocol). The effect thereof is that, unless the JIT basis is one of the above two treaties (in which case these may apply directly), it remains legally uncertain whether information lawfully obtained within a JIT when operating abroad or by foreign JIT members can be used in the United Kingdom, and, if so, only for JIT purposes or also for other purposes.[49]

1.3.3 *Belgium*

The information which a Belgian seconded member gathers in another state in the context of his participation in the joint investigation team and in accordance with the law of that state, may be used for the same purposes as spelled out in paragraph 10 of Article 13 of the EU Convention on Mutual Assistance and paragraph 10 of Article 1 of the Framework Decision (Article 10 paragraph 3 of the Mutual Assistance Act of 9 December 2004).

1.3.4 *Germany*

The German legislation has not transposed the provisions of paragraph 10 of Article 13 of the EU Convention on Mutual Assistance (literally mirrored in paragraph 10 of Article 20 of the 2001 CoE 2nd Additional Protocol).

In principle, the effect thereof is that, unless the JIT basis is one of the above two treaties (in which case these may apply directly), it remains legally uncertain whether information that has been lawfully obtained within a JIT when operating abroad or by foreign JIT members can be used in Germany, and, if so, for what purposes – for the JIT investigation only or also for other purposes.

---

[48] Guideline on the International Joint Investigation Teams, Board of Procurators General.

[49] G. Vermeulen, *Advisory Opinion, JIT and pre-JIT cooperation possibilities in the relationship between the Netherlands and other countries involved in the JIT-initiative(s) initiated under the Netherlands EU Presidency 2004, in particular Belgium and Germany*, 16 January 2005, p. 29 (not published).

2. INFORMATION EXCHANGE WITH OTHER EU MEMBER STATES NOT PARTY TO THE JIT

This type of information exchange concerns the common information exchange between EU countries, which means that the rules on such an information exchange will apply.

In the Drugs JIT, there has not been any information exchange with other EU countries not party to the JIT and therefore this section will only be a theoretical elaboration of the subject.

First, Member States will need a legal basis to be able to exchange information with other Member States. Many bilateral and regional agreements have already been signed which form the basis of a great deal of cross-border exchanges in law enforcement information. An example of such agreements is the Agreement between the Government of the Republic of Poland and the Government of the Federal German Republic on cooperation between the police and border guards in the border areas.
Beside these bilateral provisions, information can be exchanged on the basis of several international instruments such as the Europol Convention of 1995[50] and the Convention of 27 November 1995 on the use of information technology for customs purposes.[51]

Furthermore, one of the most useful provisions for police cooperation within the EU, including the exchange of information, is the Convention of 19 June 1990 applying the Schengen Agreement of 14 June 1985 between the Governments of the States of the Benelux Economic Union, the Federal Republic of Germany and the French Republic, on the gradual abolition of checks at their common borders.[52]
Article 39 concerns the supplying of information upon request.
Article 39, 1° of the aforementioned convention stipulates that police authorities from the Member States shall assist each other for the purpose of preventing and detecting criminal offences, insofar as national law does not stipulate

---

[50] Council Act of 26 July 1995 drawing up the Convention on the Establishment of a European Police Office (Europol Convention), *OJ* C 316, 27.11.1995, p. 2.

[51] Convention on the Use of Information Technology for Customs Purposes, *OJ* C 316, 27.11.1995, p. 34.

[52] Convention of 19 June 1990 applying the Schengen Agreement of 14 June 1985 between the governments of the States of the Benelux Economic Union, the Federal Republic of Germany and the French Republic, on the gradual abolition of checks at their common borders, Final Act, Protocol and Common Declaraton, signed in Schengen 19 June 1990 Schengen Convention.

that the request is to be made to the legal authorities and provided that the request or the implementation thereof does not involve the use of coercive measures by the requesting Member State.

This paragraph allows the exchange of information between police authorities from different Member States providing that the national law does not stipulate that the request is to be made by the legal authorities.
When the request or the implementation thereof involves the use of coercive measures, the police authorities of the Member States cannot exchange the information in a direct manner. Furthermore, the exchange has to take place within the boundaries of the competencies of the police authorities. In that case, they have to send the request to the competent authorities in the Member State.

Paragraph 2 of Article 39 SIC states that the written information provided may not be used by the requesting state as evidence of the criminal offence other than with the agreement of the relevant legal authorities of the requested Member State.

Finally, paragraph 3 mentions that the request for assistance and the replies to such requests may be exchanged between the central bodies responsible in each contracting party for international cooperation.

Article 46 SIC continues that each contracting party may, in compliance with its national legislation and without being asked, send the contracting party concerned any information which may be of interest to it in helping to prevent future crime and to prevent offences against or threats to public order and security. Information shall be exchanged through a designated central body. In urgent cases, the information can be exchanged directly between police authorities, save where national provisions provide otherwise and providing that the central body is informed as soon as possible.

The legal basis for the police cooperation in relation to information can also be found in Title VI of the Treaty on the European Union of 1992[53] concerning police and judicial cooperation in criminal matters.

On the basis of Article 29 TEU, the EU aims to obtain an area of freedom, security and justice. This objective shall – among other things – be achieved by closer cooperation between the police forces, customs authorities and other com-

---

[53] Treaty on European Union, *OJ* C 325, 24.12.2002.

petent authorities in the Member States, both directly and through the European Police Office in accordance with the provisions of Articles 30 and 32.
According to Article 30 TEU common action in the field of police cooperation shall include among others:

– the collection, storage, processing, analysis and exchange of relevant information, including information held by law enforcement services of the Member States on reports on suspicious financial transactions, in particular through Europol, subject to appropriate provisions on the protection of personal data.

Article 33 TEU continues that title VI TEU will not affect the exercise of the responsibilities incumbent upon Member States with regard to the maintenance of law and order and the safeguarding of internal security. This means that the national legislation will be applicable to this subject.[54]

One of the biggest impediments to information exchange between Member States is the fact that there is no obligation to share information. Despite the existing bilateral and multilateral agreements providing the basic EU framework for law enforcement information exchange and taking into consideration the recent promising agreements such as the Benelux Treaty of 8 June 2004[55] and the Schengen III Agreement of 29 May 2005, information exchange in the end still relies on the goodwill of the colleagues in the different Member States.
However, the Hague Programme of November 2004 sets out that with effect from 1 January 2008, the exchange of information should be governed by the principle of availability, which means that 'throughout the Union, a law enforcement officer in one Member State who needs information in order to perform his duties can obtain this from another Member State and that law enforcement agency in the other Member State which holds the information will make it available for the stated purpose, taking into account the requirement of ongoing investigations in that state.'[56]

---

[54] J. Verbeek, *Politie en de nieuwe internationale informatiemarkt. Grensregionale politiële gegevensuitwisseling en digitale expertise* (Police and the New Information Market. Border-region Exchange of Police Data and Digital Expertise), The Hague, SDU publishers 2004.

[55] Treaty between the Kingdom of Belgium, the Kingdom of the Netherlands and the Grand Duchy of Luxembourg concerning cross-border police intervention, 8 June 2004, URL: <http://www.benelux.be/en/pdf/rgm/rgm_Politieverdrag2004_en.pdf>.

[56] The Hague Programme on Strengthening Freedom, Security and Justice in the European Union, *OJ* C 53, 03.03.2005, p. 1.

3. INFORMATION EXCHANGE WITH THIRD COUNTRIES

A joint investigation team can exchange information with third countries. In most cases, Member States will conclude bilateral agreements with different third countries concerning the information exchange that can take place.

Next to these rules, it is of the utmost importance that the data protection principles are respected in the light of such an information exchange. The data protection guarantees that are valid for the information exchange between EU Member States and third countries will be the subject of the next section.

4. DATA PROTECTION GUARANTEES WITHIN A JIT

Data protection rules set up specifically in the context of JITs cannot be found. Consequently, no specific rules on data protection guarantees within a JIT can be found in Article 13 of the EU Convention on Mutual Assistance or in the Framework Decision on JITs. Reference to data protection can be found in Article 23 of the aforementioned Convention of 2000.

Although the agreement setting up a team could provide specific rules on data protection, the agreement setting up the Drugs JIT does not mention anything specific on data protection guarantees.

Article 23 of the EU Convention on Mutual Assistance is a general provision on data protection.[57] The Article applies 'to personal data communicated under this Convention.' The expression 'personal data' has been used within the meaning of the definition of that expression in Article 2(a) of the 1981 Council of Europe Convention for the Protection of Individuals with regard to Automatic Processing of Personal Data. Article 2(a) provides that 'personal data' means any information relating to an identified or identifiable individual ('data subject'). That definition applies irrespective of the way in which the personal data concerned are filed or processed. Article 23 consequently applies to both data processed automatically and data not processed automatically.

---

[57] The article states that: 'personal data communicated under this convention may be used by the Member State to which they have been transferred:
a) for the purpose of proceedings to which this convention applies;
b) for other judicial and administrative proceedings directly related to proceedings referred to under point a
c) for preventing an immediate and serious threat to public security;
d) for any other purpose, only with the prior consent of the communicating Member State, unless the Member State concerned has obtained the consent of the data subject.'

At the same time, the obligations of Member States under the 1981 Convention are not affected by Article 23 in any way. The definition is to be understood as implying that an identifiable person is one who can be identified, directly or indirectly, by reference to an identification number or to one or more factors specific to his or her physical, mental, physiological, economic, cultural or social identity.

The purpose for which personal data will be used dictates the conditions in which they may be used, i.e., with or without the prior consent of the Member State which forwarded them.

In three cases, the Member State to which such data have been sent may use them without the prior consent of the Member State which forwarded them:

- the first case (paragraph 1(a)) covers use 'for the purpose of proceedings to which this Convention applies.' These proceedings are those defined by the conventions mentioned in Article 1 and those referred to in Article 3 (Proceedings in connection with which mutual assistance is also to be afforded). These proceedings can obviously differ from those for which judicial assistance has been requested,

- the second case (paragraph 1(b)) covers use 'for other judicial and administrative proceedings directly related to proceedings referred to under point (a).' The words 'directly related' may include the following examples, *inter alia*:
  - Commercial proceedings related to a fraudulent bankruptcy;
  - proceedings for withdrawing parental authority related to criminal proceedings for ill-treatment of children;
  - proceedings for withdrawing a firearms licence related to criminal proceedings for violence with firearms.

In the cases referred to in paragraph 1(b), personal data obtained in the context of an international letter of request may be used without the prior consent of the Member State which forwarded them,

- the last case (paragraph 1(c)) covers the prevention of 'an immediate and serious threat to public security.' This concept must not be understood in a too restrictive manner and would cover, for example, measures taken in respect of crimes involving threats to human life, serious drug offences and similar serious crimes.

The statement made by the Federal Republic of Germany on this point should be borne in mind; this questioned the extent to which data collected by the legal authorities in one Member State may be used by the police services in another Member State for preventing serious risks and combating serious crime in the future.

As regards the use of personal data for any other purpose, paragraph 1(d) stipulates that the Member State wanting to use them must obtain the prior consent of the Member State which has sent them unless it has obtained the consent of the data subject.[58]

Paragraph 5 of Article 23 continues: 'The provisions of article 13(10) shall take precedence over this article regarding information obtained under article 13.' This last paragraph means that when information is gathered within a JIT, the rule laid down in paragraph 10 of Article 13 of the EU Convention on Mutual Assistance will apply and not the general rule of Article 23.

Since information between JIT members can only be exchanged insofar as the national legislation allows it and, within the boundaries set by this legislation, the data protection regime will also be determined by the national legislation.

At the European level, Directive 95/46/EC[59] of the European Parliament and of the Council of 24 October 1995 on the protection of individuals with regard to the processing of personal data and on the free movement of such data is the main instrument on data protection.

The main principles behind the Data Protection Directive are:

- Personal data must always be processed fairly and lawfully;
- personal data must be collected for explicit and legitimate purposes and used accordingly;
- personal data must be relevant and not excessive in relation to the purpose for which they are processed;
- data that identify individuals must not be kept longer than necessary;
- data must be accurate and, where necessary, kept up to date;

---

[58] Explanatory Report on the Convention of 29 May 2000 on Mutual Assistance in Criminal Matters between the Member States of the European Union, *OJ* C 379, 29.12.2000, p. 26.

[59] Directive 95/46/EC of the European Parliament and of the Council of 24 October 1995 on the Protection of Individuals with Regard to the Processing of Personal Data and on the Free Movement of Such Data, *OJ* L 281, 23.11.1995, p. 31-50.

- data controllers are required to provide reasonable measures for data subjects to rectify, erase or block incorrect data about them;
- appropriate technical and organisational measures should be taken against unauthorised or unlawful processing of personal data;
- personal data must not be transferred to a country or territory outside the European Economic Area unless that country ensures an 'adequate level of protection' for data subjects.

Concerning the transfer of personal data to third countries, the convention mentions in its Article 25 that the Member States can only transfer this data to third countries ensuring an adequate level of protection. Paragraph 6 of Article 25 gives the Commission the power to determine whether a third country ensures an adequate level of protection by reason of its domestic law or of the international commitments it has entered into.

The four countries discussed have implemented the directive in their national legislation.[60]

4.1 The Netherlands

Directive 95/46/EC was transposed into national law by the Personal Data Protection Act of 6 July 2000.[61] This Act (Wet bescherming persoonsgegevens; WBP) entered into force on 1 September 2001, replacing the old Data Protection Act (Wet persoonsregistraties; WPR), which dated from 28 December 1988. On the same date, the name of the supervisory authority changed from *Registratiekamer* into *College bescherming persoonsgegevens* (*CBP*). There is a great degree of continuity between the old and the new Act.

After 1 September 2001, all new processing had to comply with the new provisions. There was a one-year transition period for existing processing, ending on 1 September 2002.

4.2 The United Kingdom

The relevant national legislation is the Data Protection Act of 16 July 1998.[62] The Information Commissioner is the independent data protection supervisory

---

[60] Sixth annual report on the situation regarding the protection of individuals with regard to the processing of personal data and privacy in the European Union and in third countries covering the year 2001 adopted on 16 December 2003, Data Protection Working Party, URL: <http://europa.eu.int/comm/justice_home/fsj/privacy/docs/wpdocs/2003/2003-6th-annualreport_en.pdf>.

[61] *Wet van 6 juli 2000 houdende regels inzake de bescherming van persoonsgegevens* (Personal Data Protection Act), *Staatsblad van het Koninkrijk der Nederlanden (*Dutch Bulletin of Acts and Decrees*)* 302.

[62] Data Protection Act of 16 July 1998, URL: <http://www.hmso.gov.uk/acts/acts1998/19980029.htm>.

authority for the United Kingdom and is responsible for enforcing both pieces of legislation. She is also the United Kingdom's designated supervisory body for Europol, the Customs Information System, the Schengen Information System, Eurodac and Eurojust.

4.3 Belgium

The implementation law entered into force on 1 September 2001 (Belgian law of 8 December 1992 on privacy protection in relation to the processing of personal data, as modified by the law of 11 December 1998, implementing Directive 95/46/EC). The Royal Decree implementing the law was adopted on 13 February 2001 (*OJ* 13 March 2001) and entered into force 6 months after its publication, i.e., also on 1 September 2001.

4.4 Germany

In the course of modernizing German data protection law, the Federal Government has followed a two-phase approach. The first one was in substance directed towards implementing the Directive. On 14 June 2000 the Federal Government (Bundeskabinett) agreed on a draft law amending the German data protection law (Bundesdatenschutzgesetzes BDSG). The Chamber of State Representatives (Bundesrat) made comments concerning this draft law on 29 September 2000. On 13 October 2000, the draft law amending the German data protection law (BDSG) and other laws was submitted by the Federal Government to the Bundestag (BT-Drs. 14/4329). Discussions in the various committees of the Federal Parliament (Bundestag) started in 2000 and were concluded by the law modifying the Federal Data Protection Act and other Acts (Gesetz zur Änderung des Bundesdatenschutzgesetzes und anderer Gesetze) as of 22 May 2001, Federal Law Gazette Vol. I, p. 904.
Subsequent to this novelty, the second phase, aimed at a fundamental reform of data protection law, started on the 1st of January 2002.

5. CONCLUSIONS AND RECOMMENDATIONS

Law enforcement information exchange in the operational phase of a JIT concerns three types of information exchange: exchange between members of the JIT originating from different countries, information exchange between the JIT and EU countries not party to the JIT and information exchange with third countries.

The Drugs JIT between the Netherlands and the United Kingdom only had information exchange of the first type. Based on Article 1(9) of the Framework Decision on JITs and Article 13(9) of the EU Convention on Mutual Assistance, seconded members may provide the JIT with information from the home country as long as this is compatible with national legislation and the information is available in the home country.

According to these provisions, the national legislation still plays an important role in determining the information that can be provided to the JIT by the seconded members. As a consequence of the latter, the implementation of these provisions in the EU Member States will be of the utmost importance and will determine the possibilities for information exchange which the seconded members will have.

Taking the aforementioned into consideration, it has to be emphasised that a direct cause leading to the lack of success of a JIT concerns the legal framework. The European implementation of the JIT (consisting of the EU Convention on Mutual Assistance and the Framework Decision on JITs) into national legislation is essential. The implementation should be complete, accurate and clear, in order to avoid confusion about the application of certain provisions and the meaning of particular provisions in the national law.

Next to this obstacle, others could also be identified within the course of the Drugs JIT.
One of the most difficult problems identified in the Drugs JIT concentrated on the aspect of information exchange and was greatly affected by the British need to safeguard sensitive information.

As the Drugs JIT was located in the Netherlands in order to tackle the Dutch branch of a criminal investigation that was primarily investigated by the NCSEW in the United Kingdom, the investigation conducted by the Drugs JIT depended significantly on information being provided by the NCSEW. However, due to disclosure rules applicable in British criminal justice procedure, information stemming from investigations in the United Kingdom could only be transmitted to other countries in such a way as to avoid sensitive information being disclosed.
This principle had a serious impact on the information exchange within the Drugs JIT.

It was first of all accountable for the limited information provided in the letter of request issued by the British Crown Prosecutor in order to bring the JIT into operation, as well as the little information contained in the JIT Agreement. The JIT was also not provided with a Europol report, due to its sensitive content, derived from an AWF assessing, *inter alia,* links between the 'mother case' in the United Kingdom and Dutch suspects. As a result, the Dutch investigation started out with little information, slowly building up the investigation by collecting information that, it was felt, was available in the United Kingdom, but could not be shared.

Secondly, British disclosure rules also affected the speed of information exchange. Sensitive information, especially when stemming from British agencies apart from the NCSEW, was transmitted through the time-consuming channel via Europol. By using traditional information channels such as Europol, the potential of a JIT could not fully be used, and, as a consequence, the added value of the JIT construct as such was difficult to assess.

The seconded officers, the intended role of which was explicitly one of enhancing information exchange, were in general perceived as an additional asset for quick information exchange regarding open source information as well as tactical information. However, seconded officers were not used to their full potential. On purpose, the NCSEW selected police officers who had only limited knowledge of the 'mother case' in order not to interfere with British disclosure rules. English police officers involved in the JIT have to testify in court, which means that the information they know could become exposed.
As a consequence of this selection, seconded officers did not have a complete overview of both investigations running parallel and were thus limited in their possibilities of helping to identify information gaps and coordinate investigations.

Another issue did not so much concern legal aspects connected to the handling of sensitive information, but tactical reasons. The NCSEW was described as being very careful in the exchange of information so as not to jeopardise its ongoing parallel investigation in the United Kingdom.

The aforementioned problems can be described as differences in national legislation, lack of availability of information, differences in the categorization of information and a reluctance to share information.
These problems can be partly overcome by ensuring a thorough preparation before setting up a JIT. Considerable attention should be devoted to drafting the agreement. In this process, problems that might occur should be anticipated and solved. If such a thorough preparation does not take place, this might result in a certain reserve between the cooperating Member States, due to the aforemen-

tioned differences. It might also lead to decreasing trust between the EU Member States. However, this trust is an essential component for such a far-reaching form of cooperation without which the chances of success are rather small.

The question whether information lawfully obtained within the JIT could be used in the home country is not addressed in Dutch legislation, English legislation, or in German legislation. Consequently, Belgium is the only country involved in the THB-JIT project addressing the question and having the necessary legislation. This means that unless the basis for setting up a JIT is the EU Convention on Mutual Assistance or the CoE 2nd Additional Protocol to the 1959 European Mutual Assistance Convention in which cases the particular provisions are self-executing, it remains legally uncertain whether information that has been lawfully obtained within a JIT when operating abroad or by foreign JIT members can be used and, if so, for what purposes.

The information exchange with other Member States not party to the JIT involves an exchange of information based on the Schengen Implementation Convention of 1990, the Treaty on the European Union of 1992 and other bilateral and multilateral treaties. In fact, this form of information exchange concerns the common information exchange between EU Member States and, hence, the rules valid for such information exchange will apply. The country providing the information has to take into account that the information provided will be at the disposal of the JIT which means that the participating countries will have access to that information.[63]

Finally, the exchange of information with third countries would take place mostly on the basis of bilateral agreements.

The data protection guarantees within a JIT are composed of the traditional national and international legal instruments on data protection since there are no specific provisions on data protection concerning the JIT. Especially Directive 95/46 EC of 24 October 1995 and the implementation legislation in the countries are important in this respect.

---

[63] See also Chapter I.

CHAPTER IV
JUDICIAL COOPERATION IN CRIMINAL MATTERS: MUTUAL LEGAL ASSISTANCE

Els De Busser*

The present chapter will successively cover the context in which the instrument of a JIT was developed and should be located, as well as the specific elements that convert international police cooperation into a genuine JIT. Its background of mutual legal assistance, including the traditional mutual legal assistance requests (*commissions rogatoires*) that have dominated the scene of international cooperation between police and judicial authorities for decades and the origin and growing pains of the first JIT that was operational in the EU, will be extensively reported, thereby joining legal arguments and the views of relevant key persons working in the context of the THB-JIT project and the Drugs JIT.

For the reason that only the Drugs JIT entered the operational stage, the vast majority of this chapter will deal with this particular experience. As far as non-operational aspects are concerned, the THB-JIT project will be the additional subject of study. The difference between both is clearly indicated at all times, with the exception of paragraphs in which a general view is offered on the instrument of a JIT.

1. MUTUAL LEGAL ASSISTANCE IN CRIMINAL MATTERS

1.1 Traditional mutual legal assistance

Besides the possibility of using the instrument of a JIT, Member States of the EU have a number of other tools by which to start and enhance intensive cooperation in criminal matters with the judicial and police authorities of other Mem-

---

* Els De Busser works as an assistant at the Institute for International Research on Criminal Policy (IRCP), Ghent University (Belgium).

C. Rijken and G. Vermeulen (Eds.), *Joint Investigation Teams in the European Union*
© 2006, T·M·C·ASSER PRESS, The Hague, The Netherlands and the Authors

ber States and third states. The means provided by multilateral and bilateral conventions and agreements are plural and frequently used.

The widest-ranging convention in Europe – with regard to the number of state parties who ratified the text – regarding international cooperation in criminal matters is the 1959 European Convention on Mutual Assistance in Criminal Matters established within the framework of the Council of Europe. Together with its two Protocols (1978 and 2001), the Convention offers a range of methods of international judicial and police cooperation, such as the traditional *commission rogatoires*, the serving of documents related to a criminal case and judicial decisions, appearance of witnesses, video conferences, controlled delivery, etc. The 2001 Protocol also includes the instrument of joint investigation teams, nevertheless the aforementioned tools can be used in case the states involved do not consider the setting up of a JIT a necessity or when other means are available. For example, the police authorities of Member State A need to hear a witness in a criminal investigation. The witness, however, is residing in Member State B and is unable to travel to Member State A for the hearing due to health reasons. In that case, it is unnecessary to start up a JIT because a simple telephone conference or a video conference can be sufficient to complete the required evidence.
It is worth mentioning in this respect that although it has entered into force since 1 February 2004, the 2001 Protocol has only been ratified by a limited number of Member States.

The 2002 Framework Decision on JITs and Article 13 of the EU Convention on Mutual Assistance do not limit the use of a JIT to specific cases or crimes but refer only to the cases in which a JIT can *in particular* be established. These are the cases in which the investigation of a Member State concerning criminal acts requires difficult and demanding investigations having links with other Member States and the cases in which a number of Member States are conducting investigations into criminal acts in which the circumstances of the cases necessitate coordinated, concerted action in the states involved.

The EU Convention on Mutual Assistance also provides a range of instruments to be used in a criminal case having links with two or more Member States. Although the EU Convention on Mutual Assistance has been ratified by many of the Member States, it has not entered into force for all of them. Article 27 paragraph 5 of the Convention allows Member States to declare that until its entry into force the Convention will be applied in the relations with Member States which have made the same declaration. The Member States that have made this particular declaration are Austria, Spain, France, Lithuania, the Netherlands, Portugal, Poland and Finland. The Member States which have not ratified the Convention thus far are the Czech Republic, Greece, Italy, Ireland, Luxembourg, Malta and Slovakia.

The Schengen Agreement of 1990 contains an extensive chapter on police cooperation (Articles 39 to 47) and a chapter on judicial cooperation in criminal matters (Articles 48 to 53). The instruments included in these articles are also focused on the investigating of cross-border crime. The possibility of joint investigation teams is not included, although cross-border observation, cross-border pursuit and *commission rogatoires* are the main mechanisms to be used within the scope of the Schengen Agreement.

Important provisions on cross-border investigations are encompassed in the recent Benelux Convention on cross-border police cooperation.[1] In addition to observation and pursuit, the exchange of personal data, the use of liaison officers (complementary to Article 47.2 Schengen Agreement), cross-border protection of persons and the establishment of common police centres and patrols are mechanisms to be used in the fight against cross-border crime that go beyond the traditional mutual legal assistance tools. The instrument of a JIT was on the Benelux level already included in the Agreements of 1962[2] and 1969.[3]
In addition to the multilateral conventions and agreements, states can also conclude bilateral agreements providing instruments on international cooperation (police and/or judicial) in criminal matters, for example the bilateral agreement between Belgium and Germany on the cooperation between police and customs authorities in border areas.[4]

Traditional mutual legal assistance instruments, such as the *commission rogatoires*, have the disadvantage of being part of a rather slow process. *Commissions rogatoires* can be used when mirror (or parallel) investigations take place. Parallel investigations imply that states are investigating criminal activi-

---

[1] *Wet houdende instemming met het Verdrag tussen het Koninkrijk België, het Koninkrijk der Nederlanden en het Groothertogdom Luxemburg inzake grensoverschrijdend politieel optreden, en met de Bijlagen, gedaan te Luxemburg op 8 juni 2004* (Treaty between the Kingdom of Belgium, the Kingdom of the Netherlands and the Grand Duchy of Luxembourg concerning cross-border police intervention), 8 June 2004, *B.S,* 15 March 2005.
[2] Agreement of 27 June 1962 concerning extradition and mutual assistance in criminal matters between the Kingdom of Belgium, the Grand Duchy of Luxembourg and the Kingdom of the Netherlands, *B.S.,* 24 October 1967.
[3] Agreement of 29 April 1969 concerning the administrative and criminal cooperation in the field of the regulations related to the realisation of the objectives of the Benelux Economic Union, *B.S.,* 17 February 1971.
[4] *B.S.,* 5 March 2003.

ties at the same time that are linked to each other (for example, the same criminal network). In that context the authorities of both states can cooperate at an informal level, for example, by meeting to discuss tactics to coordinate their actions so as not to hinder or prejudice each other investigations or to discuss possibilities of sharing evidence.

The 1959 Convention requires the sending of mutual legal assistance requests through the Ministries of Justice of the Member States involved, which can be a time-consuming working method. Direct sending via the authorities involved is only allowed in cases of urgency. The EU Convention on Mutual Assistance and the Schengen Agreement have opted for the faster alternative of direct sending of mutual legal assistance requests as a general rule. However, using the new tool of joint investigation teams could offer the process another accelerating incentive. Foreign police officers working in the territory of another Member State in the investigation of a criminal case having links with the different Member States involved, can still stay in direct contact with the authorities of their home country. That working method can create a direct and permanent connection between the Member States involved in a cross-border crime case on the one hand, and their respective police officers who are part of a joint investigation team, on the other hand, which makes the sending of requests for mutual legal assistance a much faster process. Additionally, instead of travelling to another Member State in order to carry out an investigative measure (e.g., hearing a witness), police officers working within a JIT are already present in the territory of the Member State concerned.

Nevertheless, a mirror investigation can be as flexible as the instrument of a JIT. Operating in a pragmatic manner, the authorities of Member State A can send the authorities of Member State B – who are carrying out a parallel investigation – one request in which they ask for all assistance they need. Naturally, this method of working avoids the time-consuming sending of successive requests by replacing it with one 'framework request'. However, it is questionable whether this practice is consistent with the objective of *commissions rogatoires*.

1.2 Legal bases of joint investigation teams

1.2.1 *General*

Prior to the enactment of the Framework Decision on JITs in 2002, the EU Member States were able to use the mechanism of the JIT in other forms and within the scope of other legal instruments. Unfortunately, not all of the mentioned instruments are in a fully operational stage, due to problems related to the entry into force of these instruments.

The United Nations Convention against transnational organised crime[5] includes the setting up of JITs (Article 19) to prevent and combat transnational organised crime. A wide range of EU Member States have ratified this convention, implying that when transnational organised crime is concerned in accordance with the scope of the UN Convention against Transnational Organised Crime, a genuine JIT can be set up between Austria, Belgium, Cyprus, Denmark, Estonia, Finland, France, Latvia, Lithuania, Malta, the Netherlands, Poland, Portugal, Slovakia, Slovenia, Spain and Sweden.

A limited number of Member States have ratified the 2001 Protocol to the 1959 Convention. This means that a JIT, in accordance with the wide scope of this Protocol, can be set up between Denmark, Estonia, Latvia, Lithuania, Poland and Slovakia.[6]

The so-called Naples II Convention[7] allows for the setting up of JITs in customs matters according to the scope of the convention[8] by means of Article 24. However, this convention has not entered into force for all EU-Member States, more specifically because Italy has not yet ratified the convention. Ratification by Italy is necessary for entry into force by all Member States as Article 34 of the Treaty on the European Union requires ratification of all states, Member States of the EU at the time the convention was opened for signature.
Nevertheless, according to Article 32, paragraph 4 of the Naples II Convention, the convention can enter into force between the parties if they have made a declaration according to which the provisions of the convention (except Article 26) can be applied in relations with other states that have made the same declaration. These states are Austria, Denmark, Finland, France, Germany, Ireland, Portugal, Spain, Sweden, the Netherlands and the United Kingdom. The new Member States that have made such a declaration when submitting their instrument of accession are the Czech Republic, Estonia, Hungary, Lithuania and Slovenia.

The EU Convention on Mutual Assistance is the basic legal structure to the use of a JIT in criminal matters between the EU Member States. Nevertheless, not all Member States have as yet ratified it. The Framework Decision on JITs of 2002, that made it possible to use the instrument of a JIT before the entry into

---

[5] *B.S.*, 13 October 2004.
[6] Besides, Albania, Bulgaria, and Switzerland as non-EU Member States have also ratified the protocol.
[7] Convention of 18 December 1997 on Mutual Assistance and Cooperation between Customs Administrations, *OJ* C 24, 23.01.1998.
[8] Article 1 of the Naples II Convention.

force of the EU Convention on Mutual Assistance, will cease to have effect when the EU Convention on Mutual Assistance enters into force for all Member States which were members at the time of the adoption of the act by the Council (Article 27). At the end of 2005, the EU Convention on Mutual Assistance will have entered into force for 16 Member States (including 6 new Member States). However, not every state which was a member of the EU at the time the act was adopted by the Council – 29 May 2000 – has as yet ratified the text. So far, Greece, Italy, Ireland and Luxembourg – Member States at the date of the adoption of the Convention – have not made all the necessary steps for the ratification of the EU Convention on Mutual Assistance. This means that the Framework Decision on JITs is still in force at the present time.

In accordance with Article 4 of the Framework Decision on JITs, it should have been implemented by the Member States at the latest on 1 January 2003. Only one Member State, the United Kingdom, had forwarded information on the implementation in time. Denmark, Latvia and Finland had complied with the deadline, but neglected to send this information to the European Commission. Unfortunately, no compelling instrument is provided for Member States that do not comply with their duties according to the Framework Decision on JITs in time. By 31 December 2003, nine Member States (Germany, Spain, Italy, Luxembourg, Austria, Portugal, Finland, Sweden and the United Kingdom) had made efforts to implement the legislation concerning JITs and send to this information to the European Commission. In 2004 France, Austria, Belgium, Greece and the Netherlands informed the Commission that implementation legislation was pending or would enter into force in the near future.[9]

The Benelux Agreements of 1962 and 1969 created a concept similar to a JIT as described in the Framework Decision on JITs. Article 26 of the Agreement of 1962 establishes the possibility for foreign officials to assist in the investigating and detecting of criminal acts on the territory of another party provided with a *commission rogatoire*. Naturally, this only creates possibilities between Belgium, Luxembourg and the Netherlands. It is worth mentioning that Articles 17 to 20 of the 1969 Agreement includes provisions on the competencies of foreign officials operating in another state's jurisdiction.

If the establishment of a JIT is not based on the EU Convention on Mutual Assistance, the possibilities and advantages of the JIT diminish drastically. A

---

[9] Commission of the European Communities, Report from the Commission on National Measures Taken to Comply with the Council Framework Decision of 13 June 2002 on Joint Investigation Teams, 07.01.2005, COM(2004) 858 final.

JIT that is not directly based on the provisions of this text, but instead on another convention or agreement, will not have the same added value as other texts are limited to specific matters (customs matters in the case of the Naples II Convention) or crimes (transnational organised crime in the case of the UN Convention). As the scope of the EU Convention on Mutual Assistance is much wider, a JIT based on this foundation will undoubtedly have more opportunities as an instrument in the fight against cross-border crime.

1.2.2 Legal basis of the THB-JIT project

1.2.2.1 A challenging legal basis

In the interviews, those participants who were confronted with questions on legal differences emphasised that at the time of research differing legal frameworks for investigative measures were only of secondary importance as an operational JIT had not been put into practice. Instead, the paramount point of concern was whether there was a legal basis for realising an operational JIT between the participating countries. Therefore, this issue will be further explored here.

During the time the THB-JIT project tried to realise an operational JIT, the legal basis for setting up a JIT was as follows. In the United Kingdom various provisions and guidelines from 2002 indicate that joint investigation teams may be formed under the Framework Decision on JITs of 13 June 2002 and the EU Convention on Mutual Assistance. The Dutch legislator implemented Article 13 of the EU Convention on Mutual Assistance in an Act of 18 March 2004 which entered into force on 1 July 2004. In Belgium the implementation of the Framework Decision on JITs in new legislation entered into force on 3 January 2005. And finally, also Germany enacted specific legislation on 8 August 2005. Consequently, for a vast amount of the time spent on the THB-JIT project, only two of the participating countries had specific legalisation in place dealing explicitly with the establishment of JITs. However, even the issue of whether the Netherlands and the United Kingdom were in a position to forming a bilateral JIT was questioned.[10]

An overview of the project documents indicates that the issue of lacking JIT-related legislation had been a point of discussion from the very beginning. How-

---

[10] G. Vermeulen, JIT and pre-JIT cooperation possibilities in the relationship between The Netherlands and other countries involved in the JIT-initiative(s) initiated under the Netherlands EU Presidency 2004, Advisory opinion, 16 January 2005 (not published).

ever, what the documents do not show is to what extent participants considered this as either a core issue or only an indirect problem. Another important issue concerns the question of to what extent participants reached an agreement on how to proceed if a JIT was actually lacking the necessary legal basis.

In the meetings conducted during the THB-JIT project, the issue of a legal basis for establishing a JIT was addressed in a letter to the chairman of the steering group dating back to 7 October 2003. In this letter the Belgian Government addressed the issue by stating that:

> Belgium, for the time being, does not yet have a legal framework in place for the establishment of a JIT. The lack of a legal framework places us in a position where we cannot bind ourselves to an initiative for the setting up of a JIT. Therefore we were positive on the changed attitude to work in a two-phase plan. Introducing an intelligence phase before any decision on the establishment of a JIT seems a better option all the way [...].

In the Project Initiation Document, the project manager included a project risk assessment in which the lack of or a differing ratification of JIT-related legislation is explicitly mentioned as a potential risk. The Letter of Intent of 3 December 2003 comprises the consideration that 'from a practitioner's point of view there is an urgent need to establish legislation in the respective EU countries on the establishment of a JIT.' In the steering group meeting on the same day a short inventory was made of the state of play regarding the implementation of JIT legislation at the national level.

From the beginning of the THB-JIT project Germany was the country that disposed of more information on trafficking in human beings in relation to Bulgaria than any of the other participating countries.[11] As a consequence, Germany was always seen as the country with the most potential to participate in an operational JIT. At the same time Germany did not have any specific JIT-related legislation in place. Different views were adopted on how to proceed under these circumstances. For some time German delegates were of the opinion that the existing legislation allowed Germany to participate in a JIT under Article 13 of the EU Convention on Mutual Assistance. At the same time it is stated that:

> In case the legislation will not be in place (in one or more of the participating countries) a possible Memorandum of Understanding, between the parties involved, could be established. Another possibility could be to operate a JIT in the

---

[11] This is, *inter alia,* indicated by the number of contributions to the AWF Maritsa (steering group report of 10 February 2004, p. 2).

classical way (parallel investigations), although this would probably not benefit the authentic objectives of the initiative.[12]

The recommendation made during a workshop in relation to the THB-JIT project, equally included that:

> in case the judicial framework should not yet be adequate to organize a JIT as described before, the [...] case as it is now being prepared in the form of a mirror investigation by the Joint Intelligence Group should be executed (on the basis of national legislation in the participating countries).[13]

As the realisation of an operational JIT appeared to be in reach at a JIG meeting in 2004, the meeting report again dealt with a 'JIT between Germany and the Netherlands with support and parallel investigations in Belgium and Bulgaria.'[14] However, in the aftermath of this particular meeting, participants' opposite views became apparent in how far the core aim was to realise a joint investigation (which might include traditional forms of cooperation such as parallel/mirror investigations) as opposed to a JIT under the framework of Article 13 of the EU Convention on Mutual Assistance.[15] The former view was taken by Germany, Belgium and Bulgaria whereas the latter view was taken by the Netherlands and the United Kingdom. These irreconcilable viewpoints of a pragmatic approach versus a formalistic approach were explicitly formulated at a meeting on 30 September 2004 hosted by Eurojust.[16] In the subsequent steering group meeting it was concluded that due to a lack of legislation, only the Netherlands and the United Kingdom were in the position to form a 'formal' JIT. At the same time Prof. Dr. G. Vermeulen from Ghent University was requested to give legal advice on the positions of Germany and the Netherlands regarding the implementation of a JIT under Article 13 of the EU Convention on Mutual Assistance. As stated before, Prof. Dr. G. Vermeulen concluded that according to the

---

[12] Meeting Report 3 December 2003, p. 2.

[13] Meeting Report JIT/JIG workshop, Zwolle, 19 to 20 January 2004, p. 4.

[14] Meeting Report JIG Meeting in Wiesbaden, 19 to 20 July 2004, p. 2. 'Parallel' or 'mirror' investigations imply that investigations are to be started simultaneously in different countries with a common objective and a univocal strategy, on the basis of a Memorandum of Understanding or a letter of understanding. The national laws remain applicable. Transfer of evidence takes place within the framework of national legislation.

[15] Meeting Report of the steering group Meeting 7 September 2004, p. 2. At the meeting the JIG team leader explicitly stated that since Germany had not yet ratified Article 13 of the EU Convention the German delegation preferred to start with parallel proceedings. At the same time Germany offered leadership of such a joint team with the Netherlands.

[16] At the same meeting German delegates stated that meanwhile they had been informed by the German Ministry of Justice – contrary to former statements – that Germany was currently not in the position to participate in a JIT under the framework of Article 13 of the EU Convention.

Dutch implementation of JIG legislation, the Netherlands could only set up a JIT under Article 13 of the EU Convention on Mutual Assistance with countries that are equally a party to the Convention. Accordingly, at the time of research the Netherlands could not form a 'formal' JIT with Germany.

In the interviews participants criticised that the issue of lacking legislation to realise a JIT under Article 13 had been discussed too late. For most of its time the steering group had been preoccupied with issues the relevance of which was secondary and/or related to practical aspects of realising a JIT. Equally, disappointment was expressed on the unsteady position of Germany that had at first signalled a German participation in a 'formal' JIT to be possible, only to revise this position at a later stage.[17] It was specifically unclear whether Germany needed specific legislation to use the instrument of a JIT. German representatives asked the German Ministry of Justice for clarification at the start of the project and were told that this was unnecessary. However, the Ministry of Justice changed its position later. Therefore it was obvious that Germany as well as the Netherlands at first tried to establish a JIT together. This argumentation was contradicted by a Belgian delegate who emphasised that from the very beginning Germany and Belgium had made it clear that they were not – due to lack of JIT-related legislation – in the position to take part in a JIT framework, but preferred to concentrate on investigative results and to rely on traditional forms of transnational cooperation. Furthermore, the Dutch and the British participants in the steering group were criticised for not being able to clearly state the consequences of their JIT-related legislation to the participating countries. Others stated that, in general, it would have been the role of the Netherlands as the initiator of the THB-JIT project to have outlined at the beginning all the possible scenarios of a JIT or JIT-like cooperation between the participating countries.[18] In this context it was further stressed that it had been the Netherlands that was keen to realise an operational JIT in the framework of Article 13. Accordingly, the clarification of the legal possibilities should have been the first issue to address. Instead, the differing legal possibilities and expectations only showed up eventually, creating an atmosphere of uncertainty. A Eurojust representative claimed to have raised the issue of legal problems quite early but the prevailing view at that time had been to proceed with discussing practical issues

---

[17] A German delegate emphasised that in the beginning he had been assured by the German Federal Ministry of Interior that Germany was in the position to participate in a 'formal' JIT only to be told 18 months later that the additional implementation legislation of Article 13 of the EU Convention was necessary after all.

[18] A Dutch representative acknowledged that a JIT project should start by comparing the common aims as well as the differences in the legal systems and then to enter into the discussion on how to overcome discrepancies.

and leave the legal aspects to be solved later so as not to jeopardise the success of the THB-JIT project as such. In the end, in order to save one of the principal aims of the Dutch presidency a JIT was set up between the United Kingdom and the Netherlands on a drug case.

1.2.2.2 Added value

The question was raised whether the THB-JIT project, as it never entered its operational phase, had any added value or was merely an attempt to establish a form of cooperation that was especially complicated to attain.
The project certainly confirmed the idea that European cooperation is a complex issue that may encounter some obstacles on the way. It furthermore disproved the idea of some participants that when European legislation is adopted, this immediately becomes reality in the Member States by means of direct implementation. However, despite the difficulties and the fact that the end-result is not as expected, most interviewees argue that the positive outcomes of this project cannot be neglected.

The most important added value acknowledged in the THB-JIT project concerns the lessons learnt by the different states involved in how to set up a JIT and the possible difficulties that can arise during the process of setting up such an instrument in the future. It is believed that the steering group exercise can have a significant value for the Member States or other agencies and the people involved in this steering group will be of value for their own states. The participants stress that the latter does not assume that future JITs will be easier to set up. However, it is believed that the persons involved in future JITs will at least be better prepared.

For example, it was acknowledged that a feasibility study would have been an efficient instrument before the start of the project. Many problems in this project have occurred because such a feasibility study was not made. It is argued that during the project, persons involved realised that Germany and Belgium did not have the legislation to actually start a JIT with their Dutch and British colleagues. This particular fact should have been acknowledged before the project even started.

The participants continue that the feasibility study should consider the legislation of the different countries involved separately, the possibilities between the different countries involved in the project, the place where the JIT would be located, the responsibilities of the partners and, in general, everything that could jeopardize the setting up and functioning of the JIT at a later stage of the project.

Another positive consequence mentioned is the fact that the project provided a lot of support and attached importance to the questions of the representatives of the steering group for the police officers and the prosecutors in their countries. The latter were more easily persuaded to agree with proposals and actions that needed to be taken.

Furthermore, it is acknowledged that due to the close contact between several persons from different countries, the network of people involved in THB was strengthened and this might facilitate cooperation in the future. According to some interviewees, this facilitation of cooperation has already been shown between the Netherlands and the United Kingdom. They have started a JIT on drugs together, partly as a result of contacts made through the THB project.
The Bulgarian representative in the steering group argued that the THB project had a particular academic value for Bulgaria. As a country that would like to join the EU in 2007, they have gained adequate knowledge of its functioning. They have learnt how the negotiating proceedings in the Union take place, how the voting procedures work and they have in general become skilled in the fundamental rules of the international police and judicial cooperation in Europe.

Most interviewees argue that it cannot be denied that a considerable amount of knowledge has been obtained from this project. However, one interviewee commented that if all the elements learnt from one another in the EU will take this much time, not much progress will be made. He continued that in the future, we will almost certainly not have an adequate time frame to go through such learning processes.

For the reason that the THB-JIT project never entered the operational phase, its operational added value is limited. Nevertheless, efforts made by the participants had an indirect impact on the fight against trafficking in human beings. Some members stated that during the course of the project information was gathered which was beneficial for some national investigations on trafficking in human beings. Especially representatives from Germany affirmed that the contact with Bulgarian authorities has intensified. A Bulgarian representative referred to the concerted action of the German and Bulgarian Police in the course of which numerous high profile suspects had been apprehended and a number of victims had been detected. In this context the THB-JIT project had been of decisive value as it had intensified mutual cooperation. One person, by contrast, was of the opinion that information gathered in the course of this project would have been collected in any case within the framework of the Action Plan Bulgaria Working Group. Others negated any relation between information gathered within the current project and the results of national investigations.

Therefore, it is clear that although the THB-JIT project never reached its original aim, it could never be described as a superfluous operation. Gaining significant knowledge regarding the criminal justice systems of other states, on the one hand, and strengthening operational cooperation with other states, on the other, are two highly important consequences of this project that will remain to have a fundamental impact on future collaborations between the countries involved.

1.2.3 Legal basis of the Drug JIT

Two formalities needed to be fulfilled to make the JIT operational. First, an initial letter of request is needed to be able to start a JIT between the Netherlands and the United Kingdom. Although Articles 552qa-qe do not refer to it, the guideline of the Board of Prosecutors General clearly points out that a request for legal assistance is necessary to initiate a JIT. Furthermore, this is confirmed in the Home Office Circular of 1 October 2002 on the EU Framework Decision on Joint Investigation Teams section 9.[19] This requirement is furthermore prescribed in Article 13.1 of the EU Convention on Mutual Assistance and Article 1.1 of the Framework Decision on JITs.

A letter of request for mutual assistance was sent to the Department of International Legal Assistance at the Ministry of Justice in the Netherlands on 17 December 2005. The letter, originating from the Crown Prosecution Service in the United Kingdom, requested the Netherlands for assistance, under the provisions of the 1959 Convention, in obtaining evidence in relation to a sensitive and highly confidential criminal investigation being conducted by officers of the National Crime Squad of England and Wales (NCSEW).

The purpose of this letter was to ask that any evidence obtained as a result of the JIT, which was relevant to the investigation and any subsequent proceedings in England and Wales, be forwarded either to the Crown Prosecution Service or the National Crime Squad in the United Kingdom, for use in such investigation or proceedings.[20] At the same time, this letter was also aimed at being the mechanism that would bring the JIT into effect under Dutch Law.

Two aspects of this letter are rather remarkable. Firstly, this letter of request for mutual assistance does not specifically ask for the establishment of a JIT. The reason why the letter of request did not ask for the establishment of a JIT is that under United Kingdom law letters of request can only be issued in very narrow

---

[19] Home Office Circular 53/2002 of 1 October 2002 on the EU Framework Decision on Joint Investigation Teams.

[20] See Article 3 of the 1959 European Convention on Mutual Assistance in Criminal Matters.

circumstances. A letter of request asking for a JIT to be instituted *per se* cannot be issued as a matter of law. That is because it is not a request for 'evidence' which section 7 of the Crime (International Cooperation) Act 2003 requires. In order to avoid an impasse, a legitimate request for evidence was drafted which had the subsidiary effect of allowing the Dutch authorities to instigate a JIT. Currently an amendment of this section is being discussed and a parliamentary draft to this effect is being made.[21]
Nevertheless, the agreement mentions that the legal basis for the Drugs JIT is the Framework Decision on JITs and the EU Convention on Mutual Assistance (Article 13), but this was not mentioned in the letter of request.

A second remark that can be made concerning the request for mutual assistance is the fact that this formal request was preceded by an orally made request at an earlier stage. Therefore, the formal written request did not explicitly contain the request for the establishment of the JIT.

In addition to the letter of request, an agreement needs to be signed between the two countries. Parties to the agreement of 24 November 2004 were: the National Public Prosecutor's Office in Rotterdam and the National Crime Squad of the Netherlands, The Crown Prosecution Service of England and Wales and the National Crime Squad of England and Wales.

1.3 Setting up a JIT

1.3.1 *Formalities fulfilled in setting up the Drugs JIT*

According to Article 13, paragraph 1 of the EU Convention on Mutual Assistance the team working within the framework of the Drugs JIT will be set up in one of the Member States in which the investigations are expected to be carried out. As set out in paragraph 4 of the amended JIT Agreement of January 2005, the JIT is situated in the Netherlands, more precisely at the police premises in Driebergen. Accordingly, the JIT operates in the Netherlands.

The composition of the team shall be set out in the agreement (EU Convention on Mutual Assistance, Article 13, paragraph 1). The leader of the team shall be a representative of the competent authority participating in criminal investigations from the Member State in which the team operates (Article 13, paragraph 3(a)).

---

[21] Scientic Research JIT, Report on the Drugs JIT, third sub-report, Scientific Research Group under the supervision of C. Rijken, 19 December 2005, p. 7.

The JIT Agreement divides the members of the Drugs JIT into judicial authorities and police authorities (paragraph 6). Among the judicial authorities four public prosecutors are involved, two of which are from the Netherlands and two from the United Kingdom.

According to the Agreement, 13 police officers participate in the JIT, three of whom come from the NCSEW and are, therefore, referred to as 'seconded officers' (Article 13, paragraph 4 of the EU Convention on Mutual Assistance), the others are members of the Dutch NCS. Regarding the three British investigators a system of rotation applies: two seconded members are always residing in the Netherlands and one is located in the United Kingdom.

1.3.2 The relationship between the Drugs JIT and the 'mother case' in the United Kingdom

According to the Explanatory Report, the drafters of the EU Convention on Mutual Assistance anticipated that where agreement is achieved on the setting up of a JIT, the team will normally be established in the Member State in which the main part of the investigations is expected to be undertaken.[22] The wording indicates the flexibility of this guideline.

By contrast, in a circular letter on international JITs issued by the Dutch Board of Procurators General on 10 June 2004, the purpose of JITs is described as follows: to concentrate partial investigations in various countries in a single, joint investigation team, thus making sure that investigations in respect of a criminal group which is operating in several countries are not limited to just one branch of it, but that, on the contrary, the criminal group can be tackled in its entirety through coordinated investigations and actions of the various countries participating in such a team.[23]

As described above, the starting point of the JIT in question was an orally made request followed by a formal letter of request issued by the British Crown Prosecution Service to the Dutch Prosecution Service requesting assistance in a criminal investigation into drug trafficking being conducted by officers of the NCSEW. In the course of the investigation links to Dutch suspects involved in importing drugs into England from the Netherlands had been discovered.

---

[22] Council of the European Union, Explanatory Report to the Convention of 29 May 2000 on mutual assistance in criminal matters between the Member States of the European Union, Brussels, *OJ* C 379, 29.12.2000, p. 7.

[23] G. Vermeulen, JIT and pre-JIT cooperation possibilities in the relationship between The Netherlands and other countries involved in the JIT-initiative(s) initiated under the Netherlands EU Presidency 2004, Advisory opinion, 16 January 2005, p. 9 (not published).

Parallel to the Drugs JIT in the Netherlands the NCSEW continues to investigate its drug case. According to the JIT Agreement, in the course of both investigations the Netherlands and England and Wales are to provide evidence and intelligence to each other (paragraph 2). In the Agreement the reason for locating the Drugs JIT in the Netherlands is described with the aim of dismantling the Dutch branch of the criminal investigation by the NCSEW. Thus, the Netherlands is not the country in which the main part of the investigation is expected to take place, neither does the JIT contain the concentration of previous partial investigations.

In the interviews the issue of the Drugs JIT being set up to tackle the Dutch branch of a criminal organisation while the NCSEW continues to investigate the 'mother case' in the United Kingdom was addressed. It was pointed out that the question of where the Drugs JIT was best located had been intensively discussed in the preparatory phase. It could not be argued that the Drugs JIT needed to be set up in the Netherlands because a substantial part of the criminal activities took place there. In general, the interviewees confirmed the involvement of Dutch suspects in the criminal organisation investigated in the United Kingdom. Whereas one Dutch person interviewed described the Dutch suspects as key persons in the United Kingdom investigation a British interviewee described the Dutch link as an identifiable, very small part of the United Kingdom investigation. It was acknowledged by all interviewed persons that the main case was based in the United Kingdom. However, as the Dutch suspects in the United Kingdom investigation did not operate in the United Kingdom but in the Netherlands, the United Kingdom did not need Dutch officers seconded to the United Kingdom investigation. Instead, it was the Dutch side that would benefit from a JIT.

Once more, the political eagerness of the Dutch to start a JIT in the Netherlands as part of the EU Presidency and the readiness of the United Kingdom to participate in a JIT being set up in the Netherlands was pointed out. One interviewed person expressed the opinion that because experience with JITs was still lacking, the responsible persons were afraid to concentrate the entire investigation in one JIT. Instead the goal was to experiment with the JIT tool without taking too many risks.

In the interviews the general need for flexibility regarding the location of JITs in contrast to a standardised method was pointed out. Depending on the individual case a JIT could be set up in the state of the 'mother case', parallel to the 'mother case' in another state, in three different states and so on.

As evidence will be collected in both states, and proceedings are expected to be commenced in the United Kingdom as well as the Netherlands, 'parallel' investigations in both countries could be seen as an advantage. The importance of close cooperation was stressed for evidence to be admissible in both criminal procedures.

1.3.3 Model agreement for EU Member States

In May 2003, the Council of the EU published a recommendation regarding a model agreement for setting up a JIT.[24] In order to facilitate the setting up of a JIT (and hoping that the enactment of a model agreement would speed up the implementation of the Framework Decision on JITs), the Council was aware of the fact that a model agreement should be comprehensive and flexible as authorities should be able to adapt it to the particular needs and circumstances of the case at hand. Nevertheless, a recommendation still has no binding force towards the Member States and, therefore, is no guarantee that the process of setting up a JIT will run smoothly.

In general, interviewees described the model agreement as a good starting point for a JIT. One person interviewed complained that the model agreement had obviously been drafted by persons not familiar with the needs of investigators. Thus the parties to the Drugs JIT only used parts of the model agreement while deleting others. He added that the insertion of a section on the handling of sensitive information would have been useful. Instead of the requirement to insert information on the investigation in the agreement, it should be used more as a business document merely providing practical information such as the parties involved as well as the rights of the JIT members. It is evident that this concern is directly linked to the special disclosure rules applicable in the United Kingdom which oblige the responsible authorities to specifically safeguard sensitive information. However, the majority of interviewees stressed that the model agreement had to be regarded as a flexible instrument. It was pointed out that the model agreement provided only a basis that could be amended if the need for changes became evident during the JIT. This was envisaged in particular in cases of multilateral JITs. However, it was equally pointed out that the quality of the model agreement could only be fully assessed once the JIT had been terminated.

Others claim that they were not very impressed with the model agreement as it is. Partly because it was not written in perfect English, but also because it gave

---

[24] Council of the European Union, Recommendation of 8 May 2003 on a Model Agreement for Setting Up a Joint Investigation Team, Brussels, *OJ* C 121, 23.05.2003.

the impression that it would be difficult to apply in everyday practice. Consequently, some parts of it were left out, although it was followed to a considerable degree. Putting too much detail in the agreement was avoided in case the agreement would fall into the hands of persons that may not know what the case is about.

Some say that it is better to only regulate the main provisions in the model agreement and not to try to regulate all the details, because the more details are regulated, the greater the possibility that discussions will have to be held and an agreement as such would be much more difficult to obtain.
Maybe this can change in the future when there is a clearer framework for the JIT, but for the Drugs JIT simplicity was preferred in order to be able to really set up a JIT between the Netherlands and the United Kingdom. The time to re-examine the model agreement is not now, but rather at the end of this particular investigation.
It is furthermore stressed that a model is genuinely just a model that can be adapted to a specific situation that occurs in an actual case.

1.3.4 Model agreement for third states

Generally, the prevailing feeling is that a JIT with a third country is unlikely anytime in the near future. Although broadening the scope of the model agreement is regarded as useful in the theoretical sense because organised crime knows no boundaries and crime groups operate beyond borders, culture, language, etc., the police and judicial system are nevertheless restricted by their national boundaries. Consequently, a JIT also involving countries outside the EU is appreciated in principle as it allows the police to move further beyond these boundaries.

At the same time, to find suitable JIT partners would require addressing other issues particularly if the third state was known for corruption among the responsible authorities, poor training of police/judicial officers, etc. With regard to the issue of drug trafficking, the interviewees found it particularly difficult to imagine a JIT including Columbia as an important state of origin at any time soon. Interviewees felt that before states from outside the EU should be included in JITs, the instrument as such should first be tested thoroughly among EU Member States.

Practical problems regarding the model agreement with third countries include language problems, time differences, etc. Additionally, a number of supplementary problems can be expected with multilateral JITs, for example concerning the negotiations about the agreement, many different languages, etc.

It was described as an advantage to have a JIT in the EU in that there is a high quality of training and expertise, as well as trust, in each other's legal systems. Nevertheless, the level of trust of the Member States of the EU in each other's legal systems is questioned in both EU policy and literature. The European Commission and the Council adopted the Programme of measures to implement the principle of mutual recognition of decisions in criminal matters in 2000 which provided for gaining trust in other states' criminal justice systems.[25] In the same context, the Hague Programme included confidence-building and mutual trust as one of the priorities for the EU in the near future.[26] Shortly hereafter, the Commission proceeded in line with the principle of mutual recognition in order to enhance mutual trust between the Member States.[27] Researchers confirm that mutual trust between EU Member States should not been taken for granted.[28]

In the scope of the current research, one interviewee pointed out that successful joint investigations, will depend, firstly, on the parties' willingness to cooperate and, secondly, on selecting good partners for cooperation. In his opinion the chances of a JIT succeeding are just as great among EU Member States as with third states. This point of view was shared by another interviewee who felt that the current JIT agreement could be used and would only need to be moulded to fit the situation. A member of Europol pointed out that at the Europol level strategic and operational agreements with third states already exist. And in any case Europol is free to ask for information from a third state, but is limited in its possibilities to provide information in return.

1.3.5   *Scope*

1.3.5.1 Objective(s) of the JIT

The Explanatory Report on the EU Convention on Mutual Assistance states in its introduction that the primary aim of the EU Convention on Mutual Assis-

---

[25] Council of the European Union, Programme of measures to implement the principle of mutual recognition of decisions in criminal matters, Brussels, *OJ* C 12, 15.01.2001.

[26] Communication from the Commission to the Council and the European Parliament, The Hague Programme: Ten priorities for the next five years – The Partnership for European renewal in the field of Freedom, Security and Justice, Brussels, 10.5.2005, COM(2005) 184 final.

[27] Communication from the Commission to the Council and the European Parliament, Communication on the mutual recognition of judicial decisions in criminal matters and the strengthening of mutual trust between Member States, Brussels, 19.05.2005, COM(2005) 195 final..

[28] C. Rijken, *Trafficking in Persons. Prosecution From a European Perspective*, 2003, The Hague, TMC Asser Press, p. 228-229; J. Koers, *Nederland als verzoekende staat bij de wederzijdse rechtshulp in strafzaken* (The Netherlands as the requesting state in mutual assistance in criminal matters), 2001, Nijmegen, Wolf Legal Publishers, p. 458-480.

tance is to improve judicial cooperation by developing and modernising the existing provisions governing mutual assistance in order to make it quicker, more flexible and, as a result, more effective.[29] The establishment of JITs in Article 13 of the EU Convention on Mutual Assistance is recognised as a tool by which to contribute to this aim.

Article 13, paragraph 1 of the EU Convention on Mutual Assistance states that a JIT may, in particular, be set up either due to the requirement of complex, transnational investigations or the necessity of coordinated actions by several states. The wording makes it clear that the enumeration is not exhaustive. It is recognised that investigations having a cross-border dimension, particularly in relation to organised crime, can benefit from the cooperation with law enforcement personnel from another state equally affected by the offence in question.[30]

According to the Guidelines of the Dutch Board of Procurators General, by contrast, a JIT is to be used only as a last resort in cases in which the same result cannot be achieved by traditional forms of mutual (legal) assistance. The Home Office Circular of 1 October 2002 states in its introduction that 'there is no requirement to use this method for working when conducting investigations jointly with other Member States of the European Union, but there may be an advantage in doing so.'

The Agreement setting up the Drugs JIT states as formal objectives operational motivations. The JIT is to be established

> in relation to investigating the drug trafficking activities of a criminal organisation operating in the Netherlands and England & Wales. Drugs are being imported into England from the Netherlands. A joint investigation team will be established in the Netherlands to dismantle the Dutch branch of the organisation; and for the Netherlands and England & Wales to provide evidence and intelligence to each other ....

In the interviews further (unwritten) goals were added, such as the Dutch interest in the seizure of property and finance and to collect information regarding other, related, cases. It was equally hoped that the Drugs JIT would enhance

---

[29] Council of the European Union, Explanatory Report to the Convention of 29 May 2000 on mutual assistance in criminal matters between the Member States of the European Union, Brussels, *OJ* C 379, 29.12.2000.

[30] Council of the European Union, Explanatory Report to the Convention of 29 May 2000 on mutual assistance in criminal matters between the Member States of the European Union, Brussels, *OJ* C 379, 29.12.2000.

police and judicial cooperation between the United Kingdom and the Netherlands and speed up the process of mutual assistance.

In the interviews the possible advantage of a JIT for operational reasons was acknowledged and the need for close cooperation between police and judicial authorities across the EU was stressed. Whether the JIT is the best way to achieve this aim is a question that only the repeated setting up of JITs can show. At the time of research none of the interviewees argued that the construct of a JIT was absolutely essential for the successful investigation and prosecution of the drug case connected to the JIT. It was indicated that this particular case might as well have been investigated having recourse to traditional forms of mutual assistance.

It was pointed out that to answer the question whether this particular JIT provided clear benefits compared to the normal procedure of requests for mutual assistance or the construct of parallel investigations was, as yet, impossible to answer, since, at present, the necessary experience with JITs is still lacking. During the interviews, it was stated that previous efforts of joint cooperation had often failed due to the lack of a framework regulating the activities of the respective investigations.[31] Also, the question was raised whether a JIT, integrating police officers from another jurisdiction while following the laws of the state in which it was set up, was easier to manage and more flexible than parallel investigations in which the participating states could act on their own accord within their home jurisdictions.

The Drugs JIT in question was seen as a test case to help clarify the obstacles as well as possible advantages of JITs. Thus, all interviewed partners identified testing the workability of a JIT as a tool as one main objective. One interviewee summarised these arguments by stating: 'Without starting a JIT it is impossible to find out whether it is a workable tool for cooperation.' With this JIT being the first one pursuant to Article 13 of the EU Convention on Mutual Assistance and the Framework Decision on JITs, the goal was to use it as a springboard for future JITs.

It was acknowledged that the intention to test the JIT as a tool might cause problems later on in Dutch court proceedings. According to the Guidelines of the Dutch Board of Procurators General setting up a JIT requires that traditional procedures of transnational cooperation do not suffice to achieve the same goal.

---

[31] See also the Home Office Circular of 1 October 2002 stating the increasing need for clarity and consistency in the way joint investigations are conducted and information is exchanged so that evidence is admissible in the courts (paragraph 3).

A JIT gives the police more possibilities, for example foreign police officers investigating on Dutch territory. A judge could argue that this extension of police powers is to be reduced to cases in which it is absolutely necessary from an operational point of view. In the drug case in question, this precondition might not be fulfilled since it is very likely that the same results could be obtained by using the concept of parallel investigations. However, one interviewee named, as a paramount purpose, the testing of the JIT concept to find out what problems a JIT may encounter on the police as well as the judicial level. In order to do so the case will have to go to court.

All interviewed persons stressed the fact that the Drugs JIT did not only enjoy political support but that the set up of the JIT as such was to a certain extent politically driven. It was stated that politically the issue of JITs had been under discussion for years. As a consequence, the expectations towards the law enforcement agencies of both states and within these agencies themselves were rising. From the United Kingdom perspective, the political will to set up a JIT was explained by the eagerness to participate in the first THB-JIT project. From the Dutch side, the objective of instituting the first THB-JIT project under the Dutch EU Presidency was stressed.

The objective of testing the JIT as a tool also influenced the choice for the drug case. It was chosen on purpose, *inter alia,* for its simplicity: the case roughly affects only two states, thus involving only two jurisdictions. Its structure is not too complicated and it is expected to be solved in due time. It was also stated that the United Kingdom, with the help of Europol, had a clear picture of the transnational activities of the criminal organisation being investigated. Presently it is argued that experience with the JIT construct is still lacking and that joint cooperation is a complex issue in itself. The goal is not to overcomplicate the first JIT and to be able to present a successful investigation. In order to be able to promote the added value of a JIT, the case needs to be solved successfully.

1.3.5.2 Police or judicial cooperation in criminal matters?

From their statements, it can be concluded that the interviewees consider a JIT as a form of police cooperation, while in fact it is a form of judicial cooperation in criminal matters. From the British point of view, this is not surprising, since a prominent role in the criminal investigation is reserved for police authorities. Furthermore, the THB-JIT project was established under the Dutch Presidency-Police which would make it understandable for the participants to denominate the JIT as a form of police cooperation. Nevertheless, the Drugs JIT was established apart from the Dutch Presidency-Police.

This however makes a difference in the approach taken and this difference could also be clearly identified in this case, for police cooperation in criminal matters is indicated in Article 30 of the Treaty of 1992 on the European Union (hereafter referred to as TEU) as including operational cooperation between the competent authorities, including the police, customs and other specialised law enforcement services of Member States in relation to prevention, detection and investigation of criminal offences and the collection, storage, processing, analysis and exchange of relevant information, including information held by law enforcement services on reports on suspicious financial transactions, in particular through Europol, subject to appropriate provisions on the protection of personal data. The description of Article 30 TEU corresponds with what the participants indicated as the potential added value of the JIT.

A JIT is a form of judicial cooperation in criminal matters of which the description can be found in Article 31 of the TEU. The main aim of setting up a JIT is to facilitate mutual assistance in criminal matters by avoiding the time-consuming letters of request that have to be issued each time a country requests another country for action in connection with the investigation or prosecution of a punishable act. This aim clearly relates to Article 31 TEU which indicates that judicial cooperation includes the facilitating of and accelerating cooperation between competent ministries and judicial or equivalent authorities of the Member States, including, where appropriate, cooperation through Eurojust, in relation to proceedings and the enforcement of decisions.

1.3.5.3 The nature of the offence

The preamble to the Framework Decision on JITs states in paragraph 6 that JITs should apply to joint investigations into trafficking in drugs and human beings as well as terrorism. However, this list is not exhaustive.

Most participants in the Drugs JIT say that the nature of the offence does not really play an important role as such. However, it is recognised that the JIT can particularly prove its value when it concerns a form of organised crime with international links.

Others say that the nature of the offence does play a role. They argue that a JIT is more likely to be used for trafficking cases, be it human trafficking or drug trafficking, than for other offences. Naturally, a number of organised international cases concern trafficking cases.

The conclusion can be drawn that all participants in fact agree that the JIT can particularly prove its value when it concerns international organised crime, although they answer the basic questions differently.

When linking the added value of a JIT to the specific crime of trafficking in human beings, doubts are raised about the fact whether a JIT is an instrument that can be useful in the fight against this crime.

There are doubts about the presence of criminal organisations with a pyramidal structure in this crime area. Although trafficking in human beings is clearly an international phenomenon, there is reasonable doubt whether it is possible to identify one group which is active in different countries. There are indications that this type of crime is characterised by small groups active on an international scale rather than one group active internationally. If this is true, it is argued that it becomes rather difficult to identify part of the criminal organisation in the different countries and it makes human trafficking a difficult crime to be the subject of a JIT.

A number of interviewees argue that a JIT probably can have added value when it concerns other types of crime in which the criminal organisations consist of parts with a specific function. In these cases, there is more coherence in the criminal organisation, which provides more opportunities to investigate the same organisation in different states. Narcotics are a good example of such a crime, as well as terrorism, money laundering or trafficking in arms.

These crime areas are in general better understood than the complex phenomenon of trafficking in human beings. The latter becomes even more complex considering the necessary involvement of other organisations such as NGOs or IGOs, something that is not needed in other types of crime.

In the interviews the view prevailed that the topic of drug trafficking was not chosen on purpose. The purpose was to find a suitable case and the type of crime was not a deciding factor. The fact that the NCSEW had a drug trafficking investigation at hand that required international cooperation with the Netherlands was regarded as accidental. It was acknowledged that drug trafficking is a type of crime that, in general, is perfect to be investigated jointly by law enforcement from the United Kingdom and the Netherlands or any other Member States, as it is a cross-border crime regarded as a serious problem within Europe. It was further stated that in the Netherlands and the United Kingdom combating drug trafficking is high on the political agenda. Some interviewees described drug trafficking as easier to investigate than certain other fields of crime (e.g., terrorism, human trafficking). Another argument brought forward was that law enforcement agencies from both states had extensive expertise in investigating drug trafficking (regarding suspects, modus operandi, evidence gathering, etc.) and also with joint cooperation. One person interviewed elaborated on the operational aspects to explain the United Kingdom motivation for engaging in international cooperation in the field of drug trafficking. Regarding the distribution channels of criminal networks engaged in drug trafficking, the United Kingdom is – also due to its geographical location – only the end phase of the distribution chain, starting from the country of origin via other European states. Each part of the distribution chain decreases the commodity and, correspondingly, the amount of drugs confiscated in the United Kingdom is also low compared to the amount of drugs that – potentially – could be confiscated in preceding countries of distribution. For the United Kingdom to be able to tackle the distribution channels as a whole at a time when the drugs are still largely concentrated in the hands of one network, it is indispensable to cooperate with other European states. Another interviewee argued that in comparison to other crimes, drug trafficking is a topic that easily leads to operational success, since the law enforcement agencies have access to more information and covert sources. A valuable issue concerns the structure of the criminal networks: whereas organised crime groups involved in drug trafficking tend to be organised like a pyramid, the organisational structures of criminal networks engaged in human trafficking are still largely unknown. This was said to be one of the main reasons why the THB-JIT project had not succeeded.

In the interviews on the Drugs JIT the question of a separate intelligence phase, preceding the actual setting up of the JIT was answered in a negative way by all persons interviewed. The importance of avoiding the complicated and time-consuming construct of a separate joint intelligence group was stressed. Instead, a case investigation was singled out that involved the United Kingdom and the Netherlands after the NCSEW had analysed their intelligence containing links to the Netherlands. The information was shared with their Dutch counterparts who had time to consider the intelligence. In a second step it was decided to start the JIT on this target and to collect the necessary information. One decisive criterion in choosing this case was that it was expected to have a short operational life. In the interviews it was acknowledged that the Drugs JIT approach to find a suitable target, at least in theory, was not the best way to proceed. Instead, the suitability of an investigation for setting up a JIT should normally be analysed extensively beforehand (an approach applied in the JIG/THB-JIT project). Otherwise at a later stage it might become evident that the case chosen was actually not suitable for a JIT.

2. SPECIAL ASPECTS OF THE (USE OF THE) JIT

2.1 Presence of foreign police officers in a state

A significant innovation in the use of a JIT is the presence of foreign police officers in another Member State. This means they are operating within a criminal justice system that is not their own; they have – in principle – no competences within the other Member State and they have no or little knowledge of the language, the criminal justice system and criminal policy of this state. Working with the instrument of a JIT means that particular competences should be granted to these police officers in order for them to perform investigative measures and to complete their investigation in that particular state.

In the operational Drugs JIT, United Kingdom officers were assigned to work in the Netherlands with the KLPD as 'seconded members' of the JIT.

The English officers working in the Netherlands within the framework of the Drugs JIT fell under Dutch law. Foreign investigators operating within Dutch jurisdiction do not have an independent investigative competency, unless provided for by the Code of Criminal Procedure or conventions between states. The agreement setting up a JIT cannot change this; it can only limit the competences of the seconded members. The team leader can give directions to the seconded members of the team. Paragraph 9(4) of the JIT Agreement states further that seconded members attached to the Dutch tactical team must be trained in surveillance techniques and will be paired with a Dutch officer.

The article in the Dutch Code of Criminal Procedure that can be interpreted as explaining the competences of the seconded members is Article 552qb, although it does *not* explicitly refer to seconded members. As stated above, Article 552qb of the Code of Criminal Procedure of the Netherlands can be understood according to a rather strict interpretation, on the one hand, or a wider interpretation, on the other. The latter approach means that a clear indication of the competences of the English officers operating in the Netherlands is required. Consequently, they have acted in accordance with Dutch legislation.[32]

Only one convention is available at the present time that includes the entrusting of foreign officers operating on the territory of another Member State with investigative powers. The Schengen Agreement (however, not applicable to the United Kingdom) provides the right to cross-border observation and hot pursuit (Articles 40 and 41). In conjunction with Article 54.5 of the Dutch Code of Criminal Procedure a legal basis is presented for apprehending persons on Dutch territory by foreign officers in the context of cross-border hot pursuit in accordance with public international law (in this case the Schengen Agreement).[33]

---

[32] Cf., *supra*, Chapter I.

[33] G. Vermeulen, JIT and pre-JIT cooperation possibilities in the relationship between The Netherlands and other countries involved in the JIT-initiative(s) initiated under the Netherlands EU Presidency 2004, Advisory Opinion, 16 January 2005 (not published).

In case the Drugs JIT would become operational in the United Kingdom, Dutch police officers will be authorised to be present when investigative measures are taken. This principle is indicated in Home Office Circular 53/2002. The circular also points out that it will not in general be possible under United Kingdom law for seconded JIT members to exercise coercive powers such as powers of search and seizure and powers to question witnesses.

When Dutch investigators or officers of Justice act as a seconded member in a JIT established in a Member State other than the Netherlands, they are still bound by the Dutch legislation. They have no more or other investigative competences abroad than they would have according to the Dutch law.

From the aforementioned, the following conclusions can be drawn.
Firstly, concerning the competences of the English Police Officers operating as seconded members in the Netherlands, two interpretations can be given to Article 552qb, one of which is rather restrictive, while the other which is an extensive interpretation of the competences of the English seconded members. Secondly, concerning the competences of the Dutch Police Officers operating as seconded members of the Drugs JIT, a consensus exists that they are not able to independently perform investigative measures. However, they may be present when such investigative measures are being executed.

An important issue addressed in this context was the fact that in contrast to Dutch officers, British officers are generally not allowed to carry firearms. The issue of carrying arms was discussed and solved by the parties in the preparatory phase. The parties agreed that officers suddenly authorised with powers they are not trained to use, such as carrying firearms, can create dangers for themselves, their Dutch colleagues as well as civilians. Consequently, British officers seconded to the Drugs JIT were restricted to carrying arms they are allowed to carry under British law, which are a pepper spray and a baton. In addition, the seconded members undergo training with the Dutch officers to make sure that the protective equipment they use is compatible and complies with Dutch law. The Dutch Minister of the Interior granted permission for this practice.

Other issues do not concern questions of competencies, but different policies or problems arising from the fact that the seconded members do not speak Dutch. All persons interviewed described the British police officers seconded to the Drugs JIT as being an integral part of the team, on the same level as the Dutch officers. Although one seconded member remarked that even though in theory he had the same competencies as his Dutch colleagues, it is not always easy to carry these out due to language deficiencies.

Tasks were carried out under the leadership of the investigation team supervisor.[34] In order for the seconded members to be able to follow the course of the investigation all relevant contents of the police file were translated into English. The same applied to investigative measures such as telephone tapping, the products of which are summarised and translated. At the same time British investigators were included in the daily investigative work of the Dutch investigators as much as possible. In practice, seconded members were partly authorised with tasks that are not part of their job in the United Kingdom. However, this concerns only tasks that are not forbidden under United Kingdom law as such, but concern certain policies in the United Kingdom (distribution of responsibilities within a criminal investigation among intelligence and operational teams). Prosecutors from both sides discussed the issue of British investigators involved in telephone tapping by the Drugs JIT and did not identify any legal obstacles. As a consequence, the seconded officers in the Drugs JIT implemented and analysed telephone tapping, a task not conferred to them in the United Kingdom.

2.2 Investigative measures

The legal basis of carrying out investigative measures within the framework of a JIT between two countries applying divergent criminal justice systems, such as the Drugs JIT between the United Kingdom and the Netherlands, will be explained in this section. Additionally, the question whether more investigative measures will be carried out in the framework of a JIT compared to traditional mutual legal assistance is explored.

The investigative measures used in the Drugs JIT concern telephone interception, surveillance and the use of traditional police sources for information. Because the JIT was located in the Netherlands, telephone interception and surveillance have only been used on Dutch territory.

Up to the time when the interviews had taken place, the juridical regulations on the national levels with regard to choosing which investigative methods must be used, and in which country, had not influenced the activities and results of the JIT. At the time of the interviews no coercive measures had been used by the Drugs JIT. Arrests occurred in the United Kingdom in relation to the drug investigation ('mother case'). However, these arrests have not caused any problems in the functioning of the Drugs JIT.

---

[34] See Article 10, paragraph 3(b) of the EU Convention (Article 1 of the Framework Decision on JITs).

2.2.1 Problems concerning investigative measures

A JIT shall carry out its operations in accordance with the law of the Member State in which it operates.[35] The Drugs JIT Agreement states that the Drugs JIT will operate in the Netherlands, carrying out its operations in accordance with the law of the Netherlands.[36] Article 13, paragraph 3(b) of the EU Convention on Mutual Assistance (Article 1 Framework Decision on JITs) also provides that the team members, when carrying out their tasks under the leadership of the team leader, take into account the conditions set by their own authorities in the agreement on setting up the team. According to paragraph 5 of Article 13 of the EU Convention on Mutual Assistance (Article 1 Framework Decision on JITs), seconded members shall be entitled to be present when investigative measures are taken in the Member State of operation. They may also be entrusted, by the leader of the team, with the task of taking certain investigative measures where this has been approved by the competent authorities of the Member State of operation and the seconding Member State (cf., *supra*).

In the Drugs JIT, British officers are seconded to a Dutch team of investigators. Therefore, possible conflicts resulting from differences in competencies were only addressed regarding the competencies of the British on Dutch territory and not vice versa. In the interviews it was acknowledged that differences in competencies theoretically had the potential to lead to conflict. However, so far any differences had been solved through negotiations. The paramount goal was to test in practice the judicial framework of having British officers investigating alongside Dutch officers.

According to the interviewees, problems arising with regard to the use of evidence concern all sources of information classified as sensitive information, respectively intelligence due to the discussed disclosure rules in British law (see below).

Overall, the question whether different national legislation leads to conflict is answered negatively. Even though it was acknowledged that a potential for conflict is given, the differences in disclosure rules are primarily regarded as formalities. Neither the Netherlands nor the United Kingdom is prevented from using special investigative measures according to their national law. One interviewee stated that differences with regard to the use of special investigative

---

[35] Article 13, paragraph 3(b) of the EU Convention (Article 1 Framework Decision on JITs).
[36] Amended Agreement on the Establishment of a Joint Investigation Team, 17 January 2005, paragraph 4.

methods as evidence were explicitly addressed by the United Kingdom delegation from the very beginning, as the United Kingdom was well aware that its adversarial system differs from the criminal procedure of most other European Member States.

2.2.2 *Number and variety of investigative measures*

At the time of research the Drugs JIT at this point in the investigation was not perceived as leading to a greater variety in the use of investigative measures. Few interviewees felt that this was also likely to be expected in the future. A distinction was made in that there would be neither an increase in the variety nor in the number of measures used. One of the reasons was because there are a limited number of measures that can be used in an investigation. Although the lengthy process of requesting assistance through regular channels can be avoided, for example in the case of a request for a telephone interception, more information could be requested within the JIT framework and that might result in more measures. One interviewee felt the JIT construct would eventually lead to a larger number and variety of measures because of the transnational activities of criminal networks investigated, requiring the use of special investigative measures.

The main indication was that the JIT framework would allow for a quicker exchange of information and the achievement of operational results particularly because of the access to foreign systems. From a legal perspective it was stated that the JIT construct did not provide a basis for implementing more measures because no laws have been changed, but within the existing legal parameters there is an opportunity to make the investigation happen faster. For example, a lot of investigative work is being done in the Netherlands that is shared with the United Kingdom, eliminating the procedure of the prosecutor issuing a letter of request to obtain the evidence.

Another point raised by one of the interviewees was that although the Drugs JIT will not lead to further investigative measures, it seemed that the British and Dutch police forces are expected over time to become more similar to one another and it is expected that the policy at the European level will merge. This refers to the United Kingdom emphasis on keeping intelligence information, and the means used to gather it, strictly confidential.

2.3 **Evidence**

When a JIT construct is used in the international cooperation in criminal matters between two or more Member States, the issue of joining the functioning of two or more criminal justice systems will surface. In the cases described in this report, the cooperation with the adversarial system applied in the causes challenging queries to be resolved concerning the evidence to be used when a case enters the stage of court proceedings. The most significant questions arise on the level of the disclosure principle, the use of evidence stemming from telephone interceptions and the use of informers.

2.3.1 *Disclosure*

2.3.1.1 General

States that are joined in the framework of a JIT can meet severe problems when exchanging information, particularly when the states involved apply deviating criminal justice systems. In the Drugs JIT, the principle of disclosure as a feature of United Kingdom law caused practical and legal issues when the JIT entered its operational stage. As is extensively explained above, the principle of disclosure has consequences on the level of information exchange and on the level of evidence.[37]

2.3.1.2 THB-JIT project

The THB-JIT project under review did not enter the operational phase. Therefore, it could only be investigated in how far the stated differences in criminal procedure in the participating states were discussed and expected to constitute problems at a later stage and whether they in any way affected preliminary discussions on establishing a JIT.

During the steering group meeting of 3 December 2003, the Eurojust representative referred to Article 552qa of the Dutch Code of Criminal Procedure which requires a written agreement as the basis for a JIT that is to state, *inter alia,* the duty of foreign investigators to testify as a witness in a Dutch court when called upon. Accordingly, this had to be 'a point of attention when setting up a JIT'.[38] At a project-related workshop legal differences in the criminal procedure in the participating states were addressed. However, according to the minutes the legal problems addressed by the participants were not discussed in detail.

In the interviews it became clear that issues pertaining to the handling of sensitive information and the possibility to introduce them as evidence in court had

---

[37] See also Chapter III.
[38] Meeting Report, p. 3.

not been addressed in the steering group but in informal meetings and, most importantly, during the workshop in Zwolle.[39] In the interviews[40] the majority of the participants were of the opinion that in the THB-JIT project these issues had been discussed only superficially. Participants disagreed whether there had been a need to discuss them in more detail and when these issues should best have been addressed.

Some interviewees acknowledged that differences in the criminal justice system in relation to disclosure rules were discussed only superficially in the THB-JIT project and should have been discussed in more detail. Others remembered discussions on how to deal with information gathered in the participating states and their admissibility as evidence in court proceedings. Secondly, it had been discussed whether police investigations in the United Kingdom based on intelligence would meet the formal requirements for starting a formal investigation in the Netherlands. Different opinions prevailed in how far these issues had been regarded as problematic.

One interviewee was of the opinion that during the various meetings of the participants of the THB-JIT project it became clear that since it was the first attempt to implement the framework of the JIT in practice, no one knew exactly how information exchange would take place and how questions of the admissibility of evidence would be solved. Another participant pointed out that most steering group members had experience in international police cooperation and were, therefore, sensitised regarding differences in legal systems.

In the interviews a representative from the United Kingdom outlined British disclosure rules stating that every document and piece of evidence is classified according to a special system grading the level of sensitivity. Material classified as sensitive will be sanitised in such a way as to protect the sources of information. In a second step the judge will be asked to decide against the disclosure of the evidence to the defendant. It was further stressed that, in practice, investigation authorities disposed of mechanisms to solve problems evolving from states' needs to protect sensitive information. On the police level letters of intent were used to determine the purposes for which information could be used. In cases of mutual legal assistance, letters of request worked as a legal safeguard by offering the possibility to determine the extent to which evidence and intelligence from the requested state could be introduced in judicial proceedings in the requesting state. However, these mechanisms presupposed intensive contacts on the police and judicial level of the countries in question. In this regard, the JIT

---

[39] Workshop JIT, 19-20 January 2004. During the workshop the participants of the countries involved discussed the establishment of a JIT and the necessary steps to take in this process.

[40] It needs to be kept in mind that statements by the interviewees were influenced by the extent to which the interviewees had taken part in any of these forums.

construct was regarded as an asset. It was equally stated that another mechanism to protect sensitive information was to send it via Europol, the latter serving as a firewall.[41] One participant offered the explanation that differences in the handling of sensitive information between the United Kingdom on the one hand, and Belgium, Germany, and the Netherlands, on the other, did not take place because it had been clear from the outset that the United Kingdom would not make significant contributions regarding THB in connection with Bulgaria; consequently, a JIT would not have included the United Kingdom.

In this context Europol representatives made the remark that at the Europol level questions of the compatibility of legal systems as well as the handling of sensitive information were routinely dealt with in feasibility studies before opening an AWF.[42] Following from these experiences, projects like the THB-JIT project equally needed clarification on legal issues at the earliest moment possible. This had been an issue which the steering group had failed to address. However, it was believed that the overall performance of a JIT would not have been substantially impaired by differences in the handling of (sensitive) information. Even though this might slow down the information exchange, the concept of JITs which implied the seconding of officers from abroad to the team was, nevertheless, expected to speed up the information exchange. On the one hand, it was pointed out that – even though presentations on legal differences

---

[41] Information exchanged via Europol is sent through the national units of the Member States (Article 4 Europol Convention of 26 July 1995) to the liaison officers seconded by the national units to Europol (Article 5 Europol Convention). According to Article 5, paragraph 1, liaison officers are subject to the national law of the seconding Member State. They enjoy immunity pursuant to Article 5, paragraph 8 and Article 41, paragraph 2. Immunity may imply, *inter alia,* that liaison officers are not obliged to testify as witnesses in a Dutch court. The reason is to protect data files administered by liaison officers. Each Member State that provides information to Europol can decide whether the information can be disseminated or if certain conditions apply to dissemination. According to Article 10, paragraph 8 Europol Convention, the Member State that communicates the data to Europol is the judge of the degree of its sensitivity. Accordingly, sending information via Europol and the liaison bureaus, respectively, enables the United Kingdom to protect sensitive information, the disclosure of which might jeopardise ongoing investigations in the United Kingdom.
In this context one interviewed person pointed out that his country had agreements with the Europol Liaison Officers (ELO) of the different countries on how to exchange information provided by the national units. Another interviewee criticised that Europol had not been created as an 'anonymisation authority.'

[42] Issues to be covered concerned not only legislation but the compatibility of investigation measures, the position of the police towards the public prosecutor, disclosure rules as well as ownership of information (*police* v. *public prosecutor, Member States* v. *third parties*). In this context handling codes were explicitly referred to. These allowed the owner of information to classify the information in a way that it was not to be used as evidence in another country but intended only as information for individual persons.

between the Member States were a priority when setting up a JIT – the timing and the extent to which these issues needed to be discussed equally depended on the identification of a specific case and, correspondingly, the actual set up of a JIT. On the other hand, it was argued that awareness of the participating states' legal differences might influence the choice of the states actually forming the JIT.

2.3.1.3 Drugs JIT

Experience gathered from the Drugs JIT between the Netherlands and the United Kingdom showed that the need for British investigation authorities to differentiate between intelligence and operational information and the need to conceal the use of certain investigative measures as well as material stemming from it, had an impact on the nature of information the British authorities were in the position to share directly with their Dutch counterparts and on the speed with which the information could be exchanged (cf., *supra*).[43] Secondly, the disclosure rules applicable in the United Kingdom, together with the fact that officers from abroad being seconded to a JIT hosted by the Netherlands must be willing to testify in a Dutch court,[44] affected the selection process of British seconded members.[45] In the Drugs JIT the participants were sensitised to the problem of disclosure during their team-building days.

2.3.2 *Telephone interception*

Telephone interception is the subject of a special regulation in the United Kingdom. On the basis of section 17 of the Regulation of Investigatory Powers Act

---

[43] Information supplied to the Drugs JIT by the NCSEW was either exchanged directly or via Europol. Which one of the two information channels was used depended on whether the information was classified as intelligence or tactical/operational information. Due to the already described disclosure rules in the United Kingdom, a strict division was made between the sources of information (intelligence) and the information that was gathered in the course of relying on intelligence sources, e.g., informers, telephone interception (tactical or operational information). Whereas intelligence sources had to be protected, tactical or operational information could mostly be shared without restrictions. Apart from legal obligations to refrain from disclosure, another issue concerned tactical issues. British investigators described their fear that early disclosure of information in the JIT files or in court proceedings might jeopardise ongoing investigations in the United Kingdom.

[44] Article 552 qa of the Dutch Code of Criminal Procedure (CCP).

[45] In the Drugs JIT it appeared to be of paramount importance to the British that the seconded members only had limited knowledge of the ongoing drug investigation in the United Kingdom. Consequently, a decisive factor for selecting the British officers to serve as seconded members was the fact that they were never fully involved in the United Kingdom investigation. This in turn reduced the – potential – possibilities of the seconded members to support the investigation of the JIT in the Netherlands.

2000 (hereafter referred to as RIPA), evidence derived from warranted intercepts cannot be used as evidence in court. As stated above, section 18 of the Act provides for a limited number of exceptions on this principle.[46]

The aforementioned means concretely that telephone interceptions conducted in the United Kingdom cannot be used as evidence in the Netherlands. The information obtained from telephone interceptions may however be used as a basis for investigative measures in the Netherlands, for example for surveillance or wire-tapping. Nevertheless, in some cases this might have a negative consequence. For example, when the information from the telephone interception cannot be obtained by any other investigative measure in the Netherlands, one cannot use the information at all, no matter how interesting and crucial it is for the case.

The prohibition on the use of intercepted products in evidence created by section 17 of RIPA does not apply to interceptions lawfully obtained in foreign countries. This principle was confirmed in *Regina* v. *P and Others*, a judgment of the House of Lords of 8 June 2000.[47] It was argued that none of the United Kingdom Acts has a relevant extraterritorial application, which means that the Interception of Communications Act of 1985 (the predecessor of the RIPA and the act that applied during this case) could not apply a telephone interception performed in another country. Hence, the information resulting from the telephone interception in another country than the United Kingdom is admissible as evidence in the United Kingdom.

Applying to the Drugs JIT, this means that the product of lawful telephone interceptions performed in the Netherlands can be used as evidence in the United Kingdom. A telephone interception that has been lawfully obtained in the Netherlands is an interception that is conducted on the basis of Articles 126m or 126s of the Code of Criminal Procedure. But, information from a wiretap that is executed in the United Kingdom cannot be used as evidence in the Netherlands, just as mere intelligence.

It is worth mentioning that United Kingdom police officers' responsibility to prevent unlawful disclosure of telephone interception is not a problem exclusively arising in the context of the JIT. Instead, the United Kingdom routinely experiences comparable problems when engaged in transnational cooperation with other jurisdictions.

---

[46] See also Chapter III.
[47] *Regina* v. *P. and Others*, Judgment of the House of Lords of 8 June 2000, URL: <http://www.parliament.the-stationery-office.co.uk/pa/ld200001/ldjudgmt/jd001211/pappl-1.htm>.

2.3.3 *Civilian and criminal infiltration and the use of informers*

Differing provisions on the use of criminal informers can entail practical and legal difficulties in the course of an investigation by means of a JIT. The Drugs JIT cannot use information as evidence if it is collected in the course of the drug investigation in the United Kingdom through infiltration of civilian informers with a criminal record.

Criminal infiltration[48] can be carried out as an investigative method in the United Kingdom, although it is illegal in the Netherlands. This means that information obtained through criminal infiltration in the United Kingdom cannot directly be used as evidence in the Netherlands. Of course, information from a criminal infiltration can be used as a basis for other investigative measures in the Netherlands.

In conclusion, it can be stated that information that is gathered in the Netherlands and the United Kingdom within the framework of the Drugs JIT will only be admissible as evidence if it is allowed by both countries. Of course, information that cannot be used as evidence can still be used as mere information on which basis an investigative measure in the Netherlands can be carried out. In that case, it will not be mentioned what the exact origin of the information is. The only aspect that will be reassured is the fact that the information was obtained in a legal manner.

2.3.4 *Use of information gathered in the context of a JIT*

With regard to information obtained by the Drugs JIT members, a difference needs to be made between the information gathered in the United Kingdom, be it by Dutch or British police officers, and information gathered in the Netherlands, by either British or Dutch police officers.

The answer to this question only deals with the question whether information obtained by Drugs JIT members can be used as evidence for purposes of the JIT and it does not deal with the question whether the police officers from the Netherlands and the United Kingdom who are members of the JIT have the competency to execute the investigative measures used to obtain the information.

Information obtained in the Netherlands can evidently be used as evidence in the Drugs JIT. Problems might arise concerning the competences of the JIT team members, but this has been elaborated in another section.

---

[48] Criminal infiltration means using a person that is part of a criminal organisation under the authority of the police and the prosecutor. This person renders himself guilty of criminal acts with the consent of the police and the prosecutor.

The question whether information gathered in the United Kingdom by foreign members of the Drugs JIT can be used as evidence in the JIT, is a question that is not addressed in the Dutch implementation legislation, or in Dutch law in general.

However, the Guideline of the Dutch Board of Prosecutors General indicates that the public prosecutor needs to assure that the evidence is gathered in a way that does not constitute a fundamental breach of the Dutch rules of prosecution. Furthermore, Article 552qc stipulates that documents drawn up by foreign members of the JIT in the course of their investigating and prosecuting activities, will have the same evidential value in the Netherlands as actions performed by Dutch officials in the Netherlands (Article 552qc CCP). However, the weight of the evidence cannot exceed the weight attributed to the evidence in the state of origin of the foreign member.

Thus, information obtained through investigative measures executed in the United Kingdom will have evidential value in the Netherlands, but only if they are exercised and communicated in a way that is accepted by English law.

This means that the information from telephone interceptions executed by seconded JIT members in the United Kingdom cannot be used as evidence in the Netherlands due to the fact that it cannot be used as evidence in the United Kingdom itself. It is nevertheless possible to execute investigative measures in the Netherlands on the basis of the information from British wire taps. Subsequently, information obtained through these investigative measures can be used as evidence without any problems.

A similar conclusion can be drawn for, e.g., criminal infiltration. While this is not allowed in the Netherlands, in the United Kingdom it is not a problem. Consequently, information from criminal infiltration performed in the United Kingdom cannot be used as evidence in the Netherlands.

However, it was the intention that this information would be obtained by the team leader without telling him the source of the information and, consequently, further investigative measures could be performed on the basis of this information.

In short, the following conclusion can be made concerning information obtained from investigative measures in the United Kingdom that can be used as evidence. Documents or reports can only be used as evidence insofar as the investigative measures lying at the basis of the evidence are allowed by law in both states.

To overcome this problem, information coming from an investigative measure that is not permitted by one of the states involved will be used as mere intelligence on the basis of which other investigative measures will be exercised.

When the team operates in the United Kingdom and thus operates in accordance with United Kingdom law, evidence obtained within the Drugs JIT when operating abroad cannot just be used as evidence in the United Kingdom, since there is nothing in the legislation indicating that it can.

3.   PROSECUTION

Up to the time the research was carried out (and providing that the case at hand in the Drugs JIT will lead to prosecution), no binding decisions were taken concerning the place where prosecution would be initiated. The case will be prosecuted wherever the best evidence can be gathered. If this is in the United Kingdom, the case will be prosecuted by a British court. If this is the Netherlands, the prosecution will take place in a Dutch court. Therefore, the only decision that has been taken in relation to the prosecution is that it will take place wherever it is most appropriate.

The letter of request (regarding the Drugs JIT) by the United Kingdom of 17 December 2004 describes that 'it is anticipated that if proceedings are commenced against the principal targets of the JIT (meaning Dutch nationals), these will take place in the Netherlands.'

On the Dutch side, it is also anticipated that the prosecution of the suspects will take place in the Netherlands. From the point of view of the many of participants in this JIT, prosecution at the end would be a good outcome, but one of the most important objectives is to learn from the test case, finding out what the instrument of the JIT can offer us and see how it can be improved in the future.

At the current stage of the project, the different practices with regard to the principle of opportunity and the legality principle have not caused any problems. Of course, the interviewees argue that it is difficult to predict whether these different practices would cause any problems in the future and what these problems would consist of.
Both the Netherlands and the United Kingdom apply the principle of opportunity. This principle empowers the prosecutor or the police to refrain from prosecution in the cases in which prosecution is deemed unnecessary. They are thus not obliged to prosecute every person of whom it is suspected that he has committed a criminal offence. Since both countries apply the same principle, no problems can occur for the Drugs JIT due to the application of different principles.

4. CONCLUSION

The primal objective of the instrument of a JIT was intended to be the speeding up of investigations into crime(s) with links to more than one Member State. Authorities of the Member States involved working closely together, even on each other's territory, is an efficient alternative to the original practice of sending requests for mutual legal assistance to the central authorities. A drug case including connections to the United Kingdom and to the Netherlands proved to be an excellent case to implement the first JIT based on the 2002 Framework Decision on JITs in the history of the EU. The question is, however, whether the real goal of this JIT was to accelerate the process of international cooperation in criminal matters or, in fact, the purpose was to test the instrument of the JIT. It is questionable whether this is a good basis from which to start. Nevertheless, working in this manner means that growing pains of the first JIT can easily be discovered and solved to the benefit of future JITs.

Discussions concerning the legal basis of a JIT to be set up between Member States should be avoided in the future. It is essential to correctly implement the Framework Decision on JITs in the national legislation. The implementation should be complete, accurate and clear, in order to avoid confusion about the application of certain provisions and the meaning of particular provisions in the national law.

The major difficulty that will continue to surface in the EU is the cooperation between diverting criminal justice systems' authorities. The United Kingdom, being one of the strongest common law systems of the EU, clearly anticipated problems when entering into the Drugs JIT Agreement with the Netherlands. Both states have made efforts to search for creative solutions to the legal problems that arose in the Drugs JIT. In future, criminal justice systems that have a common historical, political or social (and even language) background will have stronger similarities in their respective (criminal) legislative framework and can therefore anticipate a smoother cooperation within a JIT. Naturally, the mutual trust between these states will be stronger and entail a well-organised and swift exchange of information. When thinking of the cooperation in the framework of a JIT with third states, these difficulties will need to be anticipated and solved in due time. A flexible model agreement, open to a wider range of criminal justice systems and adjustable to a large variety of situations, is indispensable.

The question whether the instrument of the JIT has added value compared to the traditional mutual legal assistance is crucial in the framework of the Drugs JIT since the 'mother' investigation in the United Kingdom was still in process.

Consequently, the Drugs JIT was really 'degraded' to a parallel investigation and could not portray its full added value as an accelerated cooperation between the authorities of the Member States involved. Additionally, the detour regarding information exchange via Europol – instead of a direct exchange between the Member States involved – did not offer the JIT a chance to fully demonstrate the swifter exchanging of relevant data. Therefore, the genuine added value of a JIT in the function of its objective to assure a smoother international cooperation in criminal matters is yet to be established.

CHAPTER V
THE ROLE OF EUROPOL AND EUROJUST IN JOINT INVESTIGATION TEAMS

Annette Herz*

1. INTRODUCTION

At its meeting on 15 and 16 October 1999 in Tampere, the European Council called upon the Member States of the European Union to initiate joint investigation teams in an effort to combat the trafficking in illicit drugs and human beings as well as terrorism. As each of these crimes typically involves a transnational dimension, they also require a cooperative transnational response. The Member States were urged to introduce the necessary provisions to enable Europol representatives to take part in these teams in a supporting role. The meeting was also the starting point for the establishment of Eurojust, an organisation created to support criminal investigations and facilitate the proper coordination of national prosecuting authorities in cases of organised crime that affect more than one Member State.[1] In the aftermath of Tampere, the Council decided upon a concept for Joint Investigation Teams (hereafter, JITs). This concept was introduced in Article 13 of the EU Convention on Mutual Legal Assistance in Criminal Matters[2] (hereafter, EU Convention on Mutual Assistance) and correspondingly in Article 1 of the 2002 Council Framework Decision on Joint Investigation Teams[3] (hereafter, Framework Decision on JITs).

---

* At the time of writing Annette Herz was a researcher at the Max-Planck-Institute for Foreign and International Criminal Law, Department of Criminology, Freiberg (Germany). Currently she is working for the management of the Bundeskriminalamt.

[1] Recommendation Nos. 43, 45, 46, *Bulletin* (Bulletin of the Press and Information Agency of the German Government) 1999, p. 793.

[2] Convention of 29 May 2000 established by the Council in accordance with Article 34 of the Treaty on European Union, on Mutual Assistance in Criminal Matters between the Member States of the European Union, *OJ* C 197, 12.07.2000, p. 1.

[3] Council Framework Decision of 13 June 2002 on Joint Investigation Teams *OJ* L 162, 20.06.2002, p. 1. The wording of the Framework Decision is identical to Article 13 of the EU Convention on Mutual Assistance.

C. Rijken and G. Vermeulen (Eds.), *Joint Investigation Teams in the European Union*
© 2006, T·M·C·ASSER PRESS, The Hague, The Netherlands and the Authors

Following on from these provisions, the initiation and creation of a JIT can take place if a criminal investigation requires difficult and demanding investigations that have links with other Member States or if a number of Member States are conducting investigations into criminal offences and the necessity for coordinated and concerted action exists in the Member States involved. The provisions contain information on the Member State in which the creation of the JIT is to be instigated, the leadership and composition of the team, the competences of the team members and, most importantly, how data is to be exchanged within the team.

In December 2003, upon the initiative of the Netherlands, Belgium, Germany, the United Kingdom, in cooperation with Bulgaria, Europol, and Eurojust, signed a letter of intent. The purpose was to initiate a JIT in accordance with the new procedures enumerated in the EU Convention on Mutual Assistance and the Framework Decision on JITs.[4] The common purpose of the project (hereafter, THB-JIT project) was to investigate criminal cases of trafficking in human beings for commercial and/or sexual exploitation, in which Bulgaria had been identified as a source and/or transit country. The project was monitored and studied from a scientific point of view in order to review how the four aforementioned countries collaborated together in applying the new concept of cooperation.[5] The overall research aim was to describe and evaluate the development and functioning of the THB-JIT project. One aspect of research was the involvement of Europol and Eurojust. With regard to their involvement, the following research questions were addressed:

- How were Europol and Eurojust formally involved in the THB-JIT project (position and responsibilities within coordinating bodies, during the intelligence phase, during the investigation phase)?
- What were the practical consequences of cooperation with Europol and Eurojust?
- What was the role of Europol and Eurojust with regard to the gathering, analysis, and exchange of information (operational and/or support functions)?
- What other tasks were fulfilled by Europol and Eurojust?
- Did problems occur that prevented the THB-JIT project from harnessing the (full) potential of Europol and Eurojust?

---

[4] In the second half of 2004, the Netherlands held the Presidency of the Council of the European Union. One priority of the Dutch Presidency was the setting up of joint investigation teams as part of improving judicial and police cooperation in the European Union.

[5] For further information on the initiation of the THB-JIT Project as well as the methodology of the research see Chapter I.

- What was the added value of including Europol and Eurojust in the THB-JIT project?
- What performance indicators can be formulated for the participation of Europol and Eurojust in future JITs?

This article is structured as follows: After a brief overview of Europol and Eurojust as institutions, the legal framework for their participation in JITs according to Article 13 of the EU Convention on Mutual Assistance and the Framework Decision on JITs as well as the respective national implementing legislation will be analysed. The fourth and fifth part of the article concentrate on the actual participation of Europol and Eurojust in the THB-JIT project as well as a JIT on illicit drug trafficking (hereafter, Drugs JIT). The main focus centres on the practical consequences of cooperation with Europol and Eurojust especially in regard to information exchange. The closing remarks will summarise the added value of, as well as the problems met by Europol's and Eurojust's participation in the projects under review, followed by recommendations for their involvement in future JITs.

2. EUROPOL AND EUROJUST AS INSTITUTIONS

At present, Europol and Eurojust provide two differing functions for cross-border Member State investigations that complement one another. Whereas Europol is charged with uncovering crimes possessing an international dimension and supporting investigations of Member States with special expertise, Eurojust seeks to coordinate and exchange information between the competent law enforcement agencies of the Member States.[6] A brief overview of both Europol and Eurojust as institutions is given below.

2.1 Europol

In the 1970s, due to fears relating to terrorism and the growing internationalisation of criminal networks, the Council of the EU increasingly concentrated on the issue of cooperation in matters of state security. The following activities, however, were reduced to intergovernmental forms of cooperation as the European Economic Community was lacking the legal competency to regulate police cooperation.[7] The legal foundation for the creation of a European Police Office

---

[6] T. Milke, *Europol und Eurojust* (Europol and Eurojust), Göttingen, V&R unipress GmbH 2003, p. 289.

[7] The Treaty establishing the European Economic Community (hereafter, EEC) dates back to 25 March 1957. For an overview of the preliminary stages of setting up a legal framework for

(hereafter, Europol) as part of police and judicial cooperation in criminal matters was introduced by the Maastricht Treaty in 1992[8] under the heading 'Provisions on Cooperation in the Fields of Justice and Home Affairs' – the so-called Third Pillar.[9] The Council Act of 26 July 1995 drew up the Convention based on Article K.3 of the Treaty on European Union on the establishment of a European Police Office (hereafter, Europol Convention).[10] However, the Europol Convention did not enter into force until 1 October 1998. In the meantime the European Drugs Unit (hereafter, EDU) was established as the forerunner of Europol.[11]

According to Article 2(1) Europol Convention, the objective of Europol is to support the competent authorities of the Member States in preventing and combating terrorism, unlawful drug trafficking and other serious forms of international crime. The latter includes Trafficking in Human Beings (hereafter, THB).[12] To trigger Europol's involvement, further indications of organised criminal structures must be present and at least two Member States must be affected by the forms of crime in such a way as to require a common approach.

Europol's core task is to support the police authorities of the Member States in their intelligence work. Accordingly, Europol not only facilitates the exchange of data between Member States, but also initiates the collection, collation and analysis of intelligence.[13] It has to notify the competent Member State authorities of the information concerning them and of any connections identified between criminal offences. Furthermore, the Europol National Units (hereafter, ENUs) are to serve as liaison bodies between Europol and the competent national authorities.[14] Each national unit is to second at least one liaison officer to represent the interests of the seconding Member State within Europol and to

---

police cooperation within the European Union, especially the work of the TREVI group (Terrorism, Radicalism, Extremism, Violence International), see T. Milke, *Europol und Eurojust* (Europol and Eurojust), Göttingen, V&R unipress GmbH 2003, p. 23-33).

[8] Treaty on European Union (Maastricht Treaty) of 7 February 1992, *OJ* C 191, 29.07.1992, p. 1. The treaty entered into force 1 November 1993 (*Bundesgesetzblatt* (Federal Law Gazette) II (1993) p. 1947).

[9] Title VI, Articles K.1 to K.9. The other pillars are European Communities and Common Foreign and Security Policy. The scope of the provisions on Europol were later specified and widened by the Amsterdam Treaty of 1 May 1999, *OJ* C 340, 10.11.1997, p. 1. Title VI, Articles K.1. to K.14 now entitled 'Provisions on Police and Judicial Cooperation in Criminal Matters'.

[10] *OJ* C 316, 27.11.1995, p. 2.

[11] *Bundesgesetzblatt* (Federal Law Gazette) II (1995) p. 154.

[12] Article 2(2).

[13] Article 3(1).

[14] Article 4.

assist in the exchange of information between the national units and Europol as well as among the national units (hereafter, ELO).[15] The most important working tool available to Europol is a computerized system of collected data, composed of an information system, work files, and an index system.[16]

2.2 Eurojust

By the end of 1990s it had become widely accepted that the successful investigation of serious transnational crime not only required close police cooperation but also the coordination of judicial proceedings.[17] This was especially because in most Member States certain investigative measures are subject to the approval of the public prosecutor who is the proper leader of investigations. Additionally, in order to further enhance police cooperation without causing distortions in the system, not only was judicial cooperation to be raised to a comparative level as police cooperation but maximum synergy was to be sought in cooperative arrangements between law enforcement agencies and the judiciary.[18] A first step in this direction was the institution of the European Judicial Network (hereafter, EJN) in 1998.[19] Here, judicial authorities in each of the Member States were appointed as contact points, serving as active intermediaries between judicial authorities of the Member States.[20] The aim was to establish the most appropriate direct contacts to improve judicial cooperation, for example, to enable judicial authorities to prepare an effective request for judicial coop-

---

[15] Article 5. The liaison officers are subject to the national law of the seconding Member State.

[16] Article 6. Title II and III contain further provisions on the stated components. Thus, the right of access to the information system is limited to the national units, liaison officers, and Europol officials (Article 9(1)). In regard to work files special procedural rules were formulated by the Council Act of 3 November 1998 adopting rules applicable to Europol analysis files, which entered into force on 1 January 1999, *OJ* C 26, 30.01.1999, p. 1. Furthermore, Europol is to develop specialist knowledge of investigative procedures, to provide advice and intelligence, and to prepare situation reports in order to support investigations in the Member States (Article 3(2)).
On the working methods of Europol see further G. Kämper, *Polizeiliche Zusammenarbeit in der Europäischen Union* (Police Cooperation in the European Union), Frankfurt a.M., Peter Lang Verlag 2001, p. 92 ff.

[17] *Bulletin EU* 4 (1997) 1.5.1. (Justice and home affairs cooperation).

[18] Council Action plan to Combat Organised Crime of 28 April 1997, *OJ* C 251, 15.08.1997, p. 1. See also W. Schomburg, 'Justitielle Zusammenarbeit im Bereich des Strafrechts in Europa: EURO-JUST neben Europol!' (Judicial Cooperation in Criminal Matters in Europe: EURO-JUST alongside Europol!), 6 *ZRP* (Zeitschrift für Rechtspolitik) 1999 p. 237 at p. 239 ff.

[19] Joint Action of 29 June 1998 adopted by the Council on the basis of Article K.3 of the Treaty on European Union, on the Creation of a European Judicial Network, *OJ* L 191, 07.07.1998, p. 4.

[20] Article 2.

eration.[21] However, the need soon arose to establish an organisation similar to the EDU that would be situated in one geographical location, enabling relationships of personal trust to occur and ensuring the better coordination of national investigations.[22] Consequently, in 2001 the Treaty of Nice[23] laid the legal foundation for the establishment of the European Judicial Cooperation Unit (hereafter, Eurojust) within the TEU.[24] The institution was finally set up by the Council Decision of 28 February 2002 (hereafter, Council Decision 2002).[25]

The purpose of Eurojust as part of police and judicial cooperation in criminal matters is to prevent and combat serious forms of crime by enhancing closer cooperation between judicial authorities of the various Member States. In particular, Eurojust aims to facilitate coordination between Member States' national prosecution authorities and their cooperation in relation to proceedings and the enforcement of decisions. Eurojust is expected to support investigations in cases of serious cross-border crime affecting two or more Member States, in particular on the basis of analysis carried out by Europol, and to cooperate with the EJN in order to facilitate the execution of letters rogatory and the implementation of extradition requests.[26]

---

[21] Article 4.

[22] T. Milke, *Europol und Eurojust* (Europol and Eurojust), Göttingen, V&R unipress GmbH 2003, p. 278.

[23] Treaty of Nice Amending the Treaty on European Union, the Treaties Establishing the European Communities and Certain Related Acts, *OJ* C 80, 10.03.2001, p. 1.

[24] Articles 29 and 31 in conjunction with Article 34(2)(c) TEU.

[25] Council Decision of 28 February 2002 Setting up Eurojust With a View to Reinforcing the Fight Against Serious Crime, *OJ* L 63, 06.03.2002, p. 1. The Decision entered into force on 6 March 2002. As a forerunner of Eurojust so-called Provisional Eurojust was instituted (Council Decision of 14 December 2000 setting up a provisional judicial cooperation unit, *OJ* L 324, 21.12.2000, p. 2.), a kind of round table of prosecutors from all Member States. This provisional unit took up its work in March 2001 and enabled concepts of Eurojust to be tried and tested.
On the preliminary stages of setting up Eurojust see further R. Zöberlein, *Auf dem Weg zu einer gemeinsamen europäischen Strafverfolgung: Eurojust als Keimzelle einer europäischen Staatsanwaltschaft?* (Towards a joint European prosecution in criminal matters: Eurojust as the starting point for a European public prosecution service?), Berlin, Logos Verlag 2004, p. 36 ff.

[26] Article 31(1)(a), (2) TEU; Articles 5 ff. Council Decision. An example of Eurojust's task is provided in Article 10(2) Council Act of 16 October 2001 establishing, in accordance with Article 34 of the Treaty on European Union, the Protocol to the Convention on Mutual Assistance in Criminal Matters between the Member States of the European Union, *OJ* C 326, 21.11.2001, p. 1. Accordingly, a requesting State may report to Eurojust any problem encountered concerning the execution of a request for a practical solution. On Eurojust's working methods see further R. Zöberlein, *Auf dem Weg zu einer gemeinsamen europäischen Strafverfolgung: Eurojust als Keimzelle einer europäischen Staatsanwaltschaft?* (Towards a joint European prosecution in criminal matters: Eurojust as the starting point for a European public prosecution service?), Berlin, Logos Verlag 2004, p. 79 ff.

Eurojust's competency extends not only to the types of crime over which Europol has competence, but also to other crimes specifically listed in the Council Decision and any other type of offence at the request of a Member State.[27] It fulfils its tasks either through one or more of the national members or as a College, consisting of all the national members.[28] Whereas national members are subject to the national law of the seconding Member State[29] the competences of the College are outlined in special rules of procedure.[30] The national members serve as points of liaison with the competent authorities of the Member States and supply and support the exchange of information among them.[31] Eurojust is to make use of an index system of data relating to investigations it is concerned with and to establish temporary work files.[32]

3. LEGAL FRAMEWORK FOR PARTICIPATION IN JITS

3.1 Europol

3.1.1 *Europol Convention*

The Europol Convention in its present form does not contain specific provisions regarding Europol's participation in JITs.[33] In fact, the Convention does not confer original investigative competences upon Europol, but restricts the institution to a supporting role. The power of decision making in respect of investigative measures remains solely within the domain of the Member States. Europol is not in the position to exchange information directly with national investigative teams but is to provide its support solely through the ENUs.

---

[27] Article 4 Council Decision.
[28] Article 5 Council Decision. In how far a national member acts as the representative of the seconding Member State or represents Eurojust in a capacity of its own depends on the seconding Member State.
[29] Article 9(1) Council Decision.
[30] Rules of Procedure of Eurojust, *OJ* C 286, 22.11.2002, p. 1.
[31] Article 13 Council Decision.
[32] Articles 14(4), 16 Council Decision.
[33] For the pending amendment of the Europol Convention by the Council Act of 28 November 2002, the drawing up of a Protocol to amend the Convention on the establishment of a European Police Office (Europol Convention) and the Protocol on the privileges and immunities of Europol, the members of its organs, the deputy directors and the employees of Europol, *OJ* C 312, 16.12.2002, p. 1, see below.

3.1.2 Treaty on European Union

The (consolidated version of the) Treaty on European Union (hereafter, TEU)[34] addresses the role of Europol as part of police and judicial cooperation in criminal matters.[35] The role of Europol is further elaborated in Article 30 of the TEU. On the one hand, the Europol Convention is reiterated in so far as Europol's tasks are described as collecting, analysing, and exchanging relevant information.[36] On the other hand, a new paragraph 2 was introduced by the Amsterdam Treaty.[37] The Amsterdam Treaty amendment was committed to widening Europol's competences within a five-year plan, thereby giving Europol a more active role in investigations. The provision contains concrete measures to promote cooperation through Europol, one of which was the use of JITs.[38] In Article 30(2)(a) TEU the Council declares its intention to enable Europol to support investigative actions of the Member States, including the possibility that representatives of Europol could become part of JITs. However, even though the provision prepares the ground for Europol to become a part of the cooperative actions of the Member States, the institution's role remains limited to one of support.[39]

3.1.3 EU Convention on Mutual Assistance/Framework Decision on JITs

A significant step towards the establishment of JITs was the aforementioned EU Convention on Mutual Assistance and correspondingly the Framework

---

[34] *OJ* C 325, 24.12.2002, p. 1.

[35] Article 29 ff. TEU.

[36] Article 30 (1)(b).

[37] Treaty of Amsterdam amending the Treaty on European Union, the Treaties establishing the European Communities and certain related acts, *OJ* C 340, 10.11.1997, p. 1. The treaty entered into force on 1 May 1999 *Bundesgesetzblatt (*Federal Law Gazette) II (1999) p. 296.

[38] Another is to put Europol in the position of asking Member States to initiate investigations in specific cases (Article 30(2)(b)). On the development of the Council's ambitions to extend Europol's support functions to taking part in operational actions of national authorities see T. Schalken and M. Pronk, 'On Joint Investigation Teams, Europol and Supervision of Their Joint Actions', *European Journal of Crime, Criminal Law and Criminal Justice,* 2002, Vol. 10/1, p. 70 at p. 71 ff.

[39] The Amsterdam Treaty shows that Member States were not willing to grant Europol executive functions of its own, as this would have required further unification of provisions on crimes and criminal procedure in the Member States. As a consequence, the new provisions do not substantially widen the scope of Europol's responsibilities but comply largely with its functions as provided in the Europol Convention. K.D. Schnapauff, 'Der Amsterdamer Vertrag – Neuregelung der Zusammenarbeit im Bereich der Inneren Sicherheit' (The Amsterdam Treaty – New regulations on cooperation in the field of state security), *ZFIS,* Zeitschrift für innere Sicherheit in Deutschland und Europa, 1998 Vol. 1, p. 6 at p. 18; T. Milke, *Europol und Eurojust* (Europol and Eurojust), Göttingen, V&R unipress GmbH 2003, p. 56-57.

Decision on JITs.[40] Even though in practice law enforcement authorities of different Member States already work together jointly in the sense of coordinating cross-border investigations when required,[41] the EU Convention on Mutual Assistance and the Framework Decision on JITs aim to provide Member States with harmonised legislation providing clear rules on the cases in which the setting up of a joint team is appropriate, how the team should be composed, the powers of the team members, the leadership of the team, the operating rules and the use of information gathered, and officials' liability (Article 13(1) of the EU Convention on Mutual Assistance, respectively Article 1(1) of the Framework Decision on JITs). Following these provisions, two or more Member States may, by mutual agreement, set up a JIT for a specific purpose and a limited period to carry out criminal investigations in one or more of the Member States that set up the team. A request for the setting up of a JIT may be made by any of the Member States concerned.[42] Most importantly, the aforementioned provisions foresee the possibility of replacing traditional mutual legal assistance arrangements between the participating countries with a simple national request emanating from the respective national member(s). Seconded members may be treated in the same manner as officials of the Member State in which they are operating.[43] Furthermore, seconded members may request their own competent authorities for investigative measures without the need for any further requests under the traditional mutual legal assistance regime.[44]

---

[40] Framework Decisions for the purpose of approximation of the laws and regulations of the Member States were introduced by the Amsterdam Treaty as a new measure to promote police and judicial cooperation in criminal matters (Article 34(2)(b) TEU). Owing to the delay in ratifying the EU Convention on Mutual Assistance, the Council adopted the Framework Decision on JITs to provide a timelier means of enhancing the operation of joint investigation teams. The Framework Decision on JITs will cease to have effect when the EU Convention on Mutual Assistance has entered into force (Article 5).

[41] For example, see Report from the Commission on national measures taken to comply with the Council Framework Decision of 13 June 2002 on Joint Investigation Teams (Commission Staff Working Paper, 07.01.2005 (COM(2004) 858)). One example of coordinated investigations are the so-called parallel investigations. They imply that countries investigating criminal activities that are linked to each other (e.g., the same criminal network) should cooperate at an informal level, for example, by meeting to discuss tactics, coordinate their actions so as not to hinder or prejudice one another's investigations or to discuss possibilities of sharing evidence. It does not imply, however, that members of law enforcement authorities from different countries work jointly, i.e., as one team allocated at one place.

[42] Article 13(1) EU Convention on Mutual Assistance; Article 1(1) Framework Decision on JITs.

[43] Article 13(6) EU Convention on Mutual Assistance; Article 1(6) Framework Decision on JITs.

[44] Article 13(7) EU Convention on Mutual Assistance; Article 1(7) Framework Decision on JITs. Such requests shall be regarded as if they were put forward on national territory within a national investigation.

The provisions also allow for arrangements for persons other than representatives of the competent authorities of the Member States setting up the JIT to take part in the activities of the team.[45] Specific reference is made to officials of international bodies set up pursuant to the TEU, which includes bodies such as Europol and Eurojust.[46] However, members of Europol and Eurojust are primarily expected to support or advise the JIT. They can take part in the activities of the JIT only to the extent that the laws of the Member States concerned or the provisions of any legal instrument applicable between them permit. Their functions do not automatically correspond with those conferred upon the members or seconded members[47] of the team by Article 13, unless otherwise expressly agreed by the participating Member States.[48]

In 2003 the Council decided upon a Model Agreement in order to facilitate the setting up of JITs and to stimulate the implementation of the Framework Decision on JITs and Article 13 of the EU Convention on Mutual Assistance.[49] Here, the participation of officials from Europol and Eurojust is specifically addressed. The Model Agreement states that their participation is not mandatory but depends on the circumstances of the investigation and their competence to participate in a JIT. It anticipates that the JIT members will agree upon the exact arrangements under which Europol and Eurojust officials may participate in the JIT. Such arrangements would, amongst other things, specify whether the rights conferred upon the members and seconded members by virtue of the Framework Decision on JITs or by Article 13 of the EU Convention on Mutual Assistance will also apply to the officials of these bodies.

---

[45] Article 13(12), respectively Article 1(12) Framework Decision on JITs.

[46] Explanatory Report on the Convention of 29 May 2000 on Mutual Assistance in Criminal Matters between the Member States of the European Union, *OJ* C 379, 29.12.2000, p. 19 (hereafter, Explanatory Report). It has to be noted that the provisions discussed in the following are evaluated in regard to Europol's and Eurojust's participation in joint investigation teams, but as far as the regulations refer to international bodies set up pursuant to the TEU as such they may equally apply to other institutions.

[47] Members of the joint investigation team from Member States other than the Member State in which the team operates are referred to as being 'seconded' to the team (Article 13(5)).

[48] Article 13(12) EU Convention on Mutual Assistance in conjunction with Explanatory Report p. 19.

[49] Council Recommendation of 8 May 2003 on a model agreement for setting up a Joint Investigation Team (JIT), *OJ* C 121, 23.05.2003, p. 1. In particular, the Model Agreement deals with the parties of the agreement constituting the JIT, the purpose of the team, the period covered by the agreement, Member States in which the team will operate, the leader, the members of the team, the participation of officials from Europol/Eurojust/the Commission (OLAF), the general conditions of the agreement, as well as specific arrangements including organisational arrangements.

3.1.4 Council Recommendations

On 28 September 2000, the Council, with regard to Article 30(2)(b) TEU, called upon the Member States to duly consider requests by Europol to initiate, conduct or coordinate investigations in specific cases, and to duly inform Europol of the results of the investigation.[50] If the Member State concerned does not comply with the request, it is to give its reasons.

Two months later the Council issued a recommendation to the Member States in respect of Europol's assistance to JITs set up by the Member States.[51] The document describes how Europol can assist JITs and urges the Member States to make full use of these possibilities. The recommendation refers to the support capacities as envisaged by the Europol Convention and specifies several advantageous aspects of incorporating Europol in a JIT, which include:

- Placing Europol's knowledge of the criminal world at the disposal of JITs;
- enabling Europol to assist with the coordination of operations by JITs;
- providing advice to JITs on technical matters;
- helping with the analysis of offences.

Again, these support functions are to be provided through the ENUs. Thus, the recommendation does not foresee additional functions being delegated to Europol, but rather clarifies its existing role and responsibilities in relation to JITs.

3.1.5 Amendment of Europol Convention

As mentioned above, the Europol Convention in its present form does not contain specific provisions on Europol's participation in JITs. Relevant changes, however, were envisaged by the Protocol of November 2002 which sought to amend the Europol Convention (hereafter, Protocol 2002).[52] The Protocol 2002 foresees the insertion of a new Article 3a which provides the legal basis for the active participation of Europol officials in JITs.[53] Even though Europol's role is

---

[50] Council Recommendation of 28 September 2000 to Member States in respect of requests made by Europol to initiate criminal investigations in specific cases, *OJ* C 289, 2.10.2000, p. 8.

[51] Council Recommendation of 30 November 2000, *OJ* C 357, 13.12.2000, p. 6.

[52] Council Act of 28 November 2002 drawing up a Protocol amending the Convention on the establishment of a European Police Office (Europol Convention) and the Protocol on the privileges and immunities of Europol, the members of its organs, the deputy directors and the employees of Europol, *OJ* C 312, 16.12.2002, p. 1.

[53] The Protocol makes explicit reference to teams set up in accordance with Article 1 of the Framework Decision of 13 June 2002 on joint investigation teams or with Article 13 of the Con-

once again described as one of support, and Europol officials are to remain explicitly prohibited from taking part in any coercive measures, Europol officials may assist in all activities and exchange information with all members of the team. Thus, they no longer have to liaise through the ENUs, and can instead work directly with the other team members to provide information from any of the components of the computerised system of collected information referred to in Article 6 of the Convention. When such direct liaison occurs, Europol is to inform the ENUs of the Member States represented in the team. Information obtained by a Europol official while part of a JIT may be included in the computerised system on condition that the relevant Member State providing the information consents.

Restrictions on Europol's involvement consist of the following: Europol officials are bound by the law of the Member State in which the JIT operates and carry out their tasks under the stewardship of the team leader. An arrangement concerning the administrative implementation of the participation of Europol officials has to be agreed upon by the Director of Europol and the Member States participating in the team, with the involvement of the national units. Equally, Europol officials committing offences are subject to the national law of the Member State of operation applicable to persons with comparable functions.[54] The immunity enjoyed by Europol officials on the basis of Article 41 of the Convention, as amended by Article 8 of the Protocol of 19 June 1997,[55] is waived in relation to official acts carried out while participating in JITs.[56]

The Protocol requires the ratification of all Member States that had EU membership status at the time the Protocol was adopted by the Council, and as yet this has not occurred and the Protocol is not in force. Accordingly, the participation of Europol in the THB-JIT project that the Netherlands, the United Kingdom, Germany, and Belgium instigated has been evaluated on the basis of the non-amended version of the Europol Convention and the Council Recommen-

---

vention of 29 May 2000 on mutual assistance in criminal matters between the Member States of the European Union.

[54] Liability of Europol officials is regulated as such, as the Member State of operation has to make good such damage as was caused during a Europol official's assistance in operational matters and may later be reimbursed by Europol (newly inserted Article 39a).

[55] Protocol on the Privileges and Immunities of Europol, the Members of its Organs, the Deputy Director and Employees of Europol, *OJ* C 221, 19.07.1997, p. 1.

[56] New paragraph added to Article 8 of the Protocol. For the justification of Europol officials' immunity as well as the need to waive immunity in cases of executive investigative actions see K. Hailbronner, 'Die Immunität von Europol-Bediensteten [Immunity of Europol officials], 6 *JZ* (Juristenzeitung) 1998 p. 283 ff.

dation of 30 November 2000. At present, Europol officials may support a JIT, but cannot directly participate in it. Instead, they have to channel their advice through the respective ENUs of the JIT states.[57] However, whereas Europol officials are still excluded from active JIT participation this does not apply to representatives of the national police forces seconded to Europol. Thus, ENU officials may be appointed as JIT members, thereby allowing the JIT to become a direct recipient of information from Europol. Equally, Member States have the possibility to incorporate their national Europol liaison officers within the JIT. The liaison officers would then be able to directly access Europol's information system and take part in analysis groups.[58]

3.1.6 Agreement between Eurojust and Europol

By an agreement dated 9 June 2004[59] Eurojust and Europol stipulated the importance of establishing and maintaining a close cooperation, in so far as their tasks, objectives, and responsibilities are complementary. The Agreement also seeks to ensure that a duplication of their efforts will be avoided. Article 6 of the Agreement addresses Eurojust's and Europol's participation in JITs upon request of one or more Member States. The Agreement states how their involvement is to be subject both to the legal framework in place at that time as well as the agreement made to establish the concrete JIT. Whereas Europol is to focus on supporting the intelligence gathering and investigative efforts of the team, Eurojust is to facilitate coordination between the judicial authorities concerned. The Agreement further outlines how Europol and Eurojust are to offer their support and expertise to national law enforcement and judicial authorities during the preliminary discussions concerning the setting up of such teams, and not only once the JIT is established. If requested, Europol and Eurojust are to facilitate the operational effectiveness of the team by providing practical support and assistance.[60]

---

[57] G. Vermeulen, JIT and pre-JIT cooperation possibilities in the relationship between the Netherlands and other countries involved in the JIT-initiative(s) initiated under the Netherlands EU Presidency 2004, Advisory opinion, 16 January 2005, p. 6 (not published).

[58] Articles 5(5), 10(2)(2) Europol Convention.

[59] Agreement between Eurojust and Europol, The Hague, 9 June 2004 <http://www.europol.eu.int/legal/agreements/Agreements/17374.pdf> (visited 02.10.2005).

[60] For the relation of Eurojust and Europol especially with regard to the need of organising supervision and control over Europol's participation in transnational and joint police activities see further T. Schalken and M. Pronk, 'On Joint Investigation Teams, Europol and Supervision of Their Joint Actions', *European Journal of Crime, Criminal Law and Criminal Justice,* 2002, Vol. 10/1, p. 70 at p. 77 ff.

3.2 Eurojust

At present, like Europol, Eurojust does not possess original competencies regarding investigations and judicial proceedings but is instead restricted to a supporting role for the competent authorities of the Member States. In the following part, the legal framework for the participation of Eurojust in JITs is outlined in as far as it has not already been addressed above.

3.2.1 *Treaty on European Union*

Article 31 of the TEU addresses the role of Eurojust as part of judicial cooperation in criminal matters without specific reference to Eurojust's role in JITs.

3.2.2 *Council Decision 2002*

Council Decision 2002 contains specific provisions pertaining to the tasks of Eurojust with regard to JITs. According to Articles 6(a)(iv), 7(a)(iv) Eurojust may – acting through its national members or as a College – ask the competent authorities of the Member States concerned to set up a JIT. When Eurojust forwards the request as a College, it may supply logistical support, including assistance for translation and interpretation, and offer support in organising and coordinating meetings.[61] If Eurojust is acting as a College and the Member States concerned do not comply with the request, they are obligated to provide their reasons for not complying.[62] National members may also forward requests for judicial assistance in order to improve cooperation and coordination between the competent authorities of the Member States.[63]

The Model Agreement for setting up JITs referred to above explicitly considers the participation of Eurojust in JITs to apply to Eurojust acting as a College. In principle, for a Eurojust member to actively participate in a JIT as a representative of Eurojust he/she would need to have a specific mandate from the organisation. At present the Council Decision itself does not foresee JIT participation by representatives of Eurojust as a College. Thus, the law of the Member States constituting the JIT and the possible lack of permission or associated restrictions in the Member States' domestic legislation must be taken into account. Regardless thereof, Member States can assign the respective national member a participatory role in a JIT, as it is the Member States which define the

---

[61] Article 7(g) Council Decision.
[62] Article 8 Council Decision.
[63] Article 6(g) Council Decision.

judicial powers granted to their national members as well as their right to act in relation to foreign judicial authorities.[64] In such cases, however, the national member would be acting on the basis of national law, comparable to other seconded members, and not as such representing Eurojust.[65]

3.3 National legislation

As stated above, both Article 13 of the EU Convention on Mutual Assistance as well as Article 1(12) of the Framework Decision on JITs make JIT participation by representatives of Europol or Eurojust dependent upon the explicit permission provided by the laws of the Member States constituting the JIT or the existence of an applicable legal instrument between them. The following section concentrates on the respective provisions of the domestic laws of the countries participating in the THB-JIT project.[66]

3.3.1 *The Netherlands*

At the time of research only the Netherlands and the United Kingdom had JIT specific legislation in place. The Netherlands did not implement the Framework Decision on JITs separately, but implemented it under the Law of 18 March 2004 concerning the EU Convention on Mutual Assistance.[67] As a consequence, a new section on JITs was inserted into the Dutch Code of Criminal Procedure (Articles 552qa to 552qe), and a third new paragraph was inserted into Article 13 of the 1990 Data Protection Police Files Act, creating the possibility to provide data from temporary police files for JIT purposes. The implementing legislation does not specify the involvement of Eurojust or Europol. However, the Dutch Board of Procurators General issued a guideline providing further implementing instructions on the setting up of JITs. In particular, the guideline states that a JIT led by the Netherlands is under the authority of a prosecutor and specifies the steps that must be taken to set up a JIT. In regard to the role of Europol and Eurojust, the guideline refers to Article 13(7) EU Convention on

---

[64] Article 9(3) Council Decision.

[65] G. Vermeulen, JIT and pre-JIT cooperation possibilities in the relationship between the Netherlands and other countries involved in the JIT-initiative(s) initiated under the Netherlands EU Presidency 2004, Advisory opinion, 16 January 2005, p. 7 (not published).

[66] The question whether at the time of research any of the Member States participating in the JIT Project were in the position to effectively set up a JIT according to Article 13 EU Convention on Mutual Assistance respectively the Framework Decision on JITs is further elaborated on in Chapter I.

[67] The law entered into force on 1 July 2004, *Staatsblad van het Koninkrijk der Nederlanden* (Dutch Bulletin of Acts and Decrees) 2004, p. 181.

Mutual Assistance. As the Dutch legislation does not specify any further special arrangements, JIT participation by the representatives of Europol or Eurojust continues to depend on the legal instruments applicable between the Member States constituting the JIT. Thus, until the amendments to the Europol Convention take effect, it will not be possible for Europol officers to fully participate in JITs.

3.3.2 The United Kingdom

In the United Kingdom there have been no comprehensive legislative enactments to implement the concept of JITs into national law. Instead, the Framework Decision on JITs is partly being dealt with by provisions and circulars. Sections 103 and 105 Police Reform Act 2002 relate to the criminal and civil liability of officials participating in international JITs. Section 16(2)(b) Crime (International Cooperation) Act 2003 implemented into domestic law Article 1, paragraph 7 of the Framework Decision on JITs, thereby permitting the execution of search powers and production orders without a letter of request.[68] The International Joint Investigation Teams (International Agreement) Order 2004[69] allows for international JITs to be formed under the Schengen Agreement of 14 June 1985 in addition to the EU Convention on Mutual Assistance and the Framework Decision on JITs. The Home Office Circular of 1 October 2002 on the EU Framework Decision on Joint Investigation Teams describes the provisions of the Framework Decision on JITs and provides guidance on matters to be covered by the constituting agreement, *inter alia,* the role of Europol and Eurojust.[70] Moreover, the Home Office strongly recommends the early involvement of Europol and Eurojust. Thus, in setting up the team and planning the team's operations, the relevant national members of the ENUs and of Eurojust shall be consulted. Otherwise, the Circular refers to Article 1(12) Framework Decision on JITs, stating that subject to the domestic law of the Member States setting up the JIT or the provisions of any legal instrument between them, the Member States may agree that representatives of Europol or Eurojust participate in the activities of the team. With reference to the Explanatory Report[71] it is stated that Europol and Eurojust will act primarily in a supportive or advisory role. Unless the agreement establishing the team expressly provides otherwise, their representatives may not exercise the functions conferred by the Framework

---

[68] See also Home Office Circular 26/2004 (Further Information on EU Framework Decision on Joint Investigation Teams).

[69] Statutory Instrument No. 1127 of 13 April 2004, which came into force on 7 May 2004.

[70] Annex A.

[71] Explanatory Report on the Convention of 29 May 2000 on Mutual Assistance in Criminal Matters between the Member States of the European Union, *OJ* C 379, 29.12.2000, p. 19.

Decision on JITs on seconded members, and may not use the information lawfully obtained by a member or a seconded member of a JIT. For Europol officials it will not be possible to be fully associated with JITs until the amendment of the Europol Convention takes affect. Nonetheless, Europol can play a crucial role in advising the JIT. It is therefore important at the early planning stages of a JIT to inform and consult Europol through the ENU at the National Criminal Intelligence Service (hereafter, NCIS).

3.3.3 Belgium

Belgium was one of the countries that did not have JIT-specific legislation in place in accordance with the EU Convention on Mutual Assistance or the Framework Decision on JITs until the beginning of 2005. The new Mutual Assistance Act of 9 December 2004 contains implementing legislation for the EU Convention on Mutual Assistance.[72] Article 8 of the Act states that JITs are set up by agreement which is to specify the purpose, the composition, the time frame, the place of action, as well as organisation arrangements. It may be agreed that representatives of Eurojust and Europol will take part in the team as experts (Article 9). The Federal Prosecutor shall inform Eurojust and Europol about the setting up of the team. The right of Europol and Eurojust representatives to be present during the execution of investigative measures on Belgian territory is dependant on the approval of the team leader. Europol and Eurojust may not carry out any investigative tasks themselves.

3.3.4 Germany

In Germany also the necessary provisions were inserted by the law of 22 July 2005 which implemented the EU Convention on Mutual Assistance.[73] The law inserted a new Article 83k into the Law on International Mutual Assistance in Criminal Matters. (Gesetz über die internationale Rechtshilfe in Strafsachen, hereafter, IRG) that deals exclusively with JITs. According to Article 83k(1) IRG upon authorisation of the German team leader seconded members may be assigned investigative powers. Other persons such as Europol or Eurojust representatives may participate in the JIT in accordance with the legal provisions of the Member States participating in the JIT or through an agreement applicable between them. Such agreements may be of an *ad hoc* nature (paragraph 2). Germany chose not to make use of the possibility provided for in Article

---

[72] The Act entered into force on 3 January 2005.
[73] The law entered into force on 8 August 2005, *Bundesgesetzblatt* (Federal Law Gazette) I (2005) p. 2189.

13(12) of the Convention 2002 to permit persons other than representatives of the competent authorities of the Member States setting up the JIT to take part in the activities of the team. Thus, the law limits the powers of Europol officials as foreseen in the future Article 3a(1) Europol Convention. Article 83k(2) IRG reduces Europol officials to a supportive role as whilst they may be present during the team's activities, they will not be allowed to take part in investigative measures, even where these do not imply any degree of coercion.[74] Regarding the participation of Eurojust, the explanatory memorandum states that Eurojust participation is possible in accordance with the competences stipulated by Articles 6 and 7 Council Decision 2002.

The table below provides an overview of the extent to which the four Member States of the THB-JIT project had enacted legislation relating to Europol's and Eurojust's participation in JITs under the EU Convention on Mutual Assistance and the Framework Decision on JITs.[75]

	The Netherlands (Bill, Prosecutors' Guideline)	United Kingdom (Acts, Circulars, Statutory Instrument)	Belgium (Bill)	Germany (Bill)
Legislation implementing EU Convention on Mutual Assistance/ Framework Decision on JITs[76]	yes	yes	yes	yes
Restrictions on Europol's/Eurojust's role[77]	Did not implement § 13	Did not implement § 13	yes	yes
- Right to be present during investigations	no	no	Upon authorisation	yes
- Right to carry out investigative tasks	no	no	no	no

---

[74] *Bundestagsdrucksache* (Official Journal of the German Parliament) 15/4232, p. 10.

[75] Note that the table refers to the present situation. However, during the time of the research, only the Netherlands and the United Kingdom had JIT-specific legislation in place.

[76] As stated above, only after the amendment of the Europol Convention will Europol officials be able to participate in JITs and liaise directly with the other team members. They will be entitled to assist in all activities of the team (except for the taking of coercive measures) and exchange information with the other team members. Eurojust representatives, at present, can represent Eurojust as a College in joint investigation teams depending on the explicit permission of Eurojust.

[77] Restrictions beyond those provided for in the EU Convention on Mutual Assistance respectively the Framework Decision on JITs.

4. INVOLVEMENT IN THE THB-JIT PROJECT

Before outlining the involvement of Europol and Eurojust in the THB-JIT project, it is pertinent to firstly provide a brief overview of the project's general structure. The project was managed and coordinated by a steering group at the police level, composed of delegates from each of the participating Member States' national police authorities. The steering group was acting as a project board at the operational strategic level, controlling the projects as a whole and responsible for reporting via the Task Force of European Chiefs of Police[78] (hereafter, EPCTF) to the Council of Justice and Home Affairs. At the outset of the THB-JIT project the participating Member States decided that a preliminary decision regarding the operational establishment of a JIT at the integrated intelligence phase was required in order to collect and analyse the available data. Accordingly, a Joint Intelligence Group (hereafter, JIG) was set up in advance. However, due to the lack of a legal basis in Germany and Belgium to bring an operational JIT into practice according to Article 13 of the EU Convention on Mutual Assistance and correspondingly the Framework Decision on JITs, a JIT was not realised at the time of research. Thus, the following remarks concentrate on the role of Europol and Eurojust in relation to management aspects of the THB-JIT project as such as well as the preliminary intelligence phase.

4.1 Europol

4.1.1 *Role and responsibilities*

As previously stated, the Europol Convention in its current form allows for Europol to participate in JITs to the extent that it does not exercise powers that go beyond providing operational support and service functions. However, this does not mean that Europol's influence on the setting up of a JIT cannot be considerable as its analytical support capacity encompasses the possibility to point out information gaps in investigations.[79] Thus, Europol can have a direct

---

[78] At Tampere the Council called upon the Member States to set up an operational task force composed of European police chiefs. The task force is to exchange, in cooperation with Europol, experience, best practices and information on current trends in cross-border crime and contribute to the planning of operative actions, Recommendation No. 44 *Bulletin* (Bulletin of the Press and Information Agency of the German Government) (1999) p. 793 at p. 798. It must concentrate its actions on the priorities established by the Council of Ministers for Europol, and its actions must depend on Europol's annual strategic reports. The EPCTF took up its duty in April 2000 and meets twice a year.

[79] T. Schalken and M. Pronk, 'On Joint Investigation Teams, Europol and Supervision of Their Joint Actions', *European Journal of Crime, Criminal Law and Criminal Justice*, 2002, Vol. 10/1, p. 70 at p. 74 f.

influence on the further course of investigations. Equally, the regulations on data protection as provided for in the Europol Convention together with adopting rules[80] were put in place not only to protect individuals in the private sphere, but also to enhance the willingness of countries to supply sensitive data without jeopardising their own national investigative interests.

In the THB-JIT project under review, Europol described its own role as a supportive one that included information exchange, analytical support,[81] and general support.[82] During the course of the project the formal role accorded to Europol was twofold. Firstly, Europol was an observer within the steering group. Secondly, Europol was responsible for the creation and maintenance of an Analysis Work File (hereafter, AWF) which served as a basis for the JIG phase. Thus, although Europol was not accorded a central management position, it was conferred a specific operational support function in the preliminary operational phase.

It has to be noted that the AWF itself was primarily not opened as a working tool for the JIG but served another project – the Action Plan Bulgaria (hereafter, APB) – which was set up by Europol upon the request of the EPCTF of 26 November 2002. The overall aim of the APB was to combat THB in relation to Bulgaria. However, it had a wider remit than the THB-JIT project as it concentrated not only on operational issues but also provided a general assessment of the extent and nature of the trafficking problem in Bulgaria, the legal gaps concerning trafficking legislation and criminal procedure, the need for a harmonisation of legal provisions and enforcement measures, and the need to ensure the political support of the relevant Bulgarian authorities. In relation to the APB, Europol not only had an important operational function but also a central management position as it was responsible for the implementation of the action plan supported by an advisory body that was composed of THB experts from the United Kingdom, Belgium, Germany, and the Netherlands (here-

---

[80] See Articles 10 ff. Europol Convention in conjunction with the Council Act of 3 November 1998 adopting rules applicable to Europol analysis files, *OJ* C 26, 30.01.1999, p. 1, hereafter, AWF adopting rules.

[81] In relation to analytical support, Europol not only referred to the analysis of information and intelligence but also to the identification of information gaps enabling a focused gathering of new information, the dissemination of analytical reports aiming at providing investigators with assembled intelligence such as an overall description of criminal organisations, modus operandi and activities, links between criminals, identification of threats, identification of new targets for investigations, assessment of evidence gathered, and, finally, the identification of new projects as a result of analysis.

[82] In relation to general support, Europol pointed out the initiation, monitoring and coordination of meetings, the offering of logistics especially meeting facilities, language support, expertise, advice on best practices and the involvement of specialised units of Europol.

after, APBWG[83]).[84] It was eventually decided to link the APB and the THB-JIT projects to the extent that both initiatives overlapped, that is, in regard to intelligence gathering activities including the AWF.

The Analysis Group, responsible for the management of the AWF,[85] included police representatives from Belgium, Germany, the United Kingdom and the Netherlands as national experts on THB.[86] The AWF was further comprised of ELOs as well as Europol analysts. To avoid the unnecessary duplication of work and to expedite the flow of intelligence, the national experts also constituted the JIG as well as the APBWG, although this did not mean that the same persons were always present. Even though the idea to appoint the same person to chair the JIG, the AWF and the APBWG, was considered, the JIG leader was finally appointed by a Member State whereas the AWF and the APBWG were chaired by a Europol official.[87]

It remains to be seen how far the linking of both initiatives actually avoided the duplication of efforts or whether in fact confusion rather than clarity was brought about regarding the respective responsibilities of both initiatives, the structure of the THB-JIT project as such and the respective roles of Europol.

4.1.2   *Information exchange/Europol as a facilitator*

During the intelligence phase, Member States participating in the THB-JIT project exchanged information bilaterally either directly between national police authorities or through the liaison officers seconded to Europol. However, most importantly information was fed into the AWF via the ENUs and the ELOs. Thus, at the heart of the JIG was the file provided by the Europol system as a standardised tool to collect and analyse intelligence.

---

[83] Action Plan Bulgaria Working Group.

[84] The working group had the same make-up as the JIT Project and consisted of representatives from the United Kingdom, Belgium, Germany, and the Netherlands.

[85] See Article 10(2) Europol Convention.

[86] The number of Member States taking part in the analysis was restricted due to the fact that the analysis was not of a general nature but concentrated on specific cases and had a direct operational aim. Moreover, the four Member States were the source of information giving rise to the decision to open the analysis file and/or were directly concerned by that information (Article 10(6) Europol Convention).

[87] Europol's rules do not allow an external candidate to chair an AWF. However, due to organisational and financial reasons the Member State appointing the JIG leader was not willing to second him to Europol.

The decision to open the AWF was based on national action plans on THB as well as the Europol Organised Crime Reports which indicated the expanding activities of Bulgarian organised crime groups and their engagement in the possible trafficking of women to the EU Member States for the purpose of prostitution.

The reasons why the THB-JIT project utilised an AWF are twofold. Firstly, Europol was expressly created for the purpose of supporting Member States to cooperate in criminal investigations and had a range of existing working mechanisms in place. Secondly, the Europol Convention, by providing for data protection, was expected to have a positive influence on the Member States' willingness to provide intelligence.[88] The Member State providing the data remains the sole judge of the further use of the information.[89] This factor was also advantageous in relation to the participation of Bulgaria, with whom Europol had instituted an operational agreement on information exchange.

According to the opening order[90] of the AWF, the purpose of the file was to support the authorities of the Member States in preventing and combating the sourcing and trafficking of human beings in and through Bulgaria. The initial focus was therefore on Bulgarian perpetrators and their victims. Depending on the interpretation of the wording of the opening order, Member States were to provide information on THB or on any other crime within Europol's mandate so long as the data had the potential of supporting Member States in preventing and combating THB.[91] To enable the implementation of an operational phase in

---

[88] The communication of stored data follows a strict procedure as outlined in Articles 10 ff. Europol Convention. Data may only be retrieved from the file by a Europol analyst who is authorised for that purpose, after which the data can be disseminated through the Analysis Group. If data is marked with a Europol Security Level the communication shall be subject to the Confidentiality Regulations and the Security Manual. Dissemination or operational use of the data needs to be decided upon in consultation with the participants of the Analysis Group. The data may only be utilised by the Member States in order to prevent and combat serious forms of crime. When communicating data, members of the analysis group should take into account restrictions on the usage made by the communicating Member State or third party. The transmission of personal data to their states or bodies can only be conducted in accordance with the provisions of the Convention and an agreement between Europol and those third states or bodies. Equally, time-limits for the storage and deletion of data files apply.

[89] Article 10(8) Europol Convention.

[90] Article 12 Europol Convention.

[91] The scope of the opening order had been a point of discussion throughout the THB-JIT project. Arguments in favour of broadening the scope pointed out the necessity of responding to changes in the course of investigations which might lead away from THB to other forms of serious crime within Europol's mandate committed by the same criminal network. Equally, a narrow opening order put Europol under pressure to ensure that the data provided by the Member

due time, the AWF was opened under the 'urgency procedure'.[92] Member States were expected to send all relevant data to Europol for analysis.

In the opening order the operational focus of the AWF was emphasised. The AWF was designated to single out suitable targets for setting up a JIT by enhancing and developing current investigations and initiating others where the need was identified.[93] Accordingly, Member States were urged to provide both existing intelligence collated as a result of recent and current investigations as well as 'live' data to the Analysis Group.

During the course of identifying a suitable target for setting up a JIT, Europol provided elements of all of its service functions as outlined above. Thus, the opportunity structures found in the legal framework of Europol were largely applied.

4.1.3 Problems met by Europol

Within the time frame set by the steering group the Analysis Group did not come to the point of producing analytical results upon which suitable target groups for establishing a JIT could be identified. As a consequence, the THB-JIT project was put on hold before the operational phase commenced. The following reasons where given as to why the AWF was perceived by the Member States and Europol as not having met its expectations.

Unclear roles and responsibilities

As the THB-JIT project originated from two initiatives that were not sufficiently linked, putting the proposed structure into practice proved more difficult than expected. The AWF served a twofold purpose. On the one hand, it was the process by which intelligence was to be collated within the THB-JIT project. On the other hand, it was an implementation tool of the APB. During the entire course of the THB-JIT project the relation between the THB-JIT project and the APB remained unclear, a situation mirrored in turn by the confusion surround-

---

States effectively had a link to THB and Bulgaria, which was often difficult to prove at the outset. Those in favour of a narrow scope of the opening order argued primarily with the overall aim of the APB as well as the THB-JIT project, i.e., to prevent and combat THB in relation to Bulgaria as a source and/or transit country and not to fight serious crimes as such. Moreover, it was argued that a broader scope would result in more data being transferred to the AWF which would eventually overstretch Europol's capacities and slow down the analysis process as a whole.

[92] See Article 12(2) Europol Convention.
[93] See Article 10(b) AWF adopting rules.

ing the role of the JIG compared to the Analysis Group. Equally, no common understanding was reached regarding the role of the JIG leader in relation to the project manager responsible for the AWF (hereafter, AWF manager).

The overall question remained why the parallel appointment to the AWF of a (separate) group responsible for the intelligence phase was considered necessary. One perspective held that the purpose of the JIG was to compensate for the common deficiencies of AWFs. Europol analysis groups were often confronted with the problem of Member States being reluctant to rapidly provide data of value without having the necessary enforcement mechanisms in place to counteract this problem. In this respect, the JIG was regarded as a compensatory mechanism to enhance the amount of intelligence going into the AWF. The national experts constituting the JIG were to forward the collection of data on the national level from local police forces to the federal police. The JIG leader was to supervise the analysis process, record information gaps and notify the steering group of relevant analysis findings. In accordance with Europol's data protection rules Europol may directly disclose research findings to the ENUs; however, this is subject to the authorisation of the Member State supplying the information. That having been said, the JIG was expected to collect intelligence from additional sources by engaging in direct consultation with Bulgaria and other contributors to the AWF. However, this argument is contradicted by the fact that Europol may receive information not only from the Member States but also from third party states as well as certain types of organisations.[94]

Other participants did not regard the JIG as having a parallel role to the AWF but instead expected it to take up its work after the Analysis Group had finalised its analysis and singled out possible target groups for the JIG to consider. In their view, the THB-JIT project never came to the point of a proper JIG phase.

From the perspective of Europol, the AWF had originally been created for the benefit of the APB and was simply extended to the THB-JIT project as a tool of support, complementing Europol's original responsibility for the APB. No added value was seen in the establishment of the JIG as an intelligence group to operate in parallel with the Analysis Group at Europol, as the latter had effectively carried out all intelligence-related work. The fact that Europol only possessed observatory status within the steering group did not add to Europol's commitment to the THB-JIT project, reflected by the fact that Europol did not consider itself bound by decisions of the steering group. The rather insignificant formal role accorded to Europol within the steering group did not correspond with

---

[94] Article 10(4) Europol Convention.

Europol's central position within the intelligence phase as the AWF remained the central tool for the collection and analysis of information.

Poor data supply

Throughout the project the amount and quality of data supplied to Europol was not considered satisfactory. Even though Europol officials identified this as a common problem experienced by AWFs which is often caused by a lack of clearly outlined capacities and differing focal points of national crime policies, in the present project Europol had expected a greater commitment from the participating Member States in accordance with the intentions they signalled at the outset of the project in their feasibility studies.[95] Furthermore, Member States were criticised for having failed to sufficiently communicate national legal restrictions on the sharing of information from ongoing investigations beforehand. Europol, on the other hand, was reproached for not having adequately communicated its role and competencies as well as its needs and expectations regarding the data to be supplied. For instance, Europol's rules do not require data to be submitted in a specific format,[96] a lenient regulation that proved to slow down the process of data analysis. Europol also pointed out the difficulty of having to analyse data that had not been graded by the Member State supplying the information. The same difficulties also applied to pre-analysed data in situations where the submitting Member State failed to provide Europol with a handling code.[97] It was also pointed out that Europol itself had no enforcement mechanism but relied on the commitment of the Member States which often depended on the dedication of individual representatives. Further points of criticism that the Member States raised included the lack of an institutionalised system through which intelligence received from Europol or to be provided to Europol could be routinely prioritised, and the late preparation of threat assessments.

Europol representatives pointed out their interest in obtaining information from Non-Governmental Organisations (hereafter, NGOs) specialised in taking care

---

[95] In their feasibility studies preceding the opening of the AWF, the Member States commented on the political and administrative support for the initiative, the legal framework and data collection mechanisms, the commitment of the law enforcement authorities as well as the amount of data available.

[96] Article 3(1) AWF adopting rules.

[97] See Articles 8 and 11 AWF adopting rules according to which data stored in analysis files shall be graded by assessing the source and the degree of accuracy or reliability of the information. Thus, data based on facts is to be distinguished from data based on opinions or personal assessment.

of victims of trafficking, in particular Bulgarian NGOs. Experience showed that the quality of the data obtained from NGOs sometimes surpassed that of data received from police forces due to their closer contacts with victims of trafficking. However, even though Europol actively encouraged Bulgarian NGOs to directly forward information, this failed to occur in practice.

Top-down approach

Another difficulty that was identified as having affected the work of the Analysis Group was the top-down approach taken by the THB-JIT project. The project was perceived as largely politically driven, stemming from the ambition of the Netherlands to test the instrument of a JIT as a means of facilitating transnational police cooperation during their EU Presidency. As a consequence, instead of beginning with a concrete investigation/a common target requiring the establishment of a JIT (a bottom-up approach), the project under review started out with the identification of a common crime problem, on which the instrument of a JIT could be tested. Only as a secondary step was the process of intelligence gathering instituted, the aim of which was to select a suitable case for realising an operational JIT. This procedure had the following negative impact: In practice, the Member States joining the APB as well as the THB-JIT project were not only chosen against the background of having experienced the phenomenon of THB in connection with Bulgaria as a pressing crime problem but also for their (political) motivation and desire to test the instrument of JIT as a tool. This in turn influenced the composition of the Analysis Group in which a number of countries that delivered data of value to the AWF were not represented while other appointed country representatives could hardly be called national experts on THB.

The top-down approach also affected the intelligence phase and the work of the Analysis Group in another way. In the absence of a concrete case, the aim of the project remained abstract which in turn made the intelligence gathering and the prioritisation of investigations on the national level more time consuming. This in turn affected the amount and quality of data supplied to the AWF as well as the speed with which it was supplied. A bottom-up approach, by contrast, would have better tied in with traditional situations of transnational police cooperation in which a common case/a common problem is present at the outset and might require an AWF as an additional policing asset.

Complex regulations

Apart from the above-mentioned difficulties, the fact that the Analysis Group did not produce the expected analytical results within an appropriate time frame was also attributed to the rules on data handling and protection as laid down in the Europol Convention. The regulations were perceived as overly bureaucratic and difficult to apply in practice. Analysis groups in general were said to take one year on average before producing analytical results. As much as Europol's standardised rules and regulations on data protection were valued for fostering Member States' trust in the Europol system, they were at the same time criticised for impeding the production of quick results that were necessary for supporting the coordination of ongoing investigations. This in turn had led to discussions at the outset of the THB-JIT project concerning whether Europol was to be included in the intelligence phase at all. The situation became more complicated because of Europol's refusal to share information directly with the steering group instead of channelling the information via the ENUs – a decision criticised by some members of the steering group and providing yet another indication that the role and competencies of Europol were not fully understood by the latter.

4.2 Eurojust

As stated above, according to Article 3 Council Decision 2002, the objective of Eurojust is to improve the judicial cooperation of the Member States, encompassing, *inter alia,* the coordinated stimulation and support of investigations and prosecutions in order to render them more effective. Specifically, Eurojust may stimulate the setting up of JITs and – when acting as a College – provide logistical support to such teams.

4.2.1 *Role and responsibilities*

Within the THB-JIT project Eurojust, like Europol, was accorded an observatory role within the steering group, with the Dutch Eurojust representative taking part in the meetings. No other role was formally agreed upon, neither in the intelligence gathering phase nor in the JIT phase, especially as the latter was never realised. Initially, it had been proposed to establish a judicial coordination group to manage the judicial aspects of the THB-JIT project. However, the steering group, largely composed of police representatives, did not have the authority to establish such a group. Secondly, the steering group did not deem it necessary to establish a judicial coordination group within the preliminary stages of setting up a JIT, particularly because the joint investigations had not actually commenced. With regard to the possibility of having national public prosecutors from the Member States involved in the THB-JIT project participate in the steering group, it was feared that this would have exacerbated the already complicated structure of the project. Others pointed out the difficulty of ascertaining the case prosecutors in the absence of a specific case.

4.2.2 *Information exchange/Eurojust as a facilitator*

As the project under review never entered the operational phase Eurojust never came to the point of coordinating investigations or prosecutions. In the preliminary intelligence phase, it was equally not involved in the gathering, exchange, or analysis of information. However, in the steering group the Dutch Eurojust representative provided legal advice in that he explained the requirements for setting up a JIT under Dutch law and pointed out how a JIT under Dutch leadership required the other cooperating countries to have implemented JIT related legislation, which at that time Belgium and Germany had not. The Eurojust representative also took over the role of facilitator by organising a meeting on the legal aspects of the establishment of a JIT. At this meeting it turned out that not all participating Member States had the requisite implementing legislation in place. It was during this meeting organised by Eurojust that the decision was taken to suspend the THB-JIT project and to turn to establishing a bilateral Drugs JIT instead.[98]

4.2.3 *Problems met by Eurojust*

As previously mentioned, the THB-JIT project was suspended after one year of trying to set up an operational JIT once it became evident that certain countries did not have the necessary legislation in place to participate in an operational JIT under Article 13 of the EU Convention on Mutual Assistance. With hindsight, the participants realised that the issue of inadequate legislation to establish a JIT under Article 13 had been discussed too late. While expert knowledge on legal issues was required, the members of the steering group, all of whom were representatives of the police, lacked the necessary legal expertise. This was especially noticeable in relation to their inability to explain the (lack of) JIT- related legislation in their own country to the other participants, and the consequences thereof.

It can be argued that Eurojust had no official mandate to provide legal advice. However, in the interviews it became clear that despite Eurojust's observatory role, the agency had nevertheless been expected to take over an active participatory role during the preliminary stages of the project. Thus, Eurojust had been expected to actively take part in the discussions of the steering group and to point out possible legal obstacles faced by the project and provide advice on how to overcome them. In this regard, Eurojust was said to have especially disappointed in that it failed to clearly point out the legal obstacles preventing

---

[98] On the joint investigation team on illicit drug trafficking see *infra* section 5.

the participating Member States from setting up a JIT under Article 13 of the EU Convention on Mutual Assistance. Instead, the steering group eventually turned to a professor of criminal law to deliver the required legal expertise.[99] According to the Eurojust representative, however, he did raise the issue of legal problems at quite an early stage but at the time the prevailing view had been to proceed with discussing practical issues and leave the legal aspects to be resolved later so as not to jeopardise the success of the THB-JIT project as such.

5. EXCURSUS: INVOLVEMENT IN THE JIT ON DRUG TRAFFICKING

Once the THB-JIT project participants became convinced that an operational JIT could not be implemented in due time because of the lack of legislation in Germany and Belgium as well as the absence of a suitable target group, the Netherlands and the United Kingdom opted to link separate investigations of their own in a bilateral manner in order to test the new concept of joint cooperation in practice.[100] As a consequence, parallel to their engagement in the original THB-JIT project, the two countries set up a JIT on drug trafficking. It was hoped that with the Drugs JIT the instrument of JITs as a new form of transnational cooperation could finally be tested. It was also hoped that the Drugs JIT could provide a benchmark for the original project. Thus, the JIT on drug trafficking also became a point of research on the basis of the research questions outlined in the introduction. This time the participating Member States succeeded in instituting a JIT composed of Dutch and British team members located in the Netherlands. The investigations were successful in that they resulted in the apprehension and prosecution of several suspects. In the following section the roles and responsibilities of Europol and Eurojust in the Drugs JIT will be addressed. Preference will be given to those aspects that differed or went beyond their respective roles in the first project. However, it has to be noted that the research covered only the investigation phase. As a consequence, the article at hand is not in the position to comment on any later involvement of Europol and Eurojust in the prosecution phase.

---

[99] G. Vermeulen, JIT and pre-JIT cooperation possibilities in the relationship between the Netherlands and other countries involved in the JIT-initiative(s) initiated under the Netherlands EU Presidency 2004, Advisory opinion, 16 January 2005 (not published).

[100] As stated before, the question whether at the time of research the Netherlands and the United Kingdom were in the position to effectively set up a JIT according to Article 13 EU Convention on Mutual Assistance, respectively the Framework Decision on JITs, is further dealt with in Chapter I.

5.1 Europol

The Drugs JIT was established in relation to an ongoing investigation on the drug trafficking activities of a criminal organisation operating in England and Wales with links to the Netherlands (hereafter, the 'mother case'). The JIT was set up in the Netherlands in order to dismantle the Dutch branch of the criminal organisation and to enable both countries to provide evidence and intelligence to each other.

As stated above, at present the Europol Convention restricts the role of Europol members in a JIT to one of support or advice. The functions of Europol members do not correspond with those conferred upon the members or seconded members of the team, unless the agreement between the participating Member States expressly states otherwise. The final agreement between the Netherlands and the United Kingdom of 17 January 2005 to establish a JIT in accordance with Article 13 of the EU Convention on Mutual Assistance and the Framework Decision on JITs (hereafter, JIT Agreement[101]) outlined that Europol officials were 'participating' in the JIT by providing 'analytical support'. Regarding the fact that neither the Dutch nor British law on JITs confers a role to Europol (or Eurojust) that goes beyond the scope of the Europol Convention (respectively the Council Decision 2002), the wording of the Agreement is to be interpreted as corresponding to these legal instruments.

In the Drugs JIT participants perceived Europol as an additional body to the JIT; a tool for processing and forwarding information. The reason for involving Europol in the JIT was not only to profit from the organisation's support functions in intelligence gathering and analysis but also to protect the interests of the Member States. The latter applied in particular to the United Kingdom which was afraid of jeopardising ongoing national investigations by joining them with investigations of the Drugs JIT. In practice, Europol was involved in the information exchange in the Drugs JIT in two ways: The United Kingdom and the Netherlands used their ELOs for exchanging information bilaterally and Europol also provided support through an AWF. In the latter case, a Europol analyst was working at the same location as the Drugs JIT.

5.1.1 *Information exchange/Europol as a facilitator*

Europol had already been involved in the 'mother case' in the United Kingdom upon which the Drugs JIT was realised, supporting the investigation with two

---

[101] The JIT Agreement used the Model Agreement of the European Council for orientation.

AWFs and intelligence reports.[102] In the course of the Drugs JIT information provided by the National Crime Squad of England and Wales (hereafter, NCSEW) on the 'mother case' to the JIT in the Netherlands was exchanged either directly between the two countries or via Europol through the ENUs and the ELOs. Equally, Europol continued to provide information to the JIT on the basis of an AWF. In the latter context a Europol analyst was partly working at the premises of the National Crime Squad of the Netherlands (hereafter, Dutch NCS) in order to improve the information being fed into the AWF and vice versa.

Which one of these two information chains was used depended on whether the NCSEW classified its information as intelligence or tactical/operational information[103] in consideration of its disclosure rules.[104] Whereas intelligence sources are protected, tactical or operational information can be shared without restrictions.[105] Thus, information of a non-sensitive nature (e.g., car registration numbers, locations, identification of suspects, previous convictions) could be exchanged directly between the investigators in the United Kingdom and the JIT.

Information classified as sensitive was exchanged via Europol through the ENUs to the ELOs. Here, advantage was taken of the fact that liaison officers enjoy

---

[102] Article 16 Europol Convention.

[103] Whereas intelligence refers to the sources of information (e.g., informers, telephone interceptions), tactical or operational information refers to information that is gathered in the course of relying on intelligence sources.

[104] Disclosure describes the extent to which the prosecution is under an obligation to disclose information pertinent to the case. In the United Kingdom disclosure is regulated very differently to the Netherlands. In principle, the prosecution has the duty to disclose the evidence which is at their disposal to the defence. However, material must not be disclosed if a court has concluded that it is not in the public interest to do. The latter can apply in relation to the protection of police operations and national security as well as the proper functioning of the government and its services. See also J. Sprack, *A Practical Approach to Criminal Procedure,* Oxford, University Press 2004, p. 137 ff. See also Chapter III.

[105] In the Netherlands, by contrast, any information used as a basis for investigative powers must be disclosed in court and may well become known by the defence. The police have to draw up official reports on the investigation measures used irrespective of whether or not the information relates to intelligence. As a consequence, all information is included in the police file as freely accessible operational information. The written records are prepared by the police under oath, and may be used as evidence by the court. The Dutch criminal justice procedure is governed by the principle that in a criminal prosecutions full disclosure will be made as to the way in which the investigation was carried out. This principle applies equally to special powers of investigation. (see also P.J.P. Tak, *The Dutch criminal justice system,* The Hague, WODC, 2003, p. 27 ff.). The JIT Agreement refers to the fact that in the Netherlands there is no disclosure procedure. As a consequence 'information given to the joint investigation team, that is used as a basis for any investigative power, must be disclosed in court and may well become known by the defence.'

immunity in Dutch court proceedings[106] which may imply, *inter alia,* that they are not obliged to testify as witnesses in a Dutch court.[107] The reason is to protect data files administered by liaison officers. Together with Europol's data protection rules applicable to AWFs – according to which the providing Member State remains the sole judge of the further use of information – exchanging data via Europol and the ELOs respectively, enabled the United Kingdom to protect sensitive information, the disclosure of which might have jeopardised the ongoing drug investigation in the United Kingdom. As far as agreed to by the United Kingdom, the information was forwarded by Europol to the Dutch Europol national unit based at the International Network Service (DIN), which in turn issued an official report to the Drugs JIT excluding sensitive information. The Drugs JIT was then in the position to use the information provided as tactical/operational information. This procedure ensured that whilst sensitive information was not to be directly provided to the Drug JIT, the information was still able to influence operational decisions in the Netherlands.

5.1.2 *Role of the Europol analyst*

For the first time in the history of Europol, the organisation assisted the investigations of Member States by providing an analyst who was not only to closely cooperate with the investigation team but also to be seconded to work with the team at the very same location. Thus, in the Drugs JIT, in addition to the team's own analyst, a Dutch analyst from Europol (hereafter, the Europol analyst) worked on-site with the JIT between two to three days a week upon the request of the Dutch authorities. Additionally, a secure data line was set up between the Drugs JIT office and Europol, which enabled the Europol analyst to transfer intelligence from the team to Europol via the Dutch ENU and ELO. Europol's interest in having a Europol analyst in the JIT working with the investigators on a daily basis was to enhance the information flow into the AWF and vice versa.

---

[106] Article 5(8) in conjunction with Article 41(2) Europol Convention. See further T. Voß, *Europol: Polizei ohne Grenzen?* (Europol: Police without boundaries?), Freiburg, edition iuscrim 2003, p. 165; K. Hailbronner, 'Die Immunität von Europol-Bediensteten (Immunity of Europol officials), 6 *JZ* (Juristenzeitung) 1998, p. 284. The JIT Agreement stated that the principle rule according to which Dutch investigators must be willing and able to testify in court as a witness or an expert (Article 552qa of the Dutch Code of Criminal Procedure) equally applied to seconded members of a JIT.

[107] T. Voß, *Europol: Polizei ohne Grenzen?* (Europol: Police without boundaries?), Freiburg, edition iuscrim 2003, p. 130. In the interview the Dutch liaison officer was of the opinion that he equally enjoyed immunity protecting him from being questioned in Dutch court proceedings regarding data files administered by him. However, according to Voß at p. 129, Dutch liaison officers at Europol do not enjoy immunity regarding their files.

According to Europol officials, Europol had been striving for some time to supply its support functions to national investigations in a more direct manner. In the analysis groups at Europol the idea of targeted working, which implied actively helping to coordinate parallel investigations in a number of countries, had already been developed. Following on from these discussions, there had been a tendency to promote the closer involvement of Europol analysts in operational teams. However, so far their involvement had been limited to paying sporadic visits to national investigators.

As stated before, the Europol Convention in its present form does not allow for Europol officials such as Europol analysts to actively participate in the activities of an investigation team. Europol officials are prohibited from exchanging information directly with members of the team.[108] During interviews the Europol analyst was described as a member of the JIT in charge of information analysis. His main task was to select information gathered by the JIT considered useful for analysis by Europol. From the perspective of the Drugs JIT, the goal of involving the Europol analyst was to help identify intelligence gaps.

To enable the Europol analyst to perform his task, all information gathered by the Drugs JIT was provided to the Europol analyst, thereby establishing a direct open information exchange the extent of which was new to the Dutch police. This form of close cooperation was described as advantageous as the Europol analyst not only knew Europol standards but, by having access both to data of the JIT as well as to data of the AWFs, was in a better position to judge the respective needs of the two, to assess the relevance of information and to select it accordingly. However, care was taken that the Europol analyst never directly received or passed on information that related to the JIT. Equally, he did not take part in meetings of the Drugs JIT. Instead, to adhere to the rules set out in the Europol Convention, all of the information was passed via the Dutch ENU and ELO. Accordingly, the Drugs JIT, even though describing Europol as 'participating' in the JIT, managed to include the Europol analyst as a facilitator in providing analytical support without violating the restrictions set out in the Europol Convention.

5.1.3 *Problems met by Europol*

JITs are regarded as a tool to expedite and facilitate mutual assistance in that the responsible police and judicial authorities are in the position to exchange information directly within the team based on one initial request issued by one state,

---

[108] This will change once the new Article 3a, inserted by the Protocol 2002, comes into effect.

without the need for repeated letters rogatory. However, in the case under review this particular intention had partly failed due to British disclosure rules as well as national investigative interests. In the Drugs JIT participants pointed out that even though the intention had been to institute a JIT according to Article 13 of the EU Convention on Mutual Assistance and the Framework Decision on JITs, the NCSEW continued to forward information to the Netherlands via Europol in order to protect its sources of information as well as not to jeopardise its ongoing national investigation. Thus, the advantage of direct information exchange as foreseen by the JIT construction had effectively been taken advantage of only to a limited extent.[109] It remains to be seen in how far this problem is only of limited informative value regarding the potential of the JIT construct in general, as it is specifically linked to British disclosure rules.

In relation to Europol, the Drugs JIT indicates how the interests of Member States in exchanging information directly is closely connected to the fact that information exchange via Europol is deemed to be too slow to effectively support an ongoing investigation concerning serious forms of crime. Team members criticised the approach of the project for continuing to rely on Europol's channels for information exchange as they were too time consuming. Against this backdrop, team members as well as Europol officials strongly supported the participation of Europol officials in JITs as foreseen by Article 3a of the Protocol 2002 as a means to speed up and enhance the information exchange via Europol. Thus, the Drugs JIT construction of having a Europol analyst working at the premises of the JIT in order to allow a quicker but nevertheless still indirect exchange of information between Europol and the team was seen as a first step in the right direction. However, even though this construction formally adhered to the present regulation of the Europol Convention concerning information exchange, the risk is evident that in practice information might nevertheless be exchanged directly between the Europol analyst and the JIT. This in turn shows the need for Member States to implement Article 3a in order to provide the legal basis for Europol's direct participation.

---

[109] T. Schalken and M. Pronk, 'On Joint Investigation Teams, Europol and Supervision of Their Joint Actions', *European Journal of Crime, Criminal Law and Criminal Justice*, 2002, Vol. 10/1, p. 70, already foresaw how the close cooperation of police authorities in joint investigation teams would automatically highlight the problems caused by differences between the various legal systems of and rivalry between the Member States. See also R. Zöberlein, *Auf dem Weg zu einer gemeinsamen europäischen Strafverfolgung: Eurojust als Keimzelle einer europäischen Staatsanwaltschaft?* (Towards a joint European prosecution in criminal matters: Eurojust as the starting point for a European public prosecution service?), Berlin, Logos Verlag 2004, p. 16 ff., on differences in the role of the public prosecutor in Germany – which is comparable to that under Dutch law – compared to England and Wales.

Finally, the bilateral JIT under review was not regarded as the ideal test case for assessing the added value of Europol's involvement. The necessity of involving Europol in the gathering and analysis of intelligence was said to depend upon the number of participants involved, with a high number of participants automatically rendering the intelligence phase more complicated. Only in this scenario is the exchange of information via Europol deemed to be more preferable to the creation of a bilateral agreement on information exchange.

5.2 Eurojust

As pointed out before, Eurojust may fulfil its tasks either through one or more of the national members or act as a College. In the Drugs JIT, the national representatives of the United Kingdom and the Netherlands at Eurojust offered their support by hosting meetings, acting as facilitators, monitoring discussions as well as providing legal advice. As already stated, the decision to set up the bilateral Drugs JIT between the United Kingdom and the Netherlands was taken at a meeting at the Eurojust premises. Eurojust also chaired discussions in relation to the drafting of the underlying agreement of the Drugs JIT. In the final version of the JIT Agreement Eurojust officials were referred to as participants in the JIT. At the same time, they were described as national members of Eurojust and accorded a supportive role as facilitators and coordinators, thereby acting on the basis of their national laws. It can be concluded that despite the somewhat confusing wording of the agreement, the listed Eurojust members were acting as national members and not representing Eurojust as a College. The JIT-Agreement mentioned two further prosecutors from each country.

5.2.1 *Information exchange/Eurojust as a facilitator*

The Eurojust members were not involved in the day-to-day work of the Drugs JIT. Thus, they did not actively take part in the coordination of investigations and/or in the exchange of information. However, throughout the project, Eurojust stayed in the background, ready to provide advice upon request.

Eurojust was described as having stimulated cooperation between the United Kingdom and the Netherlands by contacting prosecutors and the relevant representatives from the police in both countries. Thus, the Dutch Eurojust representative advised the Dutch coordinating prosecutor and team leader in discussions with the Dutch Board of Procurators General in the preparatory phase. His role was not so much described as being more experienced with international cooperation on a practical level but on a theoretical level. Equally, he was described as facilitating the realisation of the Drugs THB-JIT project through activating contacts in the judiciary thereby 'pulling the strings in the background'.

Eurojust subsequently hosted meetings in the preparatory phase at which the JIT Agreement was drafted. Eurojust further introduced the relevant authorities to each other and helped in clarifying and coordinating their different roles. Apart from providing legal advice in the process of setting up the JIT, Eurojust continued to be involved in subsequent evaluative meetings. The purpose of these meetings, attended by Dutch and British members of the police as well as public prosecutors and the respective ELOs, was to monitor the progress and state of affairs of the JIT and the progress of the 'mother case' in the United Kingdom. The meetings were also used to discuss the flow of information between both investigation teams. In particular, possibilities of providing the JIT with intelligence from the United Kingdom investigation without violating United Kingdom law or compromising the United Kingdom investigation were discussed. Participants realised the need for further expertise especially on differences between the competencies and the relation of the police and judicial authorities in England and Wales compared to the Netherlands.

5.2.2 *Problems met by Eurojust*

The national Eurojust members provided their support to the Drugs JIT primarily during the preparatory phase. After the national prosecutors had been introduced and the JIT Agreement had been signed, their role as legal advisors became less important. Communication between Eurojust and the responsible persons on the national level primarily took place at meetings hosted by Eurojust. Apart from these meetings Eurojust continued to be a point of liaison but only for the prosecutors from both countries on an irregular basis. In general, especially police team members described the role of Eurojust as minor. It can be concluded that Eurojust never rendered direct assistance to the Drugs JIT, but remained in the background. As a consequence, its role and functions remained largely unclear to the police members of the team.

From the perspective of Eurojust a bilateral JIT was not the ideal test case to evaluate the potential performance of Eurojust in a JIT. This is principally because in bilateral forms of cooperation the responsible judicial authorities are themselves in a good position to engage in direct close cooperation without the need for a facilitator or advisor. Thus, Eurojust would be expected to take over a more prominent role in a multilateral JIT. However, as already stated, a central problem encountered by the Drugs JIT during the investigative phase was how to organise the information flow between the 'mother case' in the United Kingdom and the JIT in the Netherlands. This problem was highly juridical in nature, and concerned the differences in laws of criminal procedure, especially questions pertaining to the admissibility of evidence in court proceedings. Even though participants in the project acknowledged their need for legal advice, it was felt that it was not Eurojust's primary task and that the respective national prosecutors should overcome these difficulties by directly communicating between themselves. However, it is questionable whether the national prosecutor's knowledge of their own legal systems automatically qualified them as experts in transnational judicial cooperation. This question will become even more acute in JITs when more than two countries are involved. Secondly, in the Netherlands as well as in most other Member States, ultimately public prosecutors are responsible for investigations. Therefore, understanding the role and potential of Eurojust to act as a facilitator of judicial cooperation is important not only to the judicial authorities but also to the police of the Member States. It can be concluded that in the Drugs JIT this opportunity was missed.

6. CONCLUSIONS AND RECOMMENDATIONS

The participants in the two THB-JIT projects largely agreed that the question of whether the JIT construction was a suitable tool for supporting transnational cooperation in criminal matters primarily depended on its added value compared to traditional forms of cooperation (parallel investigations, letters of request). The added value in turn depended on whether information exchange was improved, and whether better investigative as well as procedural results could be achieved, thereby balancing the additional costs caused by the JIT construct.

These considerations also apply to the question of whether the involvement of Europol and Eurojust is of added value to transnational cooperation in general and JITs in particular. In the long run, both institutions will only be justified and accepted by the Member States if it becomes evident that their involvement renders Member State investigations more effective and successful compared to bilateral forms of cooperation. When asked whether they considered the involvement of Europol and Eurojust necessary for the successful operation of the JIT under review, most participants were of the opinion that their involvement had not been a conditio sine qua non for the functioning of the JIT. The participation of Europol, but especially of Eurojust, was primarily seen as politically driven. Their participation was nevertheless deemed advisable as both institutions had been created for supporting transnational cooperation in criminal matters, a support function that was only to be achieved and tested by repeated practical involvement. At present, countries still bypass these agencies and deal with numerous obstacles on the local level that could and should effectively be dealt with by Europol and Eurojust. In regard to JITs, participants advised against automatic involvement of Europol and Eurojust in every case due to the necessity to keep the structures as lean as possible. Instead, the added value of their involvement was to be determined in every case anew.

In the following, specific conclusions and recommendations regarding Europol and Eurojust are formulated.

6.1 Europol

Both projects under review indicated the potential of Europol to provide information upon which a JIT could possibly be established. At the same time, numerous obstacles prevented Europol's services from being used to their full potential:

The THB-JIT project demonstrated the problems caused by linking two initiatives with different goals and responsibilities. This concerned especially the role of Europol and the purpose of the AWF. A dual approach, as occurred in the present project when the Action Plan Bulgaria was run alongside the JIT initiative, should be avoided. In general it remains questionable whether an intelligence body of its own like the JIG is needed besides an AWF and an Analysis Group as provided for in the Europol Convention. Whereas the JIG construction is lacking a basis in law, the information gathering and analysis by Europol is subject to a detailed legal framework on data protection. Moreover, providing a mandate for two bodies to carry out very similar tasks always runs the risk of a duplication of efforts as well as rivalry. Instead of implementing new instruments it is advisable to improve the effectiveness of existing instruments. Very likely, the functions accorded to the JIG could also have been performed by the members of the JIT in cooperation with Europol. It also remains questionable whether it was wise to limit Europol's status in the steering group to an observatory role when, in actual fact, it was effectively Europol's AWF that was the central tool for intelligence gathering in the preliminary phase.

Connected to the problem of linking two initiatives was the fact that right up until the end of the THB-JIT project, the roles and responsibilities of the different bodies such as the steering group towards the APB as well as the JIG towards the Analysis Group remained a matter of discussion. Thus, the roles and responsibilities of different bodies should be clearly and realistically defined and agreed upon from the outset.

For a THB-JIT project to be successful, participating countries have to start from the assumption that they share a common problem that is worth being solved by a joint effort. Political issues should not be the main driving force as they do not necessarily correspond to practical necessities. Thus, a bottom-up approach is to be favoured. It is less time-consuming and almost inherently implies a common starting point for joining investigations.

With regard to the somewhat disappointing data supply to the AWF, the following issues are worthy of consideration. To avoid unrealistic expectations, Europol as well as the participating countries should clearly state their possibilities, needs, and expectations at the outset. A standardised format for data supply to AWFs is needed to facilitate the analytical work of Europol. On the national level, effective lobbying is of paramount importance. Local and regional police forces should have been informed about the THB-JIT project and its developments as they are commonly the original suppliers of data and intelligence sourced from ongoing investigations. Equally, the relevant public prosecutors have to be involved as they are often responsible for authorising the transnational exchange of (sensitive) data.

Even though Europol would have welcomed receiving data from NGOs, this did not take place in practice. According to Europol officials, a standardised procedure is lacking on the format in which NGOs could provide information and handling codes that would enable Europol to assess the intelligence supplied. Equally, Europol is not in the position to further distribute information from NGOs in the absence of a link to a specific Member State or an operational agreement. A Memorandum of Understanding and some basic guidelines are needed about how the information is to be dealt with by Europol and how Europol is to assure NGOs that the information they provide will not eventually be introduced as evidence in criminal proceedings without their prior consent. As a consequence, Europol is to set up a standardised procedure in order to encourage NGOs to directly supply data to Europol.

Moreover, comprehensive feasibility studies should precede the opening of the AWF, in which Member States are to realistically describe their commitment to the project, including political and practical support as well as possible legal impediments regarding data supply in order to avoid later frustration.

The involvement of Europol has proven its potential for enhancing the working relationships between police authorities of the Member States with those of non- Member States such as Bulgaria.

The relevance of involving Europol in JITs as a form of transnational cooperation is likely to increase with the complexity of the team. Thus, in a bilateral JIT the necessity to involve Europol is less obvious.

In both projects the regulations applying to the involvement of Europol were criticised for being too complex and time-consuming. Thus, even though Europol's standardised rules and regulations on data protection have to be adhered to, timelier means of support have to be considered for Europol to be of value to ongoing investigations of serious forms of crime. It remains to be seen in how far the direct information exchange as provided for in Article 3a of the Protocol 2002 properly answers this problem.

6.2 Eurojust

As previously mentioned, the decision to institute Eurojust was heavily influenced by the intention to elevate judicial cooperation to a comparable level as police cooperation. Regarding the fact that in most Member States it is the public prosecutor who is the leader of investigations, mutual assistance in criminal matters is primarily an issue of judicial cooperation. The hitherto existing focus on police cooperation is understandable as it is commonly the police that are responsible for the day-to-day activity of effectively carrying out investigative measures and collecting and analysing intelligence. Nevertheless, in most Member States certain investigative measures remain subject to the approval of the public prosecutor. Equally, the issuing of letters rogatory as well as the authorisation of the transfer of (sensitive) data are judicial tasks. Thus, the coordination of investigations is as much a question of police cooperation as judicial cooperation. Against this background, the potential of Eurojust to coordinate communications between responsible judicial authorities has to be assessed.

It has to be remembered that the THB-JIT project under review originated from the Dutch EU Presidency, respectively the Dutch representative of the EPCTF, and that the steering group was responsible to the EPCTF. It started out as a 'police project' corresponding to the fact that JITs were primarily perceived as a working tool for the police. However, participants – by and large representatives of the police – eventually came to realise the need to involve the legal expertise of judicial authorities. This concerned primarily the lack of a legal basis for setting up a JIT in the first project on THB, but also the central question in the second project of how to exchange information without jeopardising the evidential value of that information. Equally, it became clear how national prosecutors only partly possessed the necessary legal expertise. Throughout both projects, however, the involvement of Eurojust was minimal in comparison to Europol.

Both legal obstacles to the realisation of a JIT and possible future complications that may arise during the JIT have to be clarified from the outset. Legal analysis is especially required to understand the different legal traditions of the countries involved and the varied ways in which the Member States have implemented JIT-related legislation. This implies, for example, understanding the different arrangements regarding who the competent authorities are for setting up a JIT as well as the competencies of seconded members. The latter in turn has the potential of causing 'JIT shopping', i.e., the location of a JIT is selected according to the country in which seconded members are granted the most far-reaching powers. In this regard, it seems advisable to follow the example of the Drugs JIT and to arrange introductory courses in which representatives from the participating countries present their legal system to each other and provide specific manuals on legal issues to the team. In both projects Eurojust made neither its role nor its potential transparent. Especially in the first project, Eurojust did not actively engage in addressing and helping to overcome legal obstacles. In the second project it limited its role to that of a point of liaison for the judicial authorities, thereby failing to successfully address police authorities. As a consequence, Eurojust's role and functions remained largely unclear to the police members of the team. Considering the expectations regarding the role of Eurojust, the decision of the first project to accord Eurojust only an observatory status in the steering group remains questionable.

The view that Eurojust should only become actively involved at the moment investigations are commenced cannot be upheld. Instead, for a JIT to be realised effectively, an early involvement of the national judiciary as well as Eurojust – especially in the preparatory phase – can be recommended. This view is supported by Article 6(a)(iv) of the Council Decision 2002 which states that Eurojust may ask the competent authorities of the Member States to consider setting up a JIT. Furthermore, according to Article 3(1)(c) Eurojust is to provide support to the Member States not only in the context of prosecutions but also in the context of investigations. On the basis of these articles, it can be argued that Eurojust should be involved in the preparatory phases of a JIT.

It has to be remembered that the projects under review constitute the first attempts to set up a JIT in accordance with Article 13 of the EU Convention on Mutual Assistance and respectively the Framework Decision on JITs. Furthermore, the Council Decision setting up Eurojust only entered into force in 2002. Thus, it is still a very young institution meaning both its role and corresponding best practices still need to be tested in practice. However, as stated before, the projects at hand demonstrate the need for thorough feasibility studies to occur preceding the actual setting up of JITs. These assessments should, among other things, focus on legislative aspects, existing possibilities of mutual assistance between countries, and a clarification of JIT-related legislation. In this regard, Eurojust can play the prominent role it has yet to develop.

CHAPTER VI
SOCIOLOGICAL ASPECTS REGARDING THE SET UP AND MANAGEMENT OF A JOINT INVESTIGATION TEAM

Markus Mayer*

The following reflections are based on experiences gathered from two separate projects that both aimed to create a functional Joint Investigation Team (JIT) according to Article 13 Convention on Mutual Assistance in Criminal Matters between the Member States of the European Union.[1] In the first project, four Member States were involved: the Netherlands, the United Kingdom, Belgium, and Germany. The focus of this project was on Trafficking in Human Beings related to Bulgaria (THB-JIT project). The second project was set up between the United Kingdom and the Netherlands in order to carry out investigations into trans-border drug trafficking (Drugs JIT).[2] The scientific research in these projects allowed for a deep insight to be gained into several problems relating to the creation of a working JIT. The problems encountered, as well as the ensuing answers, will, where possible, be discussed from a sociological and organisational point of view in this chapter in order to make the gathered experiences available to the broader public.[3]

1. THE THREE CORNERSTONES FOR THE ESTABLISHMENT OF A JIT

For the establishment of a functional JIT it is necessary to address three major questions: First, a legal basis must exist. While the EU Convention on Mutual

---

* Dr. Markus Mayer was formerly a researcher at the Max-Planck-Institute for Foreign and International Criminal Law, Freiburg (Germany), and is now working for a German welfare organisation.
[1] Convention on Mutual Assistance in Criminal Matters between the Member States of the European Union, *OJ* C 197, 12.07.2000 p. 1.
[2] See Chapter III.
[3] The reflections in this chapter refer to bilateral JITs. If the results differ considerably for multilateral JITs, it is mentioned in the footnotes.

Assistance provides for a legal framework at a European level, it is still necessary to clarify in which way the Convention is implemented on a national level in the participating countries. Second, a criminal case has to be selected and the JIT has to be set up. Regarding the latter question, three approaches to set up a JIT can be distinguished: bottom-up, top-down and outside-in. Third, the ongoing JIT must be managed.[4]

It is obvious that each step involves different institutions or actors dependent on their respective authorities and competences; a fact that does not necessarily accelerate the implementation of the JIT concept.

2. LEGAL BASIS

2.1 Implementation of the EU Convention on Mutual Assistance on a national level

Before a JIT is set up it has to be clarified whether the respective national legislation allows for the establishment of JITs according to Article 13 of the Convention. This issue has already been discussed from a judicial point of view.[5] From a sociological point of view it must be stated that the institutions or actors which are concerned at the national level with the legal framework – the legislature or high governmental authorities – are not likely to be identical to the institutions responsible for the process of setting up a JIT as such and, therefore, might focus on different aspects of the JIT concept. This gives rise to the supposition that in each country the first JITs will take a certain amount of time to be established. Furthermore, new laws or regulations have to be carefully projected and analysed.[6] Thus, the first JITs must have a rather long term strategic orientation instead of being pressed by current investigation needs. Finally, the criminal investigators – both the police as well as the public prosecutor – need to have certainty surrounding the question of whether the legal basis for setting

---

[4] In some respects, these questions reflect the terms of the macro, meso and micro level of police cooperation proposed by Benyon. See J. Benyon, et al., 'Understanding police cooperation in Europe setting a framework for analysis', in M. Anderson and M. den Boer, eds., *Policing Across National Boundaries,* London, Pinter Publishers 1994, p. 46 at p. 65.

[5] See Chapter I.

[6] An example may show that this issue is not easy to answer: At the beginning of one of the THB-JIT projects, the German representatives received the official opinion of the Ministry of Justice stating that the existing legislation was sufficient. About one year later, the Ministry of Justice withdrew its opinion and informed the German delegation that the existing laws were insufficient for Germany to participate in a JIT under Article 13 Convention on Mutual Assistance in Criminal Matters and that the necessary amendments had only been started.

up a JIT is in place in order not to compromise their investigations. As long as this question is not answered in a definite way, the investigation agencies will not gain confidence in the JIT concept and will hesitate to make use of it.[7]

2.2 Review of the possibilities to cooperate with other countries

Another question that has to be addressed is in how far the participating Member States have legislation for police and judicial cooperation in place and the way in which the participating countries have implemented the Convention domestically.[8] This question will not always be easy to answer, since it requires specialised judicial knowledge. Additionally – taking into account the number of 25 Member States of the European Union – this question has to be answered 576 times all over Europe. Therefore, it is rather probable that the use of JITs as an everyday tool of transnational police cooperation will be limited if the respective implementing legislation differs too much. Furthermore, it has to be clarified on a practical level which regulations might be useful for the cooperation of police officers from different countries, especially taking into account specific police traditions.[9]

The question as to how far Member States are in a position to cooperate under the Convention demands specific knowledge that cannot be expected to be available in any police department or public prosecution agency. Therefore, it seems to be beneficial to install a commission or agency on a national level which informs the local agencies about the possibilities available through the JIT concept, provides for training on that topic and gives advice in actual investigations. Since the JIT concept is still new and far from being common police knowledge, its diffusion in everyday police work will largely depend on its ease of use for the local investigators in charge of a case.

---

[7] The question remains whether the national implementation will accelerate as soon as the Convention is ratified. However, the need to have clear regulations for the investigation agencies will persist in either case.

[8] The Dutch implementation of JIT legislation – for example – only allows for JITs under Article 13 Convention on Mutual Assistance in Criminal Matters with countries that have implemented the Convention into national law. See also Chapter I.

[9] British police officers are – for example – usually not trained to use firearms. If they are seconded to another country it has to be decided whether they will receive additional training on that issue or how their safety can otherwise be provided for.

3. SELECTION OF A CASE – THE SETTING UP OF A JIT

3.1 Specifications made by the EU Convention on Mutual Assistance

Although Article 13 of the Convention gives some criteria that criminal cases have to meet in order to become the object of a JIT, it does not specify in which way and by whom a specific criminal investigation should be selected. It only states that 'the competent authorities of two or more Member States may set up a joint investigation team'[10] without further specifications concerning the selection at a national level. The Explanatory Report on the Convention of 29 May 2000 on Mutual Assistance in Criminal Matters between the Member States of the European Union[11] also does not mention this topic.

3.2 How can a JIT be initiated?

JITs can generally be set up in three different ways. First, a case can be selected after having identified a field of crime assessed as requiring a transnational investigation (top-down). Second, an ongoing national investigation may require support from abroad (bottom-up). Finally, a country can be asked by another country to join a JIT (outside-in). Each type has its own characteristics and demands for specific provisions.

3.2.1 *Top-down: identifying a field of crime and selecting a case*

The top-down approach was used in one of the two projects (THB-JIT project) from which our experience derives. In the top-down approach, investigative agencies on a national level or even governmental institutions (Ministry of Justice, Ministry of Home Affairs) identify a field of crime to be targeted by a JIT. Thereafter, the national police are to establish cooperative arrangements between the other countries supposed to join a common JIT as well as to charge local agencies with the investigation.[12]

As already mentioned, this approach seems to be suitable as long as JITs are not very common. It cannot be neglected that at a European level the JIT initiative has been politically motivated in the first instance. Therefore, the JIT concept

---

[10] Convention on Mutual Assistance in Criminal Matters between the Member States of the European Union, (*OJ* 2000 C 197/9).

[11] Explanatory Report on the Convention of 29 May 2000 on Mutual Assistance in Criminal Matters between the Member States of the European Union, *OJ* C 379, 29.12.2000, p. 18.

[12] In some particular cases the national police themselves might carry out the operational investigation.

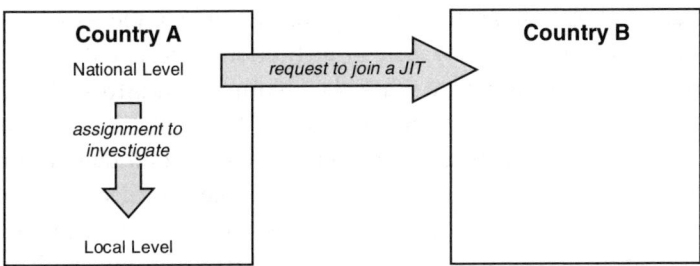

has to be promoted by either political or high governmental actors in order to make the new tool for cooperation known amongst prosecution agencies. A top-down approach will usually provide for sufficient political support and financial funding. However, the top-down approach also entails some problems which showed up in the above-mentioned project.

First, the top-down approach risks involving too many actors. In the respective project 50 persons from four countries were members of a so-called steering group, with most of them only involved for a certain period of time instead of attending the project from the beginning to the end. Consequently, the cooperation is likely to lack flexibility, particularly if political interests have to be taken into account.

Second, the representatives of the participating countries might change during the course of a top-down THB-JIT project as necessitated by the tasks to be fulfilled at different stages of the project.[13] This will lead to a certain loss of information even if this problem is taken into consideration by the delegation, and even when a briefing has been given to the succeeding representative. Furthermore, it has to be asked in how far the discontinuity of representatives is beneficial to the development of mutual trust and confidence. During the interviews with members of both projects almost every participant outlined the fact that mutual confidence was a very important and necessary factor in transnational police cooperation. Since confidence always depends on a personal relationship – and not on the function a person fulfils – it is very plausible that the discontinuity of representatives can lead to uncertainty among the project members. Moreover, effects on group dynamic can be expected. The theory of group dynamic assumes that every new group member initiates the group dynamic

---

[13] While the beginning of a top-down JIT requires high-ranking representatives on a national level able to make more general decisions concerning the framework of the project, at a later stage most probably local (and lower-ranking) forces will carry out the investigation on a day-to-day basis.

processes anew.[14] A new group member can be understood as a new person joining a group but also as a new state or institution represented in the group.[15] Every new group member has to learn the – formal and informal – rules that apply within the group and find his/her own – functional and hierarchical – position. This will in turn change the rules and the social structure of the group. This process is an effort any group has to undertake in order to establish and improve its functionality. Normally, this process takes place during the constitution of a group and is completed after a certain time. If group members change constantly, the group dynamic has to readjust again and again which will affect the overall performance of the group.

Third, the structure of a top-down project will tend to be more complex than intended by the EU Convention on Mutual Assistance. The THB-JIT project comprehended three bodies – a steering group, an Analytic Work File located at Europol and a Joint Intelligence Group – without even having a functional JIT. None of these bodies is mentioned by the Convention. It is evident that the initiators of a top-down JIT want to control the further steps of the project. However, the three cornerstones for the establishment of a JIT mentioned above – the implementation of the Convention at a national level, the selection of appropriate investigations or fields of crime and the proper management of ongoing JITs – should be seen as different challenges to be carried out by different institutions and not be merged into a single body.

Fourth, a top-down approach can highlight differences between the policies pursued by the participating countries and institutions. In the THB-JIT project, for example, some countries involved focussed on the achievement of a concrete investigative success, whereas others were predominantly interested in testing the JIT as a tool in whatever field of crime. If these differences are important or not disclosed and discussed among the initiators of a JIT, they risk considerably affecting the outcome of the project.

Fifth, a possible problem of top-down JITs relates to the lack of motivation within the local agencies charged with the investigation. The initiators of a top-down approach are more likely to be high-ranking representatives of the national prosecution agencies, rather than local investigators. It is unclear whether local authorities – police officers as well as public prosecutors – have the same

---

[14] Barbara Langmaack; Michael Braune-Krickau: Wie die Gruppe laufen lernt. Weinheim 1998. p. 70f.
[15] In each steering group meeting of the THB-JIT project 27% of the participants, on average, assisted for the first time.

view on a given situation as the representatives of national agencies or the government.

3.2.2 Bottom-up: processing a demand related to an ongoing investigation

Bottom-up JITs will usually be instigated due to the need for an ongoing local investigation that requires additional support from abroad. In this case, the local agency will request the national level to establish contact with one or more countries to facilitate the creation of a JIT.

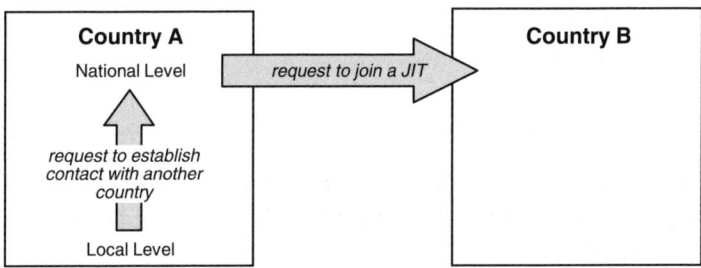

The bottom-up approach requires a functional institutional structure at a national level that is able to process the demands from a local level and to promptly make transnational contacts. It cannot be expected that local police officers have knowledge of international regulations like the EU Convention on Mutual Assistance. Therefore, they have to be supported by competent national institutions and the prosecution service concerning the creation and the management of a JIT. From a sociological point of view, this structure seems to be one of the most vital issues for the functionality of the JIT concept.

Unlike top-down JITs, bottom-up JITs will most probably have leaner structures, since only those institutions will be involved that are necessary for the setting up of the JIT and the investigation of the case. Therefore, bottom-up JITs will also be less affected by political or governmental issues. Initiated by local agencies already in charge of the respective investigation, the issue of motivation on the local level seems to be of minor concern. In contrast, bottom-up JITs risk having less support and funding, since political interests might be lacking.

3.2.3 Outside-in: processing of a demand from abroad

The outside-in approach focuses on the perspective of the receiving country regardless of whether the initial intention to set up a JIT by the requesting country goes back to a top-down or bottom-up approach. From the perspective of the requesting country, the first hurdle to take is to find out which institution is responsible for processing such a request in the requested country. Usually the head of the national police or a person from the national prosecution service will be the institution to address the demand. However, this issue is not specified in Article 13 of the Convention.

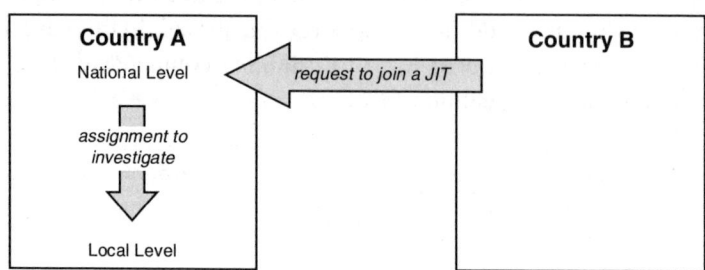

The requested country in turn has to have an institutional structure which allows for the processing of the demand: Identifying a local agency that can be assigned to join the investigation and supporting this agency while the JIT is ongoing. In this respect the processing of a demand from abroad always requires a functional top-down structure in the requested country. If this structure does not exist or is dysfunctional, this country will hardly become a member of a JIT.

3.3 Conclusion

Regarding the different ways to set up a JIT, it seems to be useful to install a competent agency or institution at a national level which is able to

- accumulate the necessary knowledge on legal as well as managerial questions concerning JITs.
- assign local investigation agencies to carry out a JIT.
- advise local investigation agencies as to the management of a JIT.
- process requests from local authorities and forward them to other countries.
- process and forward requests from abroad.

Taking into consideration the amount of specialised judicial knowledge and experience that is necessary to carry out JITs, it seems beneficial for the further advancement of the JIT concept to assign these tasks to one agency at the national level.

4. MANAGEMENT OF A JIT

4.1 Location and organisational structure

Article 13 Convention on Mutual Assistance in Criminal Matters provides for the setting up of a JIT 'in one or more of the Member States setting up the team.'[16] The Convention does not further specify the location of a JIT within one country. Thus, the JIT might either be linked to the national police or to local police forces. Most likely this issue will be determined by the police agency in charge of the investigation.

The Convention foresees that 'the Member State in which the team operates shall make the necessary organisational arrangements.'[17] It appears useful to orient the organisational structure of a JIT to the common organisational structures in the hosting country as long as the JIT concept does not require the adaptation of existing structures. This in turn will help the domestic police officers to introduce their seconded colleagues to their police structures.[18]

For analytical and managerial purposes it is useful to differentiate between Inner and Outer JIT. While the Inner JIT only includes the (domestic and seconded) police officers as well as the public prosecutor in charge of the ongoing investigation[19] on an everyday basis, the Outer JIT might include high-ranking representatives of the police and the judiciary.[20] For the members of the Outer JIT, the work related to the JIT is only one aspect of their overall duties.

The leader of the JIT serves as a link between the Inner and Outer JIT. While the leader's main function with respect to the Inner JIT is the management of the personnel and the ongoing investigation, the major challenge regarding the Outer JIT is to keep the higher-ranking representatives informed of the judiciary and the police in both the country hosting the JIT as well as the country seconding its members. The members of the Outer JIT can also be seen as a 'steering board' of the JIT and, therefore, should meet regularly in order to coordinate the objectives of the JIT.

---

[16] Convention on Mutual Assistance in Criminal Matters between the Member States of the European Union, *OJ* C 197, 12.07.2000, p. 9.

[17] Convention on Mutual Assistance in Criminal Matters between the Member States of the European Union, *OJ* C 197, 12.07.2000, p. 10.

[18] This approach was carried out very successfully in the British-Dutch JIT.

[19] In most Member States the public prosecutor is the head of the investigation.

[20] Further representatives of other institutions might join the Outer JIT according to Article 13(12) Convention on Mutual Assistance in Criminal Matters between the Member States of the European Union, *OJ* C 197, 12.07.2000, p. 11.

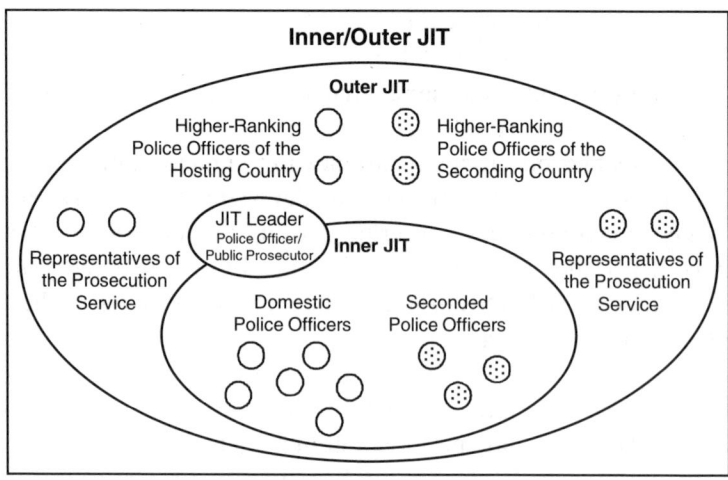

4.2 Finance and funding

The EU Convention on Mutual Assistance does not address financial aspects related to the establishment of a JIT. Only the Explanatory Report on the Convention of 29 May 2000 on Mutual Assistance in Criminal Matters as well as the Model Agreement for Setting up a Joint Investigation Team[21] mention costs as a topic to be addressed in an agreement between the Member States establishing a JIT. However, no further suggestions are made. The costs related to a JIT basically result from the involvement of seconded officers. The salary agreements of police officers usually provide for overseas allowances and the reimbursement of travel expenses. Furthermore, the lodging of the seconded members of a JIT has to be covered.

Major expense factors	Minor expense factors
• Overseas allowances for seconded members • Travel expenses of the seconded members • Overtime premiums for seconded members • Lodging costs and utility bills for the seconded members	• Office and work resources for the seconded members (e.g. mobile phones, computers) • Transportation costs for the seconded member within the hosting county (e.g. police car)

Other facilities like office and work resources for the seconded members or the use of police cars will normally be covered by the existing budget of the host police agency and, therefore, will only play a minor role. Consequently, the

---

[21] Model Agreement for Setting up a Joint Investigation Team, *OJ* C 121, 23.05.2003, p. 5.

total amount of money spent for a JIT will depend on the number of seconded members and the duration of the JIT. If these factors do not change during the course of the JIT the costs of the project will be quite predictable and, therefore, no unexpected increase should occur. Further expenses may result from the training of the seconded members or from team-building activities. These can be considered as investment costs for the set up of the JIT. Another possible issue is the cost of additional insurance for the seconded members.

The question remains how the costs related to a JIT should be divided between the countries involved. One possibility consists of adding up the total costs at the end of the project and dividing them into equal shares among the participating countries. Another – probably easier – alternative consists of allocating specific expense factors to the countries: While the seconding country covers overseas allowances, travel expenses and overtime premiums for the seconded members, the hosting country provides for the lodging of the seconded members as well as office resources and transportation facilities.[22]

4.3 Labour law aspects

Labour law aspects like working hours and compensation for overtime are usually regulated at a national level for all police officers. If a JIT is set up, it must be clarified in how far these regulations apply for the assignment of seconded members in a foreign country. The easiest way seems to be to maintain the regulations applicable in the home country. However, this obliges the team leader of the hosting country to adapt to this regulation and – probably – to apply different regulations for the members of the same team.

4.4 Other legal aspects

Another important topic is the investigative powers which the seconded members are able to dispose of in the hosting country. The EU Convention on Mutual Assistance states that 'the team shall carry out its operations in accordance with the law of the Member State in which it operates. The members of the team shall carry out their tasks ... taking into account the conditions set by their own authorities in the agreement on setting up the team.'[23] One possible implementation of this provision is to provide the seconded members with the same powers as the domestic officers, as long as these powers do not exceed the powers

---

[22] This division of costs was applied in the British-Dutch JIT.
[23] Convention on Mutual Assistance in Criminal Matters between the Member States of the European Union, *OJ* C 197, 12.07.2000, p. 10.

which the seconded members have in their home country.²⁴ In so doing, the powers of the seconded members might be less extensive than the powers of the hosting country's police officers.

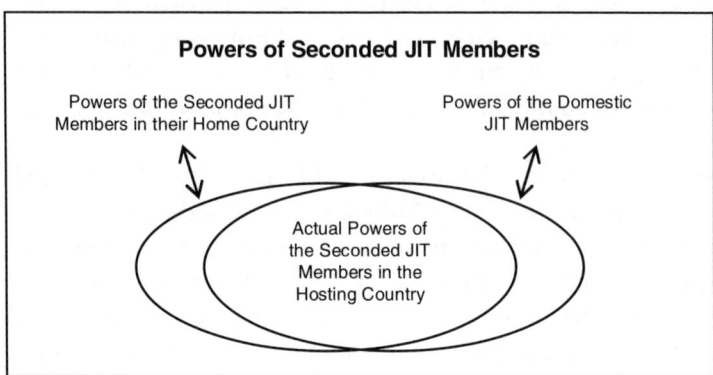

The restrictions on the powers of the seconded JIT members are of particular importance for the leader of the JIT: On the one hand, the restrictions might prohibit the seconded members from carrying out certain tasks.²⁵ On the other hand, the team leader has to ensure that the seconded members do not exceed the powers assigned to them by the host country. Furthermore, the execution of actual powers is highly dependent on the implementing legislation in the countries involved in the JIT.²⁶

4.5 Hierarchical structure

The EU Convention on Mutual Assistance states that 'the leader of the team shall be a representative of the competent authority participating in criminal investigations from the Member State in which the team operates. The leader of the team shall act within the limits of his or her competence under national law.'²⁷ Consequently, the seconded members are under the authority of the team leader. He can entrust the seconded members as well as excluding them from carrying out certain investigative measures. However, the seconded members remain part of the hierarchy in their home country. In this respect they have two superiors: The leader of the JIT as well as their superior in the home country.

---

²⁴ See Chapters III and IV.

²⁵ In the British-Dutch JIT the British members were not allowed to carry firearms, since British law generally prohibits police officers from doing so. While their Dutch colleagues carried firearms in the JIT, the British members were restricted to carrying arms that they are allowed to carry under British law, which are a pepper spray and a baton.

²⁶ See also Chapter I

²⁷ Convention on Mutual Assistance in Criminal Matters between the Member States of the European Union, *OJ* C 197, 12.07.2000, p. 10.

The graph shows at which point hierarchical conflicts might occur (dotted arrow): The seconded members might receive orders from two sides. In cases where these orders differ or even contradict one another, the seconded members

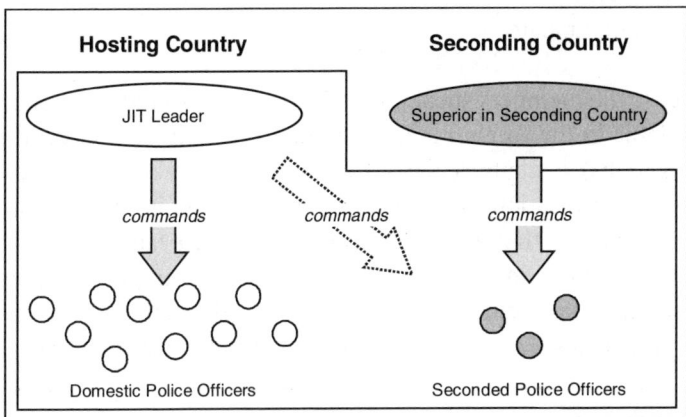

will face a dilemma. The 'collective leadership' requires that the leader of the JIT stays in close contact with the superiors of the seconded members of his team in order to coordinate the strategy of the investigation and to avoid contradicting orders. If this coordination is not carefully realised, the outcome of a JIT can be seriously affected.

4.6 Language and culture in JITs

In the two projects from which our knowledge is derived, according to the actors neither language nor differences in culture were insurmountable obstacles. However, the collaboration of persons from different countries implicates certain challenges to be taken into account. Neither the EU Convention on Mutual Assistance nor the Explanatory Report on the Convention of 29 May 2000 on Mutual Assistance in Criminal Matters address the question of language within a JIT. Only the Model Agreement for Setting up a Joint Investigation Team mentions the 'language to be used for communications'[28] as a topic to be defined in an agreement between Member States establishing a JIT, although no further suggestions are made.

4.6.1 *Emergence of subgroups*

One of the issues related to language is the risk that the JIT will be divided into subgroups according to the respective languages of the members. Two constel-

---

[28] Model Agreement for Setting up a Joint Investigation Team, *OJ* C 121, 23.05.2003, p. 5.

lations are possible: First, the seconded members are able to speak the language of the hosting country or the domestic members speak the language of the seconded members.[29] Second, the seconded members do not understand the language of their domestic colleagues and vice versa. Therefore, they use a third language to communicate.[30]

In the first case the members speaking both languages can directly access information available in the foreign language (e.g., files, phone interception protocols, interrogations). In contrast, the other members – speaking only one language – are in need of translation assistance in obtaining this information and easily risk being excluded if the bilingual members use their native language. If so, the members will not gain a complete insight into the ongoing investigation. In this case the bilingual members have a strategic advantage since they can exclude their colleagues by means of language while the others cannot.

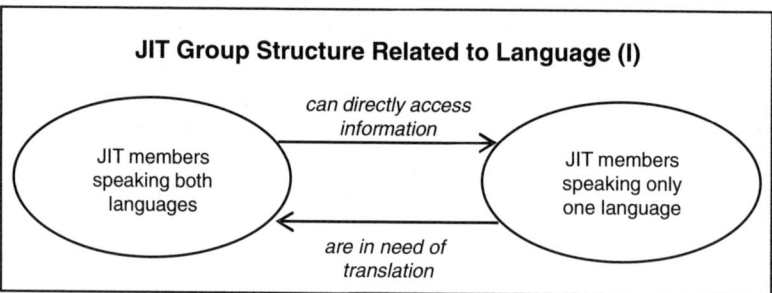

In the second case, both groups are able to exclude each other by using their native language. Any information has to be translated into a third language spoken by all team members.

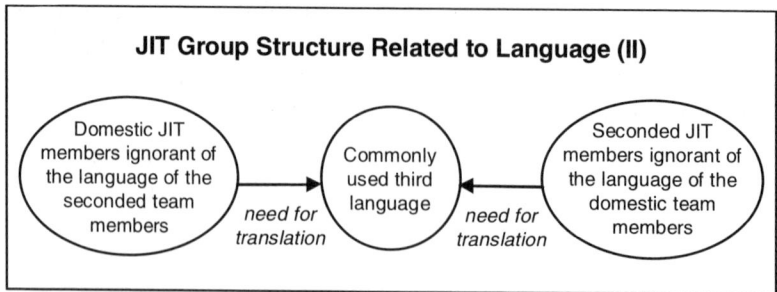

The experiences gathered within the research project show that the problem of exclusion can be solved as long as – in case one – the bilingual members consis-

---

[29] That was the case for the British-Dutch JIT.
[30] In multilateral JITs both circumstances can occur simultaneously.

tently use the language that can be understood by the monolingual members or – in case two – a common third language is consistently used by both groups. Otherwise, the use of a language not spoken by other team members can easily cause mistrust which is certainly not beneficial to the cooperation.

4.6.2 The need for translation

Another challenge consists of the need to translate files, documents and protocols of phone interceptions or interrogations. In both of the above-mentioned cases, certain investigation data have to be translated. On the one hand, translation requires time and additional resources.[31] On the other hand, the JIT members – unable to speak the foreign language – might be confronted with incomplete and improperly translated records, since the selection of data to be translated will usually depend on the country providing the data. This might be another source of mistrust. The members of the bilateral Drugs THB-JIT project analysed in the framework of this research project outlined that the efforts relating to the translation of information were considerable but not impossible to undertake. However, the issue of a common language could be an argument to keep the number of countries involved small.

4.6.3 Restrictions due to a lack of language skills

The concept of a JIT implies that the seconded team members have the same powers as the domestic members as long as these do not exceed the powers they have in their home country. However, further restrictions might exist due to lacking language skills on the part of the seconded members: If they do not speak the language of the country they are seconded to, they will not be able to carry out certain investigative tasks like interrogations, phone tapping or the analysis of written sources. The above-mentioned graph concerning the powers of seconded team members can consequently be amended to the graph shown on the top of the next page.

This can lead – as one of the recent THB-JIT projects has demonstrated – to a division of tasks between domestic and seconded team members.[32] This division of tasks is not necessarily disadvantageous as long as all team members agree to it. However, even if this concern has been clarified between the team

---

[31] It is easy to imagine that this effort will considerably increase in the case of multilateral JITs.

[32] In the British-Dutch JIT, the British team members – unable to speak the Dutch language – were charged with tasks not related to language like observation. In return, they were responsible for the evaluation of English intercept material.

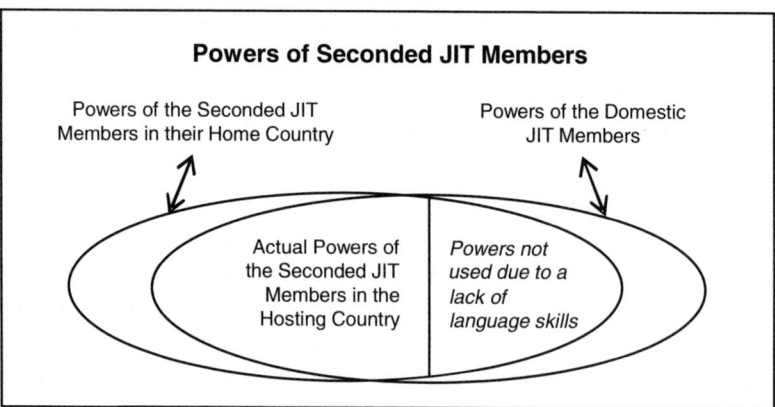

members, the situation might arise in which the seconded members feel 'less effective as they would like to be.'[33]

4.7 Team building

The official documents do not mention the issue of team building. However, the issue seems to be relevant for the successful management of a JIT. As soon as new (seconded) members join an existing investigation team, a specific change in the group dynamic has to be expected.

4.7.1 *Inauguration of new team members*

In the Drugs JIT an extensive team-building phase was carried out for several days at the start of the project. This team-building phase did not only involve the domestic and seconded police officers and public prosecutors in charge of the investigation but also higher-ranking police officers and public prosecutors from both countries. First of all, this event aimed at familiarising the JIT members with their new colleagues in a formal as well as informal context. Furthermore, the seconded members were introduced to the legal system of the hosting country and obtained instructions concerning the work equipment like computers and other technical devices. As a result, the seconded members felt appreciated right from the start of the project and easily integrated into the investigation team. The members of this JIT unanimously agreed that the team-building phase at the beginning of the project prepared the ground for the open-minded and friendly atmosphere within the JIT. The question remains whether future JITs will dispose of the necessary resources to carry out a team-building event. How-

---

[33] Interview held with a seconded JIT member of the British-Dutch JIT.

ever, team building seems to be an indispensable aspect for the successful initiation of a JIT.

4.7.2 Pairing

Another strategy to integrate the seconded members consists of pairing them off with domestic police officers, as was the case in one of the analysed projects. This procedure has several advantages. First, the domestic officer can translate in case the seconded officer does not understand what is said or written. Second, the seconded officer can rely on a person who is familiar with the local situation in the hosting country. Third, the domestic officer can advise his seconded colleague in case of legal or procedural questions. Finally, the close cooperation will intensify the personal relationship within the team.

5. CONCLUSION

The members of the two THB-JIT projects analysed in the framework of the current research project unanimously agreed that the JIT concept provides for new and interesting opportunities to improve transnational investigations. One of the projects also proved that the management of an ongoing JIT does not entail insurmountable obstacles as long as the JIT is carefully managed by a leader taking into account the various challenges related to this type of cooperation. These challenges include:

- integrating the seconded team members in the host country and introducing them through team-building events and pairing them with domestic officers
- taking into account the powers of the seconded members as restricted by legal regulations and the possible lack of language skills
- ensuring that important information is available in the language to be used for communication
- preventing the emergence of subgroups created by language or cultural barriers
- considering the issue of collective leadership in order to avoid contradicting orders

The Outer JIT – established to supervise the JIT – should be kept as lean as possible and concentrate on clearly defined issues in order not to compromise the advantages of the JIT concept by creating an overly complex structure.

Another issue concerns the question of whether the countries participating in a JIT under Article 13 Convention on Mutual Assistance in Criminal Matters have implemented the necessary legal provisions domestically. The most vital issue from an organisational point of view seems to be appointing a functional structure or agency at the national level to support and advise local authorities willing to set up a JIT, and to process requests from abroad. As soon as such a structure is established and operational in each Member State, the JIT concept can and will become a useful tool for law enforcement agencies Europe-wide, exactly as was intended by the authors of the EU Convention on Mutual Assistance.

CHAPTER VII
CONCLUSIONS AND RECOMMENDATIONS

Conny Rijken

1.   CONCLUSION

This book demonstrates that the establishment of JITs can greatly contribute to closer cooperation in criminal matters, at least when certain requirements are fulfilled. The two JIT projects that formed the practical input for the analysis made in this book are valuable steps in finding the right way in the jungle of criminal cooperation in the EU. They also show that criminal cooperation is a complex matter and that its success is dependent on many factors, not in the last place the presence of mutual trust between the players in the field. It was furthermore shown that criminal cooperation is not a static event but a process which is constantly under revision and improvement. Although the adoption of legislation on the EU level is, for some people, the final step in the process of improving cooperation, for most of those dealing with criminal cooperation in their daily work, it is the beginning of a new phase or a new road in the whole event of criminal cooperation. Only when people are prepared to learn from each other and have an open mind towards other rules, other systems, and other states, can this new road be taken. The people involved must be able to appreciate the new challenges created by this new legislation and they must have the courage to take the necessary steps towards further and closer cooperation. Like many other things we have to learn in life, learning by doing is a well-established method of becoming familiar with new possibilities.

A JIT is an instrument adopted in such new legislation and the projects under research in this book are examples of the method 'learning by doing'. As was learnt from the THB-JIT project and the Drugs JIT, there is not one single way to establish a JIT. When considering the text of Article 13 of the EU Convention on Mutual Assistance, a first impression may be that the concept is well-defined and clear. However, when trying to translate the provision into a practical level, it becomes clear that there are many ways to use the instrument of a JIT. In the

C. Rijken and G. Vermeulen (Eds.), Joint Investigation Teams in the European Union
© 2006, T·M·C·ASSER PRESS, *The Hague, The Netherlands and the Authors*

past, law enforcement officers have undertaken many attempts towards closer cooperation, in which they have tested the boundaries of the legal framework on this matter. Some of those may welcome the legal framework of a JIT as the necessary basis to intensify cooperation. Especially in border regions, law enforcement officers are used to closer cooperation with colleagues on the other side of the border, and special agreements are concluded for that purpose. Such forms of cooperation have the appearance of a JIT. The great advantage of these agreements is that they are flexible and can be tailored to the specific situation of that region. We should learn from those experiences and use the instrument of a JIT in a similarly flexible way.[1] The projects analysed in this book must therefore be considered **a possible** way in which JITs can be set up or prepared and not as **the only** way to establish a JIT. Nevertheless, the conditions for a successful JIT indicated in this book are applicable for all types of JITs, also for future JITs that might be set up in a different way. This book, furthermore, makes it clear that the adoption of a legal framework for a JIT at the EU level is an important condition. However, it is only a first step in achieving the intended added value of a JIT. The adoption of clear and unambiguous national legislation by the EU Member States as well as guidelines and interpretations on the use of JITs in the specific Member States intensively analysed in the first chapter, are other important preconditions for JITs to be established. The conditions on the operational level are of major importance before a JIT can be established and achieve its desired effect. If these conditions are not met, the JIT may even frustrate the cooperation. These conditions, therefore, must not be underestimated but be given considerable attention when establishing a JIT. This book also provided an insight into the factors that played such an important role on the operational level. Based on the previous chapters, a concluding overview of the conditions for a successful JIT is made. These conditions on the operational level are divided into conditions in the preparatory phase of a JIT, conditions in the operational phase of a JIT, and conditions regarding the role of Europol and Eurojust. Subsequently recommendations specified to the different disciplines involved in JITs are formulated. But before these conditions are discussed some concluding remarks on the results of the THB-JIT project and the Drugs JIT are made.

1.1 The evaluation of the results of the projects under research

The results from a law enforcement perspective, especially for the THB-JIT project, can be considered limited. The reasons for this limited effect for the

---

[1] Taking into account that border-region cooperation has the advantage that law enforcement officers often know each other and work together on a more regular basis.

THB-JIT project are the lack of sufficient legislation in Germany to enter into a JIT, the lack of a case suitable to start a JIT, and the absence of a new common goal once it became clear that a JIT on THB could not be set up in a short time. In addition to these reasons, the limited success of the THB-JIT project must mainly be sought in the way it was organised and practical matters that emerged during the project. The instrument of a JIT as such could not influence these aspects. As a result of the Drugs JIT, some suspects were convicted and some cases are still pending before the courts. The division between the United Kingdom part and the Dutch part of the investigations, combined with the use of the JIT concept, are two more reasons why the case was postponed several times. The significance of both projects for the further development and improvement of criminal cooperation, however, is considerable. This mainly concerns the lessons learnt by the different states involved in how to set up a JIT and the possible difficulties that can arise during the process of setting up such a team in the future. People involved in future JITs will at least be better prepared. Closer contacts might facilitate cooperation in the future. Gaining essential knowledge regarding the criminal justice systems of other states and strengthening operational cooperation are two important effects.

1.2 Conditions on the operational level for the establishment of a successful JIT

In this section the conditions for a successful JIT are described before recommendations are made. The difference between the two is that the conditions are more focused on the process of running a JIT while the recommendations are made from a more analytical and abstract perspective. The link between the two is that the recommendations can be considered as a further elaboration of the conditions.

1.2.1 *Conditions in the preparatory phase of a JIT*

In all forms of cooperation, the willingness to cooperate must be present among all persons involved in the cooperation. A JIT is no exception to this. A common interest (whether operational or differently) to use the instrument of a JIT is a condition which increases willingness. If such a common interest and therefore willingness is not available, efforts towards closer cooperation will fail to be successful. Structures set up to compensate for the lack of common interest or built to identify this common interest may not be taken seriously as a result.

Before a JIT can be established, proper legislation, which is an adequate implementation of the international framework, must be in place. This implementation should be complete, accurate, and clear in order to avoid confusion about the application of certain provisions and the meaning of particular provisions in national law. If such legislation has not (yet) been adopted, it is not impossible to run a JIT. However, the problems that may arise as a consequence of inadequate legislation must be taken into account as a factor that is weighed in determining whether a JIT is the right instrument for cooperation in a particular case.

As is stated in Article 13 of the EU Convention on JITs, a JIT should only be set up in large transnational and complex cases as this instrument is complex and time-consuming and requires an extra effort on the part of all participants involved. In general, it would be too great an effort for relatively straightforward investigations. Furthermore, limited financial resources will force practitioners to use this instrument only in cases where other less expensive ways of cooperation are not expected to succeed. If the necessary financial resources are not available, a JIT should not be set up. However, it cannot be excluded that, in less complex cases, a JIT may be the most effective form of cooperation, especially if this cooperation takes place on a more regular basis, as in border regions. In these cases, the framework of a JIT may also be used to the benefit of these particular forms of cooperation. But in all cases, the 'need' basis for all states involved must determine whether to start a JIT. A JIT should only be set up when a criminal case or a common problem in which there is a need for establishing a JIT is identified.

The joint investigation and prosecution of such a case should reflect the common interest of the states involved in establishing a JIT. If there is a common problem but not a common case, the information exchange with the aim of identifying such a common case should follow the normal procedures, which must be adjusted if necessary. Especially if more than two states are involved, Europol seems to be best suited to create the overall picture and to help identify a case. At this stage, the well-known problems of information exchange are an obstacle in the rapid identification of a case. In order to be able to select a JIT-worthy case, information gathering in the states concerned should take place on a central level in order to facilitate a quick exchange of information.

Before a JIT becomes operational, its structure must be agreed upon and set out in a JIT agreement. In order to be able to make the necessary adjustments while operating a JIT, a flexible agreement, open to a wider range of criminal justice systems and adjustable to a large variety of situations, is indispensable.

It is advisable that the structure of a JIT is as simple as possible and linked to the system of the country where the JIT is located. In order to overcome the problems of working with different legal systems in a team, members of a JIT should have or obtain basic knowledge of the system and procedures of the country in which the JIT operates. This process of becoming familiar with different legal systems within the EU will take quite some time but seems to be a necessary stepping-stone for more complex cooperation with the involvement of a larger number of states and operations in various countries and thus with different team leaders. This means that the coming years should also be used for experience building and becoming familiar with different legal systems and cultures. To this end a functional structure or agency on the national level that is to support and advise local authorities willing to set up a JIT and to process requests from abroad should be established. Such an agency should collect the necessary experiences in this field. Recently, an expert group with national JIT contact points has been established within the EU. This group is composed of experts on JITs from all the EU Member States from the police, the judiciary or the Ministries. The aim of this group is to collect information on experiences with JITs and to enhance the awareness and use of JITs. This expert group had its first meeting on 23 November 2005 at Eurojust.[2] The national contact points in the Member States can well serve as the national agency on experience building.

1.2.2 Conditions in the operational phase of a JIT

The instrument of a JIT has been established in order to bypass the difficulties in the normal process of information exchange by avoiding the sometimes long and complex structures of requests for mutual assistance. That does not mean that all these difficulties disappear when a JIT is established. In a JIT information exchange should be compatible with national legislation, which means that national laws still play an important role in determining the information that can be provided to the JIT by the seconded members. Differences in legislation may continue to be a factor that prevents immediate information exchange, as the experience of the Drugs JIT made clear. In the Drugs JIT, the labelling of information as confidential and the refusal of the agency providing the information to share it in the JIT led to a reduction of the effect of the JIT. Such rules existing in the different Member States must be taken into account in advance and the consequences must be calculated. In order to make a JIT effective, relevant information from the states involved must be available to all members of a JIT.
Information from states not party to a JIT can be obtained by a normal request. However, the requested state must be informed of the fact that the information is used for a JIT and it must be informed of the members of the JIT. Strictly speaking, the requested state must again be asked permission when the composition of the JIT changes. To make this system more flexible, a standardised

---

[2] Council of the European Union, Conclusions of the First Meeting of the National Experts on JITs, Brussels, 2 December 2005, 15227/05.

statement should be used in which it is indicated that the information provided can be used for the purpose of the JIT regardless of changes in its composition in the future.

The way in which law enforcement is organised differs between the criminal justice systems. Here again it is important to have inside information on these structures of the participating states when operating a JIT. Information exchange on these matters is therefore of major importance.

Although often underestimated, language can constitute a major obstacle in the cooperation outside a JIT. This is even more the case within a JIT. It seems inevitable that a common language is spoken and understood by the team members. Furthermore, it must be underlined that communicating in a different language includes risks of misunderstanding and loss of information.

Only when the requirement of mutual trust between the participants and the countries involved is met should a JIT be set up. If this mutual trust is lacking, people will not be able to cooperate with each other.

1.2.3 *Conditions for the involvement of Europol and Eurojust in a JIT*

It is widely known that Europol has to deal with the reluctance of Member States to provide it with accurate data. This was no different in the cases under research. Europol should be more involved but its participation is complicated by the strict rules to which it is bound. Only with the consent of the providing state is it allowed to share information with other states. These strict rules were set up in order to motivate Member States and to guarantee that they would provide Europol with operational information. However, States remain reluctant to do so and Europol is saddled with the strict rules on data protection.

As stated above, the role of Europol in helping to identify a common case seems to be indispensable if a common problem is experienced by more than two states. In those cases, the instrument of an AWF should be used. In order to overcome the problem of not providing Europol with the requested information, a more binding request from Europol to provide information should be adopted in some cases. Furthermore, a standardised format for data supply to AWFs should be adopted to make an analysis of data more reliable.

The output of an AWF should bring an advantage for the states by providing essential information following from the analysis made by Europol. In that way, AWFs can prove their right of existence. Besides, Europol should set up a standardised procedure in order to encourage NGOs to directly supply data to Europol.

It seems that Eurojust is less hindered by such strict rules. As an institution set up to facilitate judicial cooperation, its role is different from that of Europol. Usually, a question for assistance to Eurojust is more definite. Furthermore, the common interest of states asking Eurojust for assistance is in general already apparent because the states involved are working on a particular case. This common interest is often not clear when Europol is involved because its involvement usually concerns the pre-operational phase.

Representatives of Eurojust can be involved in a JIT in two different ways, namely, as a representative of the state they are representing at Eurojust, and as a representative of Eurojust as an institution. It must be determined in what position members of Eurojust participate because this can have serious consequences for their competences. In the THB-JIT project, Eurojust was given an observatory role. Although Europol was formally also limited to this role, it was much more active in facilitating the THB-JIT project than Eurojust.

2. RECOMMENDATIONS FOR THE USE OF THE JIT INSTRUMENTS

The THB-JIT project and the Drugs JIT involved authorities from many levels and origins. The research underlying this book was conducted by academics from different disciplines. This resulted in a broad insight into how these two initiatives were established and how they operated. Consequently, recommendations on these various issues are made. The recommendations that are discussed in this chapter flow from the previous chapters as well as the research underlying this book and will be divided into recommendations for the police, the prosecutors, the policy makers, and the legislator. Of course, a number of these recommendations are applicable to more than one discipline. For reasons of readability, these will be discussed in the section on the discipline that will be affected the most by that particular recommendation.

2.1 Recommendations for the police

To meet the problems of gathering information on a national level, effective lobbying is of paramount importance. Local and regional police forces should be informed about the concept of the JIT and the establishing of a JIT in a particular case, when applicable, as they are usually the actual suppliers of data and intelligence from ongoing investigations. In that regard, the police should take a more proactive role in selecting and promoting potential cases for which setting up a JIT is advisable, for instance, for cases requiring constant and intensive collaboration during which the presence of foreign police representatives is necessary.

Institutions such as Europol, that already have analytical and supportive possibilities, should be used more effectively to strengthen the operational cooperation between countries in the EU. Besides, Europol should make it easier to share information with JITs and to share the information from AWFs more broadly.

In order to avoid complex structures, a JIT should be managed by the police unit which is either already concerned with the actual criminal case or usually responsible for a particular type of crime. It appears to be more productive if the establishment of a JIT relies on ongoing investigations in one or more countries, provided that a common legal basis exists. This helps to avoid a complex and time-consuming intelligence phase and ensures that the persons involved have a high motivation to support the JIT.

Following the positive experiences in the Drugs JIT, an extensive orientation and team-building phase seems to be beneficial to the atmosphere among the JIT members and, therefore, for the efficiency of the project. This team-building phase must be used especially to exchange information on the team members' legal system, the law enforcement organisation, and the way of operating. If such a team-building phase is successful, it may create a solid basis in which a reluctance to share information can be identified and the reasons for this reluctance can be discussed openly.

If it is expected that investigative measures are undertaken in different countries, it should be considered to establish a joint leadership in order to avoid frequent shifts of leadership and possible contradicting orders.

2.2   Recommendations for the prosecution

One of the most important lessons from the JIT experiences concerns the realisation that a feasibility study needs to be carried out before a JIT can be set up, in order to identify the possibilities and the risks involved in establishing a JIT. This assessment should focus on, among other things, legislative aspects, existing possibilities between countries, location and responsibilities. Eurojust can and should play a prominent role in this feasibility study.

In order to build experience, the structure of JITs in the coming period should be kept as simple as possible. It seems to be appropriate to use the existing structures and instruments of the hosting country as much as possible, rather than building new networks of communication, such as the JIG. However, when the authorities involved are more familiar with this form of cooperation, other forms of performing a JIT are, of course, possible.

The factor of necessity plays an important role. A JIT should only be set up if this instrument can be useful in the fight of several countries against crime. It is important that a case is identified in which the use of a JIT can have added value. A bottom-up approach is to be favoured. It is less time-consuming and almost inherently implies a common starting point and a commonly shared interest. Furthermore, the form that is chosen to set up a JIT should be tailored to the particular situation. For instance, it will not always be necessary to have the seconded member of a JIT on a permanent basis in the accommodating country. This means that the instrument of a JIT should be used in a flexible way.

For a JIT to be realised effectively, the early involvement of the national judiciary (as well as Eurojust) is recommended. The early involvement of the prosecution is natural when taking the existence of a case as a starting point for a JIT. Article 13(1) of the EU Convention on Mutual Assistance states that a JIT may, in particular, be set up where 'the investigations require difficult and demanding investigations having links with other Member States or where the case necessitates co-ordinated, concerted action in the Member States involved.' In general, the prosecution is already involved in such complex cases.

2.3 Recommendations for policy makers

The issue of language has to be taken into account in a double perspective. On the one hand, the use of different languages can complicate group building within the JIT, which can compromise collaboration. On the other hand, the need for translation will always be a potential source of misunderstanding and also slow down the exchange of information. Therefore, language training should be widely available.

Furthermore, a willingness and awareness for cooperation and the use of a JIT are connected to mutual trust and are recognised as important factors. As the Drugs JIT showed, mutual trust on the operational level seems to be greater than with the persons more indirectly involved in a JIT such as the tactical level. Policy makers should also create opportunities for increasing this mutual trust for these levels which are indirectly involved in a JIT as they often have decisive powers concerning the establishment of a JIT.

An institutionalised procedure for the realisation of JITs has yet to evolve within the Member States. In the ideal situation, such a procedure is preceded by a coordination phase and an experience building phase, during which the key players involved in transnational cooperation in criminal matters (Ministry of Justice/Home Affairs, national and local police forces, national and local prosecution services) will participate. Within the framework set up by the national legislator, they determine suitable ways of realising a JIT in practice. Since this topic is new for most of the Member States of the European Union, the establishment of JITs in the near future will most likely be actuated by the will to test the concept. Only when national routines for the establishment of a JIT are in place will it become the easy, flexible, and efficient tool aspired to by the authors of the EU Convention on Mutual Assistance. Besides the experience-building phase, further research on the added value of a JIT and the circumstances under which it can best be achieved must be conducted. Such a study should also focus on the value of seconded members to make a direct examination of whether the collecting of information and the execution of investigations meet basic (human rights) standards in this field.

2.4 Recommendations for the legislator

The national legislator should realise that the adoption of binding instruments on the European level, also in the area of the third pillar, is only a first step in the facilitation and improvement of police and judicial cooperation. The national legislator has to support this process. He should, within the given time frame, adopt clear and unambiguous implementing legislation which fulfils the requirements on a European level.

In this respect, the main performance indicator and the necessary condition is the legal framework in the countries involved in a THB-JIT project. The legal framework can be seen as the essential basis for a JIT because, in its absence, the instrument is useless. Although the EU Convention on Mutual Assistance has now entered into force, the Framework Decision on JITs can still play an important role regarding states that are not a party to the Convention. With regard to the legislator in the Member States involved in the THB-JIT project, the following is recommended. The Netherlands should amend its Article 552qa CCP and change the word 'treaty' into 'treaty or binding decision of the Council of the EU'. Furthermore, Article 552qb CCP should be formulated more clearly or a statement by the Minister of Justice on how to interpret this article should be requested. In order to avoid confusion, the United Kingdom should consider implementing the Framework Decision in a legally binding instrument.

In Belgium, the Framework Decision has been properly implemented in general, although seconded members can never execute operational tasks without the presence of a Belgian officer and the agreement of the team leader. Furthermore, the text must be completed and explained in circulars since some provisions cannot be used in practice without problems.

Germany did not have the necessary legislation for cooperation in JITs until 8 August 2005. The new Article 83k Mutual Assistance in Criminal Matters Act, implementing Article 13 of the EU Convention on Mutual Assistance, is also a rather minimal supplementary implementation to enable Germany to apply international treaties allowing for the setting up of JITs.

3. FINAL REMARKS

A JIT can have added value and make a difference in fighting transnational crime, at least when some considerations are taken into account. First, the role a JIT can play must not be overestimated. In the first instance, the instrument is meant to facilitate judicial cooperation rather than police cooperation, although the largest effort to establish a JIT is expected to come from the police. Second, the difference a JIT can make must not be expected in the short term. Given the difficulties that were encountered by the THB-JIT project and the Drugs JIT, many more difficulties must be expected for future JITs before a solid basis for the establishment of JITs materialises.

It clearly follows from this book that the adoption of legislation on the EU level is only a first step for police and judicial cooperation within the EU. It seems that the European level is aware of the necessity for intensified cooperation and is able to translate this awareness into creating a legal framework for police and judicial cooperation. In the recent history of the EU, proposals in policy documents have been increasingly repeated in various other policy documents without an effort having been made to adopt such proposals in legally binding instruments. This seems to have changed as, for instance, the Tampere conclusions are monitored every six months and proposals are taken seriously and more often transformed into legally binding instruments. However, is the national level ready for a JIT? When comparing the THB-JIT project and the Drugs JIT, it can be concluded that cooperation in the field of crime is strongly dependent on the willingness of states to cooperate and the mutual trust between the persons involved in the cooperation. In the THB-JIT project, each and every (possible) hurdle was discussed in detail and considered an obstacle to the establishment of a JIT. Meanwhile, the Netherlands and the United Kingdom managed to start the Drugs JIT, although this road was not smooth either. The authorities directly involved in cooperation on the operational level seem to have more confidence in each other than those indirectly involved in a JIT, for instance the tactical level. Much improvement can be made in building confidence also on this latter level. Furthermore, the role of the national legislation in implementing European law should be given more attention. Finally, it is to be welcomed that the initiators of the THB-JIT project and the Drugs JIT had the courage to make an effort to use the JIT instrument. It must be realised that police and judicial cooperation will only move forward when initiatives such as those underlying the analyses in this book are courageously undertaken.